D1203408

SOCIAL ETHICS IN A CHANGING CHINA

THE THORNTON CENTER CHINESE THINKERS SERIES

The John L. Thornton China Center at Brookings develops timely, independent analysis and policy recommendations to help U.S. and Chinese leaders address key long-standing challenges, both in terms of Sino-U.S. relations and China's internal development. As part of this effort, the Thornton Center Chinese Thinkers Series aims to shed light on the ongoing scholarly and policy debates in China.

China's momentous socioeconomic transformation has not taken place in an intellectual vacuum. Chinese scholars have actively engaged in fervent discussions about the country's future trajectory and its ever-growing integration with the world. This series introduces some of the most influential recent works by prominent thinkers from the People's Republic of China to English language readers. Each volume, translated from the original Chinese, contains writings by a leading scholar in a particular academic field (for example, political science, economics, law, or sociology). This series offers a much-needed intellectual forum promoting international dialogue on various issues that confront China and the world.

Also in this series:

Yu Keping, *Democracy Is a Good Thing: Essays on Politics, Society, and Culture in Contemporary China,* 2009

Hu Angang, *China in 2020: A New Type of Superpower,* 2011

He Weifang, *In the Name of Justice: Striving for the Rule of Law in China,* 2012

SOCIAL ETHICS IN A CHANGING CHINA

Moral Decay or Ethical Awakening?

HE HUAIHONG

BROOKINGS INSTITUTION PRESS

Washington, D.C.

The Brookings Institution is a private nonprofit organization devoted to research,
education, and publication on important issues of domestic and foreign policy. Its
principal purpose is to bring the highest quality independent research and analysis to
bear on current and emerging policy problems. Interpretations or conclusions in
Brookings publications should be understood to be solely those of the authors.

Library of Congress Cataloging-in-Publication data
He, Huaihong, 1954–
    Social ethics in a changing China : moral decay or ethical awakening? /
He Huaihong. — 1st [edition].
        pages   cm. — (The Thornton Center Chinese Thinkers series)
    Includes bibliographical references and index.
    ISBN 978-0-8157-2573-2 (hardcover : alk. paper) —
    ISBN 978-0-8157-2572-5 (ebook : alk. paper) 1. Social ethics—China.
2. Social change—China. I. Title.
    HN740.Z9M633 2015
    303.3'720951—dc23   2014047638

9 8 7 6 5 4 3 2 1

Typeset in Adobe Garamond

Composition by Peter Lindeman
Arlington, Virginia

CONTENTS

FOREWORD

JOHN L. THORNTON

He Huaihong's subject is no less than the soul of his country. Anyone who has met this renowned professor of philosophy and ethics can only be impressed by the depth of his learning and understanding of the human condition. In Professor He's view, China has reached a moral crossroads. He is troubled by the paradox of post–Cultural Revolution China, the period that has spanned his adult life. On the one hand, by almost any material measure, China has never been more prosperous or strong. Reform and Opening have moved hundreds of millions from poverty into the world's largest middle class. China's influence on world affairs is arguably broader and more consequential now than at any point in its long history. Yet, as Professor He observes, "Those achievements do not seem to have generated solidarity and cohesion among China's citizens; they have not built up our confidence in ourselves or each other" (see chapter 1).

Professor He attributes the "moral miasma" that he sees pervading Chinese society to a century of chaos and violence—the "tragic collision with the West," the fall of the Qing dynasty, decades of warlordism, the war with Japan, and the nihilism of the Cultural Revolution—that eviscerated 3,000 years of tradition and belief without nominating something lasting to take their place. And this process of destruction has only been abetted during "thirty years of heavy erosion by the market economy," leaving the country in a state of transition in which the old is gone, but the new has yet to take clear shape.

Nevertheless, despite his unblinking assessment of the state of China's social ethics, Professor He is not prone to despair. He has faith "in humanity and in particular the humanity of the Chinese people." And it is within this particular Chinese humaneness, established over millennia of continuous civilization, that he locates the sources and the possibility for an updated morality that could galvanize a confused society. In the volume's first essay, "New Principles: Toward a New Framework of Chinese Social Ethics," Professor He appropriates the structure and language of Confucianism familiar to all Chinese to propose a renewed set of "guidelines and constants" to govern proper behavior within a society.

Professor He's interests are as broad as his learning is deep. This rich volume of some of his finest essays includes his thinking on the Cultural Revolution's Red Guards, his moral argument against the death penalty (in a country that carries out more death sentences than any other country in the world), and the influence of the American moral philosopher John Rawls on the evolution of He's own thinking.

Two of his subjects, I believe, will be of particular interest to the Western reader. The first is his essay on the "selection society" (chapter 3), by which he refers to the examination system that China used for 2,000 years to select the officials who served the emperor and governed the country. The practice began in the Qin and Han dynasties (221 BC–220 AD) and became institutionalized over the centuries into a truly unique system for choosing a ruling class. While the integrity of the process could vary with a dynasty's fortunes, the truly remarkable characteristic about the system was how consistent and powerful it remained over time. Professor He points out that the highest government position of *zaixiang*, or chancellor, was overwhelmingly filled by officials who had risen through the examinations—sixty-four of seventy-one *zaixiang* during the Northern Song Dynasty, for instance. The process was even more rigorous in elevating only the very highest test scorers during dynasties such as the Ming and Qing.

The result was not only a ruling class that was intellectually capable and highly learned—it was a society that placed the highest value on scholarship, because influence and resources flowed from success in the examinations. The all-important examination system had effects far beyond the court and officialdom. It pervaded every corner of society and every aspect of life, even for ordinary people. The marriage of social mobility to learning made the Chinese "the most bookish culture in world history. Even those who could not read themselves understood that ink on paper was precious, and there was a universal reverence for literature and the written word" (see chapter 3).

Professor He wonders if a combination of the Western modern election system and the Chinese traditional selection system might produce a better solution to the challenges of modern governance. He notes that the strength of election systems is their ability to handle *egress*—"very successful in arranging peaceful transitions of power, but not as successful in selecting capable people to hold office." By contrast, the Chinese selection system has been more concerned with *ingress*—"highly successful in selecting people but not so successful in replacing them." He wonders if a synthesis of the two, combining their distinct strengths, might be feasible.

A second particularly topical essay in the volume is titled "On Possible Ways to Contain the Corruption of Power" (chapter 12). Although first published in 2005, it is prescient in anticipating many of the issues that confront President Xi Jinping and the unprecedented anticorruption campaign he is leading. Professor He advocates a combination of punishments and inducements to make corruption unattractive to officials. But, with the philosopher's focus on human nature, he also argues that the ultimate goal of external pressure must be to effect a fundamental change in character: "Rules constrain only those who are willing to be ruled; threats deter only those who are willing to be deterred; incentives work only on those who want to be motivated."

The analysis of social ethics in today's China presented by Professor He in this volume is formidable. It is natural to wonder if the new ethics he proposes is powerful enough to uproot and supplant the old. In the end, however, He's ultimate optimism derives from his rejection of the notion that "current problems mean that Chinese people are especially bad or that our national character is bad. Human nature does not vary much in this world" (see chapter 8). For the true causes, he points to the unique circumstances of history, culture, and political systems that created a particular ethical vacuum that afflicts society today. While in Professor He's view history may be immutable, culture and political systems are very much malleable, and thus it remains firmly within the control of the Chinese people to define a moral system that is at least the equal of their country's other remarkable achievements.

ACKNOWLEDGMENTS

China is now on the path to realizing the dream of prosperity and power that it has sought for nearly a hundred years. But in order to achieve sustainable economic growth, make progress toward the rule of law and democracy, and have its people obtain universal happiness, China still urgently needs to rebuild its social and ethical foundations—including its commitment to social justice and individual morality. Therefore I thank the scholars at the Brookings Institution for their interest in and concern about China's economic, social, political, and demographic transformation, and for publishing and promoting the Chinese Thinkers Series, including this volume on ethics.

First and foremost, I thank John L. Thornton, co-chairman of the Brookings Institution Board of Trustees and professor and director of Global Leadership at Tsinghua University. Soon after the plan for this book began, he and I had a heart-to-heart talk in Beijing, and it is because of his confidence and support that this book is being published. I greatly admire his foresight and boldness. I also thank the leadership at the Brookings Institution, including President Strobe Talbott, Executive Vice President Martin Indyk, and Acting Vice President and Director of Foreign Policy Bruce Jones, for their support of this project.

I am deeply grateful to Dr. Cheng Li, director of the John L. Thornton China Center at Brookings. He has continuously supported and contributed to this book project at every stage from organization to promotion, providing guidance in the selection of the book's key topics and essays and shepherding their translation, editing, and publication. Even before we met, I had heard from my wife, Shao Binhong, that Dr. Li is an honest, warm, enthusiastic, and wise person. After our many meetings and deep conversations in Beijing, I can attest to the accuracy of this description. He brings a valuable international perspective and tremendous insight to his research on China, and all of his academic work reflects a diligent, careful, enthusiastic, and rigorous attitude. During these last few years, each time Dr. Li visited Beijing he would always arrange to meet with me, often racing, travel-weary, from one side of Beijing to another.

My thanks also go to the strong team at the John L. Thornton China Center for their great assistance in the production of this volume. This has been a long process, and I appreciate the patience, diligence, and rigorousness of their work. Meara Androphy, the center's translation and publications coordinator, merits heartfelt thanks for her constant communication with me and her meticulousness and consideration during all stages of the book's publication, including her detailed revision of the translation, and her editing and proofreading of the English version. I thank Tony Zhao for creating the explanatory English notes for the Chinese names, events, and terms that appear in the volume, which are very helpful to the general readership. I also appreciate the editorial and other assistance of the center's remarkably capable Ryan McElveen, Vincent Wang, and Lucy Xu, and very talented interns Ming Ching Chai, Yuxin Zhang, and Jeffrey Zhao. I would like to also acknowledge Woo Lee for his help and input on the project.

I thank the entire team at the Brookings Institution Press who worked on this volume: Janet Walker, managing editor; Eileen Hughes, staff editor; and Vicky Macintyre, copy editor. Particular thanks go to Philip Hand, the primary translator of this volume, for his solid understanding of the original Chinese and the authenticity of his translation. If this book can inspire readers to consider and understand China's ethical issues, his translation will have played an important part in that effort. I would also like to thank Daniel Wright, a nonresident senior fellow at Brookings China Center, for his friendship with my family over the years, and for his support of this volume from start to finish.

My doctoral student and research assistant Pan Bin deserves special thanks for his enthusiastic support of my work, for collecting materials, editing articles, providing commentary on the book, and reviewing the translation. Wang Qiong of SUNY-Oneonta and Cai Zhen of East China Normal University are thanked for their comments on the translation, and Tan Ankui of Zhongshan University for his general remarks. In addition, several professors generously offered commentary on and endorsement of this book: Chen Lai, of Tsinghua University, Roger T. Ames of the University of Hawai'i, and Aloysius Patrick Martinich of the University of Texas at Austin. For any deficiencies and errors that might have survived all the above assistance, I, of course, bear sole responsibility.

I thank my family, especially my wife, Shao Binhong, for her continuous, enthusiastic support of this book project from the very beginning. She and our son Andy are the source of happiness in our daily lives, and they helped me at last finish this volume.

Finally, I want to thank this book's readers in advance for their interest in my book, and for any comments they may have.

He Huaihong
Beijing
June 2015

INTRODUCTION
Bringing Ethics Back into Chinese Discourse

CHENG LI

Civilization is a stream with banks. The stream is sometimes filled with blood from people killing, stealing, shouting and doing the things historians usually record, while on the banks, unnoticed, people build homes, make love, raise children, sing songs, write poetry and even whittle statues. The story of civilization is the story of what happened on the banks. Historians are pessimists because they ignore the banks for the river.
—WILL DURANT, *The Story of Civilization*

I first met Professor He Huaihong at a small café near the Law School of Peking University on an autumn afternoon in 2011. Actually, I came not to meet with him, but with his wife, Shao Binhong, executive editor of the journal *International Economic Review* and researcher at the Chinese Academy of Social Sciences (CASS). Shao is a former CCTV anchorwoman, best known for her primetime feature program, "Oriental Portraits."[1] We wanted to discuss Sino-American economic relations on the tenth anniversary of China's

Thanks go to Ming Ching Chai, Yinsheng Li, Yuxin Zhang, and Tony Zhao for their research assistance; and Meara Androphy, Ryan McElveen, Lucy Xu, and Jing Jing Zhang for their very helpful comments on an early version of this introductory chapter. I am also grateful to Daniel B. Wright for arranging my first meeting with He Huaihong and his wife, Shao Binhong, in Beijing in October 2011.

1. Shao Binhong produced about 300 episodes of the CCTV feature program "Oriental Portraits" (东方之子) in the 1990s and became a household name in the country.

accession to the World Trade Organization (WTO). Shao brought her husband He Huaihong to the meeting.

While fully engaged in the conversation, Professor He only occasionally made comments. He struck me as a soft-spoken, humble, gracious, and very knowledgeable gentleman. At the end of the meeting, he gave me his two recently published volumes, *The Hereditary Society* and *The Selection Society*. These two books served as the expanded version of his famous "dual study" of Chinese elite selection in ancient history and the ethical foundation of the governing structure of pre-1905 China.

I came to more fully appreciate He Huaihong's scholarship and his intellectual contributions, especially in the field of ethics, almost a year later. In the autumn of 2012, I began to solicit recommendations from scholars in China for a volume on ethics for the Thornton Center Chinese Thinkers series published by the Brookings Institution Press. To my surprise, the three distinguished Chinese public intellectuals I contacted—political scientist Yu Keping, legal scholar He Weifang, and philosopher Xu Youyu—all singled out He Huaihong as the most influential ethicist in China today.[2] I spent the following months reading He's writings and was deeply enthralled by his philosophical and historical narratives on ethical perplexity in present-day China. Fascinated by the depth and breadth of his intellectual inquiry, I often meet with Professor He whenever I visit Beijing. He and I have had several substantial discussions and numerous e-mail exchanges during the past three years.

It was hardly a coincidence that the three aforementioned prominent Chinese scholars, though strikingly different in terms of academic field, political status, and worldview, all regard He Huaihong as the country's leading ethicist. Combining masterful expertise on Chinese philosophical tradition with a deep knowledge of Western ethical theories, He Huaihong has produced a steady stream of widely respected scholarly publications on ethics and morality for almost three decades. He Huaihong is not an academic who isolates himself in an ivory tower and produces research that can only be understood

2. Yu Keping and He Weifang are the authors of the two earlier volumes of this series: Yu Keping, *Democracy Is a Good Thing: Essays on Politics, Society, and Culture in Contemporary China* (Brookings, 2009), and He Weifang, *In the Name of Justice: Striving for the Rule of Law in China* (Brookings, 2012). Both were named by the U.S.-based *Foreign Policy* magazine as among the World's 100 most influential thinkers in 2011. *Foreign Policy* website, November, 28, 2011 (http://foreignpolicy.com/2011/11/28/the-fp-top-100-global-thinkers-4/). Xu Youyu offered me the recommendation through his wife, Professor Yang Gonghua, China's leading epidemiologist.

by a handful of peers. On the contrary, He is known for his role as a public intellectual who is keenly interested in linking past with present, bridging East and West, and blurring academic boundaries.

As early as 1989, for example, He Huaihong translated *Meditations,* reflections of Marcus Aurelius, emperor of ancient Rome (161–180 CE) and one of the most important Stoic philosophers. *Meditations* is a monumental work in ethics that focuses on following nature as a source of guidance, peace, and inspiration at a time of tremendous physical tension and moral pressure. In November 2007, during his visit to Singapore, then Premier Wen Jiabao told journalists that *Meditations* was his "bedside book," and that he had read it more than 100 times.[3] The first Chinese version of this Marcus Aurelius masterpiece, translated by He Huaihong and published by the China Social Science Press in 1989, has sold more than 500,000 copies.[4]

Over the past three decades, through scholarly publications of both original works and translations, frequent lectures at academic conferences and in public forums, commentaries, and featured interviews in print, on television, and on social media, He Huaihong has emerged as one of the most influential thinkers in the country. These endeavors have transformed the Chinese public's understanding of the moral predicament underlying many news headlines and controversial issues in this rapidly changing country. Perhaps more effectively and constructively than anyone else, He Huaihong is bringing ethics back into Chinese discourse.

During the past half-century, the People's Republic of China (PRC) has experienced several incredible human-made dramas: Red Guard fanaticism, a loss of education for a whole generation during the Cultural Revolution, the Tiananmen tragedy, an economic miracle and the subsequent rise of money worship, rampant official corruption and the resulting legitimacy crisis of the Chinese Communist Party (CCP), and the ongoing and painstaking search

3. Qui Yang, "Pandian lingdaoren jianshu" [Review the books recommended by leaders], Xinhua Newsnet, December 17, 2013 (http://news.xinhuanet.com/book/2013-12/17/c_125870261_4.htm). There are over two dozen Chinese translations of *Meditations,* most of them from English versions. Probably the earliest one was translated by Liang Shiqiu. See Liang Shiqiu, *Chensi lu* [Meditations] (Taipei: Hsieh-chih Industrial Library, 1958). Liang's volume was a Chinese translation from the English translation by C. R. Haines, *Communings with Himself of Marcus Aurelius Antoninus, Emperor of Rome* (London: William Heinemann, 1916).

4. This number was provided by He Huaihong. See also Wang Jingjing, "He Huaihong: Rang wenhe chengwei zhuliu taidu" [Let the moderate attitude be the mainstream one], *Huanqiu renwu* [Global characters], No. 24, 2013.

for modern virtues in an ancient civilization. He Huaihong was not only an intimate witness to all of these extraordinary experiences; he also played a key role as a philosopher, historian, and social critic exploring the deeper intellectual and sociological origins of these events and their profound impacts on society's moral codes.

What, then, is the current status of ethics and morality in China? What are the causes of the widely perceived moral decay (*daode huapo*) and crisis of trust (*xinren weiji*) in Chinese society? Why is ethical discourse critically important to an assessment of China's reemergence in the twenty-first century? Does an analysis of ethical issues suffice to reveal the sociopolitical challenges and the ideological vacuum that China now confronts as a nation? What is the relationship between individual moral standards and social ethical norms, or between moral principles and the political system in a given country? How can China reconstruct a forward-looking and globally oriented moral order from the broken shards of the traditional ethical code? How should the Chinese rebuild their ethical norms? What kind of contemporary values and beliefs should the Chinese embrace? How should they tread the fine line between preserving Chinese ethical norms and promoting universal values at a time of unprecedented multidimensional, fast-paced globalization?

This volume, which includes some of He Huaihong's most important and representative works, will shed valuable light on all of these important questions. In a broader sense, the volume not only highlights the imperative for ethical discourse in a country that is increasingly seen by many as both a materialistic giant and a spiritual dwarf, but also demonstrates an innovative effort to rebuild the Chinese collective consciousness and social norms necessary for an ethical awakening. The ramifications of the reestablishment of systems of beliefs and ethics will be felt beyond China's national borders, especially now that the country is reemerging as a global power.

Chinese Concerns and Debates about Moral Decay

It seems a paradox—an irony—that the growing Chinese concerns about moral decay are occurring in a period when China is perceived by many people both at home and abroad to be rising, or reemerging, on the world stage. Top Chinese leaders—from Jiang Zemin and Hu Jintao to Xi Jinping—have often linked China's remarkable economic development in the reform era with what they have called "cultural advancement" (*wenhua zhenxing*) and "spiritual civilization" (*jingshen wenming*). At the turn of the century, Jiang

Zemin claimed that the CCP in the new environment of the twenty-first century should represent the "progressive course of China's advanced culture," "advanced productive forces," and "fundamental interests of the overwhelming majority of the Chinese people."[5] This so-called Theory of Three-Represents constituted a guiding ideological framework for this course.

In the Hu Jintao era, the CCP even claimed that China had reentered its "booming and golden age" (*shengshi*), similar to that of the Tang and Song dynasties.[6] For many years, the political establishment and official media used that phrase to characterize the achievements under Hu's leadership, especially in referring to landmark events like the 2008 Beijing Olympics and the 2010 Shanghai Expo. This complacent notion was met with much criticism in the country, however, not only from liberal public intellectuals but also from some senior officials.[7]

Ever since he became the top CCP leader in 2012, Xi Jinping has advocated the "Chinese dream" and "the great rejuvenation of the Chinese nation."[8] In a widely reported speech delivered in the fall of 2014 at an international conference in Beijing on the 2,665th anniversary of the birth of Confucius, Xi claimed that the CCP does not adhere to cultural nihilism but instead greatly values Confucianism and other important aspects of Chinese tradition.[9] For Xi, China's rise to prominence on the world stage should not lie solely in its economic accomplishments but also in public confidence in its cultural values and social ethics.[10]

5. "Sange daibiao zhongyao sixiang" [Important thoughts on the Three Represents], Xinhua Newsnet, January 21, 2003 (http://news.xinhuanet.com/ziliao/2003-01/21/content_699933.htm).

6. "Shengshi dayuebing" [Parade in the booming and golden age], People's Net, October 1, 2009 (http://022net.com/2009/10-1/502335113149597.html).

7. For example, Zi Zhongyun stated bluntly that underneath this superficial "booming and golden age," there is a profound sense of crisis in the making and deep concern about the moral decay of the regime. Hao Yu, "Zi Zhongyun: Zhongjian Zhishifenzi dui 'daotong' de dandang" [Resuming the role of intellectuals in ethics], *Jingji guancha bao* (Economic Observers), December 25, 2010. See also http://chinaelections.com/article/101/180995.html.

8. Xi Jinping, *Guanyu shixian zhonghua minzu weida fuxing de Zhongguo meng lunshu zhaibian* [Excerpts on the realization of the great rejuvenation of the Chinese dream] (Beijing: Central Literature Publishing House, 2013).

9. *Shijie ribao* [World Journal], September 25, 2014, p. A5.

10. For more discussion of Xi Jinping's effort to promote Confucian values, see Evan Osnos, "Confucius Comes Home," *New Yorker*, January 13, 2014.

The emphasis of top Chinese leaders on cultural and ethical advancement does not necessarily imply they would completely deny the moral predicament in reform-era China. Deng Xiaoping, for example, acknowledged on a number of occasions in the late 1980s that the greatest mistake during the first decade of post-Mao reforms was in the domain of education, referring not only to young students in schools, but also to the general public and the inadequacy of its ideological and ethical development.[11] Probably the Chinese leadership's most candid acknowledgment of their failures in reestablishing a belief system and reconstructing social ethics came from Wen Jiabao. In 2011 then premier Wen made an astonishingly forceful statement about the poor status of ethics in the wake of several horrifying food and drug safety scandals in the country: "These scandals are strong enough to show that the moral decay and loss of trust have reached an extremely serious point."[12] Wen further argued: "A country that fails to embody the high moral standards of its citizens can never become a truly powerful country or a respected nation."[13] Xi Jinping, expressing a similar sense of foreboding at the Politburo's first meeting under his leadership in 2012, referred pointedly to the rampant corruption among officials and its terrible impact on public confidence in the CCP: "Many facts tell us that corruption has become so widespread that it will ultimately destroy the party and the nation."[14]

Chinese public sentiment offers a more comprehensive explanation of the aforementioned concerns of the CCP leadership. The crises of trust and morality, which are commonplace in Chinese daily life, are reflected today in general empirical facts, as observed by Gao Zhaoming, professor of ethics at Nanjing Normal University.[15] In a large survey on "social diseases" in China

11. Xinhua Newsnet, February 23, 2015 (http://news.xinhuanet.com/ziliao/2005-02/23/content_2608913.htm).

12. Wen Jiabao, "Jiangzhenhua, chashiqing" [Examine the facts, and tell the truth], China Newsnet, April 14, 2011 (http://china.com.cn/policy/txt/2011-04/18/content_22381581_2.htm). It should be noted that some Chinese officials publicly rejected Wen's notion about the moral landslide. Fang Ming, "Wen Jiabao nuchi Zhongguo chengxin queshi yinqi renmin buman" [Premier Wen Jiabao angrily stated that the loss of trust causes resentment among the people], Sina Global News, October 22, 2011 (http://dailynews.sina.com/gb/chn/chnnews/ausdaily/20111022/20172861650.html).

13. Ibid.

14. Xinhua Newsnet, November 19, 2012 (see http://news.cntv.cn/18da/20121119/103379.shtml).

15. Gao Zhaoming, *Daode wenhua: cong chuantong dao xiandai* [Moral culture: From tradition to modernity] (Beijing: Renmin chubanshe, 2015), p. 53.

conducted in 2014, the "loss of trust" was ranked the top such condition. As many as 88 percent of respondents (60.2 percent fully agreed and 27.8 percent agreed somewhat) believed that China has been beset with a "social disease of moral decay and the loss of trust."[16] The country's ethical and moral problems are all too clear from the long list of widely occurring phenomena such as commercial fraud, tax fraud, financial deception, shoddy and dangerous engineering projects, fake products, tainted milk, poisonous bread, toxic pills, and decline in professional ethics among teachers, doctors, lawyers, Buddhist monks, and especially government officials.

These seemingly anecdotal social phenomena are actually symptomatic of what He Huaihong calls two "worrying aspects of our moral miasma": the "level of severity" and "the scale of the moral disruption." The first concern is that corruption is widespread among all levels of government. It has infected not only senior leaders such as former minister of railways Liu Zhijun, former head of the State Energy Administration Bureau Liu Tienan, former police chief and Politburo Standing Committee member Zhou Yongkang, and former vice chairman of the Central Military Commission Xu Caihou, each of whom was charged with stealing an exorbitant amount from state coffers. But even at lower levels, civil servants such as village heads, town heads, and local bank managers "are able to accumulate tens or even hundreds of millions of *yuan* in bribes. A district bureau chief may own dozens of houses" (see chapter 8).

As for the second worrying aspect, He Huaihong believes that corruption is not just a problem of governmental officials; it is a "failure of society" and signifies the collapse of ethical codes in the nation. Over the past decade, the Chinese media have reported countless terrible stories from daily life: in fear of legal liability or blackmail, bystanders offer no help when a little girl is hit by a car or an elderly person falls in the street (see chapter 1).[17] As chapter 9 ("Chinese People: Why Are You So Angry?") illustrates, the behavior on the streets can even turn savage. People who behave like this have one common characteristic: "They attempt to relieve their anger through violence. They try to use violence to solve their problems." Even worse, when a female driver

---

16. Xu Yanhong, Yuan Qing, and Tan Feng, "Dangqian shehui bingtai diaocha fenxi baogao" [Survey report on the social diseases of present-day China], *Renmin luntan* [People's Forum], September 1, 2014 (http://paper.people.com.cn/rmlt/html/2014-09/01/content_1476497.htm).

17. Xu Jilin, "Ruhe chongjian Zhongguo de lunli yu Xinyang" [How to rebuild China's ethics and faith], *Jinrongjia* [Financier], August 10, 2014 (http://chuansong.me/n/593505).

was severely beaten by a male driver in a recent road-rage incident in Chengdu and a video of it was posted online, a large number of social media commentaries blamed the female driver for her poor driving habits. As He Huaihong argues, all of these troubling phenomena indicate "fundamental trust and fundamental kindness are being lost in our society" (see chapter 8).

The breakdown in society's value system is reflected in a nationwide survey on the spiritual life of contemporary Chinese people conducted in 2014 by the Modern Chinese Thought and Culture Research Institute at East China Normal University. Nearly 60 percent of the respondents agreed that "people's values differ and therefore there should be no good or bad, right or wrong regarding moral issues." As Xu Jilin, a prominent historian of Chinese thought who helped design this research tool, observed, this staggeringly high figure reflects the crisis of moral standards in today's China.[18]

Similarly, a large number of Chinese scholars from diverse fields—law, sociology, politics, economics, and philosophy, as well as history—have expressed serious concern about moral decay and the loss of trust in contemporary China. According to Zhang Weiying, a prominent economist and former dean of the Guanghua School of Management at Peking University, "What China needs most is not law, but heavenly principles (*tianli*). There can be no genuine rule of law if its law neither complies with heavenly principles, nor does it speak to conscience."[19]

In place of heavenly principles and law, some observers find present-day China sadly filled with "hidden rules" (*qian guize*, 潜规则), a term coined by Wu Si, a prominent historian and former chief executive editor of the popular magazine *China through the Ages* (*Yanhuang Chunqiu*).[20] According to Wu Si, at a time of moral decline and loss of trust, "hidden rules" based on connections, favoritism, and unethical dealmaking tend to replace ethical codes and social norms. For example, as can happen in other countries, a young aspiring actor might follow such rules to his or her advantage to get a role in a film, on television, or in a play by granting sexual favors to the casting producer. "Hidden rules" have now penetrated virtually all aspects of Chinese public life.

---

18. Ibid.

19. Zhang Weiying, "Dangjin Zhongguo zui que tianli" [What present-day China needs the most is heavenly principles or ethics], *Wenzhai* [Digest], October 6, 2013. See also Duowei Net, http://opinion.dwnews.com/news/2013-10-06/59335074-all.html.

20. Wu Si, *Qian guize: Zhongguo lishi zhong de zhenshi youxi* [The hidden rules: Real games of Chinese history] (Shanghai: Fudan daxue chubanshe, 2009).

Even the field of education has been infected by corruption, as pointed out by Zi Zhongyun, former director of the Institute of American Studies at CASS who served as an interpreter for both Mao Zedong and Zhou Enlai. In a widely viewed 2014 media interview in China, she recounted an extraordinary story about a middle school student who was caught cheating but whose father accused the school of being unfair to his son. In a quite bizarre (but also thought-provoking) fashion, the father reasoned: for a kid from a nonofficial family who had no privileges or special access, cheating was the only "fair game." The father claimed the school's crackdown on cheating meant "there would be no fairness at all for kids who come from humble families."[21] According to Zi, the moral decay of the Chinese nation, especially as it has already penetrated into the critically important domain of education, is "very sad and enormously frightening."[22]

For Sun Liping, a distinguished professor of sociology at Tsinghua University, the defining predicament that confronts the country is rooted in "social decay" (*shehui kuibai*).[23] In his view, the greatest threat to China is not social unrest, but social decay. Whereas most analysts of China (both domestic and foreign) are concerned about mass protests and serious tensions between interest groups, Sun is more worried about social decay, which at its core indicates the abuse of power. In China today, argues Sun, power is neither constrained by external forces in society nor controlled by any internal mechanism. As a result, corruption has not only reached an unprecedentedly large scale among officials but has also spawned a wide assortment of social phenomena such as unrestrained interest groups, serious erosion of social equity and justice, the convergence of money and power, the loss of professional ethics, and a decline in basic moral standards. All of these problems, says Sun, reflect the fundamental flaw of China's market reform: the failure to reestablish value objectives for a renewed civilization.

21. Zi Zhongyun, *Xiansheng cengjing zheyang shangxue: Zi Zhongyun he tade xiaoyuan* [When I was attending school: Zi Zhongyun and her experience on campus] (Beijing: CITIC Publishing House, 2014).

22. Ibid.

23. Sun Liping, "Zuida weixie fei shehui dongdang ershi shehui kuibai" [The greatest threat to China is not social unrest, but the social decay of the country], *Nanfang ribao* [Southern Daily], February 28, 2009. See also 21CN Net, http://news.21cn.com/today/zhuanlan/2009/02/28/5930537.shtml. For more discussion of Sun Liping's notion of social decay, see Sun Liping, *Shouwei de dixian: Zhuanxing shehui shenghuo de jichu zhixu* [Minimal responsibility: The basic order of social life in a transformational Chinese society] (Beijing: Shehuikexue wenxian chubanshe, 2007).

Two main factors—or historical circumstances—have contributed to moral decay in present-day China. First, Mao's philosophy of violent class struggle, especially the violent Red Guard movement during the Cultural Revolution, had a detrimental effect on the country's ethical foundation. By way of illustration, in his discussion of Red Guard violence, He Huaihong mentions an incident that might be incomprehensible to those unaware of the details of the Cultural Revolution: "Another Red Guard group had caught someone that they claimed was an 'old conservative boss.' They shot him in the head in front of a hotel and then went to eat inside, leaving the body in the street. All evening, going in and out of the hotel, they just pretended not to see it" (see chapter 6). It was astonishing that this sort of humiliation, torture, and murder occurred in public, before the eyes of so many people. The Cultural Revolution was an extraordinary period during which children condemned parents, husbands betrayed wives, and students tortured teachers—all for political and ideological reasons. In its aftermath many Chinese asked themselves how they could believe or trust anyone in authority after such a dark age in recent Chinese history.

The intellectual ferment in the post-Mao era from the late 1970s to the late 1980s, especially its critical reflection on the decade-long political fanaticism and human suffering of the Cultural Revolution, led to the subsequent call for humanism.[24] In a sense, the Chinese discussion of humanism represented a search for an ethical and moral awakening. Unfortunately, this movement toward enlightenment did not last long, partly because of the government's crackdown on large-scale public discourse on the political and ethical sources of the turmoil. The famous writer Ba Jin's appeal for the establishment of a Cultural Revolution museum, for example, was sadly rejected. The search for ethical awakening came to a halt mainly because the nation was caught up in another overwhelmingly rapid socioeconomic transformation—market reform, also recognized as the era of money worship (see chapter 7).

Money worship, He Huaihong believes, is another factor contributing to the crisis of faith and moral decay.[25] Today, four decades after Mao's death, China is very different, not only in its national character but also in that of

24. The call for humanism in the post-Mao era was most evident in the literature. Representative works include Dai Houying "Ren a ren" [Stones in the wall], *Huacheng* [City of Flowers], No. 11 (November), 1980; Dai Houying, *Shiren zhisi* [Death of a poet] (Shanghai: Taibai wenyi chubanshe, 1994); and Lu Xinhua, "*Shanghen*" [Scar], *Wenhui Daily*, August 11,1978.

25. Gao, *Daode wenhua*, p. 538.

its individuals. As a nation, China is set to become an economic giant on the world stage; perhaps it is one already (see chapter 4). But it fails to show the world its true values and beliefs. As individuals, "Chinese now have drummed up their purses, but their spirit tends to be empty," in the words of Zi Zhongyun.[26] Extensive interviews with Chinese people in various walks of life led Evan Osnos, former foreign correspondent in Beijing for the *New Yorker*, to a similar observation: "The Cultural Revolution dismantled China's ancient belief systems, and the economic revolution that followed could not rebuild them. Prosperity had yet to define the ultimate purpose of the nation and the individual. There was a hole in Chinese life that people called the *jingshen kongxu*—'the spiritual void.'"[27]

A well-known Chinese saying vividly captures the ramifications of the spiritual and moral decay in present-day China from a historical perspective: "China lost its Middle Kingdom with the end of the Ming; its Han ethnicity with its conquest by the Qing; its faith with the Cultural Revolution; and its morality with economic reform."[28]

Not all Chinese ethicists and public intellectuals agree with the negative assessment of the current status of ethics. As some point out, moral decay was talked about even back in the ancient time of the Middle Kingdom. As early as the Spring and Autumn Period (770–476 BCE), when etiquette and a code of ethics were closely observed, the "disintegration of propriety" (*libeng yuehuai*) was a growing concern. And throughout the entire twentieth century, if not earlier, writers in both China and abroad described the "deep-rooted bad habits" of the Chinese people (*guomin liegenxing*).[29] These are most evident in some of Lu Xun's well-known fictional characters. The provocative writings of the Taiwanese author Bo Yang, especially his famous book *The Ugly Chinaman*, reaffirmed this long-standing criticism of China's

26. Zi Zhongyun, "Renxing, wenhua zhidu" [Humanity, culture, and institution], Consensus Net, August 2, 2012 (http://21ccom.net/articles/zgyj/gmht/article_20120 80164907.html).

27. Osnos, "Confucius Comes Home." For his work that won the 2014 National Book Award, see Evan Osnos, *Age of Ambition: Chasing Fortune, Truth, and Faith in the New China* (New York: Farrar, Straus and Giroux, 2014).

28. "Mingwang zhihou wu huaxia, manqing zhihou wu hanren; wenge zhihou wu xinyang, gaige zhihou wu daode" (明亡之后无华夏，满清之后无汉人，文革之后无信仰，改革之后无道德).

29. "Guomin liegenxing: yige wenhua de huangyan" ["Deep-rooted bad habits" of the Chinese people: A lie about the Chinese culture], *Tushuguan* [Library], March 1, 2012 (http://360doc.com/content/12/0301/16/904434_190857084.shtml).

ethical and cultural norms.[30] According to some PRC critics, the influential works of Lu Xun, Bo Yang, and others have helped create a value-laden and biased dichotomy between Confucian ethical rubbish and Western ethical essence. This, they say, has given rise to "a die-hard lie" both about Chinese culture and about the status of ethics in China today, for the Chinese are neither better nor more abhorrent than any other nationals in terms of barbarism, ignorance, tyranny, and cruelty. As an anonymous Chinese scholar concludes, "The crimes conducted by the Chinese during the past century could not be worse than the crimes and atrocities inflicted on various groups of indigenous populations by colonial racists in world history."[31]

Some other Chinese scholars have tried to downplay the extreme depth of moral decay in today's China by pointing out that major socioeconomic transformation and political change are bound to have an impact on a country. As world history makes clear, a nation in the throes of rapid socioeconomic transformation is likely to experience some sort of spiritual and ethical crisis.[32] As one Chinese scholar has observed, the former Soviet Union and other post-Communist Eastern European countries all experienced such a crisis and saw the cult of money worship take hold during their socioeconomic and political transitions.[33] The same could be said of many European countries in the fifteenth to seventeenth centuries and the United States from 1865 to 1914, when Americans went through the periods of Reconstruction, the Gilded Age, and the Progressive Era, marked by rapid industrialization and a surge in immigration.[34]

Tu Weiming, former director of the Harvard-Yenching Institute at Harvard University and currently a professor of philosophy at Peking University, believes that the ongoing Chinese discourse on morality could not only bring ethics back into critical focus but also encourage the Chinese to rethink their tradition, especially Confucianism, in a more positive light.[35] According to

30. Lu Xun, *The True Story of Ah-Q* (Beijing: Foreign Languages Press, 1960); and Bo Yang, *Choulou de zhongguoren* [The Ugly Chinaman] (Taipei: Yuanliu chuban, 2009).

31. "Guomin liegenxing."

32. Gao, *Daode wenhua*, p. 99.

33. Li Xiaohong, *Zhongguo Zhuanxingqi shehui xinyong huanqing yanjiu* [Study of social credit and trust in China's transitional period] (Beijing: Economic Publishing House, 2008), p. 1.

34. Ibid.

35. Tu Weiming, "Rujia renwen jingshen de pushi jiazhi" [Universal values of the Confucian human spirit], *Renmin luntan* [People's Forum], August 11, 2014. See also People's Net, http://theory.people.com.cn/n/2014/0806/c112848-25414997.html.

Tu, of the five spiritual leaders who shaped civilizations around the world—Confucius, Socrates, Buddha, Jesus, and Mohammed—only Confucius has suffered constant maligning in contemporary China. Among the civilizations existing at the same time, according to Tu, only the Chinese civilization has continued for 5,000 years without interruption.[36] In Tu's view, this remarkable continuity stems from the Confucian tradition, and Confucian ethical codes for individual behaviors will likely become part of the common language of citizens of the world in the twenty-first century.[37]

Some Chinese scholars find that the ongoing intellectual discourse on morality in China is itself a very encouraging development. While the field of philosophy has been largely marginalized around the world in recent decades, its subfield of ethics seems to have attracted an increasing number of Chinese scholars and students.[38] Li Zehou, Chen Jiaying, and Li Meng, for example, represent three different generations of distinguished Chinese philosophers whose important works in ethics have enriched this subfield.[39] For He Huaihong, critical views of ethics, culture, politics, and history (as exemplified in the above discussion) have significantly broadened his horizon.

This review of Chinese concerns and debates about the country's ethical status provides a broad context in which to assess He Huaihong's scholarly work. The intellectual journey that He has undertaken is understandably very challenging. He needs to address tough questions, both politically and intellectually, regarding individual moral standards versus social ethics, morality versus legality, personal responsibility versus institutional accountability, and cultural pluralism versus universal values. More important, He Huaihong strives to reconstruct a new intellectual framework of Chinese social ethics. A discussion of the personal and professional experiences of this leading Chinese ethicist will provide more clues about what he hopes to accomplish in China's search for a new ethical order.

36. Tu, "Rujia renwen jingshen de pushi jiazhi."

37. Ibid.

38. Gan Shaoping, *Lunlixue de dangdai jiangou* [Modern construction of ethics] (Beijing, China Development Press, 2015, p. 22).

39. For their representative works, see Li Zehou, *Lunlixue gangyao* [Outline of ethics] (Beijing: Renmin ribao chubanshe, 2010); Chen Jiaying, *Hewei lianghao shenghuo* [What is the good life?] (Shanghai: Shanghai Wenyi chubanshe, 2015); and Li Meng, *Ziran shehui* [Nature society] (Shanghai: SDX Joint Publishing Company, 2015).

He Huaihong and His Search for a Philosophy of Life

He Huaihong was born in a rural area of Qingjiang County (now Zhangshu City), Jiangxi Province, in December 1954. The Cultural Revolution began just as he was entering middle school. As a teenager, he worked as a porter in Nanchang County, Jiangxi Province, for a year. He belongs to the so-called lost generation, the age cohort born in the 1950s, and his formative years coincided with the "decade of political turmoil" (1966–76). In his pre-college education, which included classical Chinese and history, He Huaihong was largely self-taught. In 1972, at eighteen, He was recruited to the People's Liberation Army (PLA) and was stationed in an economically disadvantaged region of Inner Mongolia for six years.[40]

In 1979 he was transferred from Inner Mongolia to Shanghai, where he later attended an eighteen-month program at the Political Institute of the Air Force. There he spent most of his time studying English and reading scholarly works by both Chinese and Western authors. Like most of his generation, He Huaihong never had formal training in any foreign language, but he was very fond of languages. Reading foreign language materials, especially literature and intellectual history, served as the wonderful window, or in He's words, "a magnificent door," opening into to an entirely new world.[41] As a young man who had just escaped the "long imprisonment in an intellectual desert filled with dogmatic worship," He Huaihong was thirsty for knowledge and was very receptive to anything foreign and fresh.[42] As he later recalled, at that time he could even recite many parts of Ernest Hemingway's novel *The Old Man and the Sea* in English. In the late 1980s, He taught himself Latin, French, and German.

After graduating from the Political Institute of the Air Force, He Huaihong began teaching at the Air Force Academy in Beijing in the fall of 1980. When he was demobilized in the early 1980s, he briefly worked as a researcher at the Academy of Social Sciences of Jiangxi Province in Nanchang. In 1984 he took the entrance examination for graduate school and enrolled in the ethics program (first for a master's degree and then for a doctoral degree) at Renmin University in Beijing. The university was very strong in the social sciences and humanities, including philosophy and ethics.

40. Part of this discussion about the personal and professional life of He Huaihong is based on He Huaihong, *Zixuan ji* [Selected works] (Guilin: Guangxi Normal University Press, 2000).

41. He, *Zixuan ji*, p. 338.

42. Ibid.

The post–Cultural Revolution years were an exciting period in which young Chinese were extremely enthusiastic about absorbing Western liberal ideas. This was a time when the old faith and attitudes had collapsed while new ones were yet to be established. Unlike their counterparts in today's China who may not be bothered by the lack of ideological beliefs, college students and young professionals at that time often felt something important missing in their lives. During that period, He Huaihong became profoundly interested in the works of Western philosophers, including Socrates, Plato, Immanuel Kant, and John Rawls. He was curious about many long-standing issues: how the interaction between human beings and the environment shapes human relationships, the differences between moralities across cultures, the true meaning of Chinese national character, how to evaluate ethics through cross-cultural comparisons, and the circumstances in which a new set of ethical codes in a given country can be established.[43]

During this time, He Huaihong began to think he would devote his career to the study of ethics. What attracted him to the field is its concern with the "philosophy of life" (*rensheng zhexue*) and focus on people.[44] His first book, titled *Contemplating Life: Comments on Pascal* and published in 1988, is about the seventeenth-century French mathematician, physicist, and philosopher Blaise Pascal. This legendary intellectual giant not only made great contributions to science but also produced some groundbreaking works for the important philosophies that emerged in the following centuries, such as existentialism, pragmatism, and voluntarism. He Huaihong was particularly intrigued by the way in which Pascal dealt with philosophical paradoxes such as between infinity and limit, faith and reason, and death and life. The following remarks make clear the impact of Pascal's work on He Huaihong's own philosophical view: "Human beings are finite space-time existences, but they seek to reach beyond their own limitations to become infinite. It is when people feel limited in the face of [the] infinite, that they sense their trivialness, and feel a mysterious fear and trembling. Yet, people will never give up and relax their efforts."[45] Pascal's notion of human beings' three hierarchical levels of greatness—in order of lower to higher: the greatness of an emperor or a head

43. Ibid., p. 349.

44. Ibid.

45. He Huaihong, "Kewang wuxian" [In search of unlimited], Xilu Net, October 23, 2002 (http://club.xilu.com/hnzqz3/msgview-135899-24174.html).

of state, the greatness of sprit and thought, and the greatness of benevolence and kindness—has greatly influenced He Huaihong's philosophy.[46]

Throughout He Huaihong's career—whether in his academic writings or wider public outreach, whether in his painstaking efforts to reestablish a new ethical order for China, or in his call for a Chinese ethical dialogue with the West and the world—the philosophy of life, or the principle of life, is always a central theme (see chapter 11). He believes that "whether Chinese or foreign, ancient or modern, life should always be the first and foremost concern."[47] He Huaihong highlights three reasons for his pursuit. First, "life is the primary and most fundamental value of humanity; it is the precondition for all other human values." Second, "life is precious in itself—that is, it is precious as an end in itself, not just as a means." And third, "the life of every person is equally valuable" (see chapter 18).

In the summer of 1982, He Huaihong read the English translation of Jean-Paul Sartre's *Being and Nothingness* and became fascinated with existentialism, particularly Sartre's two types of being: "being-in-itself" and "being-for-itself." While "being-in-itself" can only be approximated by human beings, "being-for-itself" is the being of consciousness. This concept has greatly influenced He Huaihong's own work, especially his theory of conscience and the notion of "minimum moral standards." Over the following years, He delved more deeply into the works of other important proponents of existentialism such as Gabriel Marcel, Karl Jaspers, Martin Heidegger, Albert Camus, and especially two of its pioneers in the nineteenth century, Friedrich Nietzsche and Søren Kierkegaard. Their works helped He Huaihong eventually depart from Sartre's more extremist views of self-being in the realization that Sartre's philosophy is "too far away from reality, and too far from the lives of real people."[48]

In his early professional career, He Huaihong made an exceptional contribution to the dissemination of Western ideas and values in China through translation. He translated nine important classic books on ethics into Chinese, totaling approximately 1.6 million words.[49] In addition to the aforementioned *The Meditations* by Marcus Aurelius (1989), he translated or cotranslated *Introduction to Ethics* by Frank Thilly (1987), *Moral Maxims* by

46. Hu Huaihong, *Bi tiankong geng guangkuo* [Wider than the sky] (Shanghai: SDX Joint Publishing Company, 2003), p. 3.

47. Hu Huaihong, "Cong 'zunzun qinqin xianxian' dao 'ziyou pingdeng boai'" ["From 'respect, love, and virtue' to 'freedom, equality, and fraternity'"], Chinese Studies Net, November 16, 2014 (http://bbs.gxsd.com.cn/forum.php?mod=viewthread&tid=962524).

48. He, *Zixuan ji*, pp. 343–44.

François de La Rochefoucauld (1987), *A System of Ethics* by Friedrich Paulsen (1988), *Anarchy, State, and Utopia* by Robert Nozick (1991), and *On Tyranny* by Leo Strauss (2006). Among Chinese scholars and students of ethics and philosophy, He Huaihong is widely considered the primary translator who introduced John Rawls's masterpiece *A Theory of Justice* (1989, 2001, 2009) to Chinese readers. Besides his scholarly contributions and translations in the field of philosophy and ethics, He Huaihong has published a large number of commentaries for general Chinese readership on a wide variety of topics such as Fyodor Dostoevsky's novels, Jean-Paul Sartre's plays, and José Ortega y Gasset's essays.

Despite his extensive research and publications on Western philosophy and foreign cultures as a young scholar in the 1980s, He Huaihong did not forsake his study of Chinese philosophy and traditional culture. He was keenly aware of the need to make up for all of the lost years in his educational development due to the Cultural Revolution. He called his age cohort "the generation growing up with a deep fracture in Chinese tradition and culture."[50] He undertook a strictly planned study of important Chinese classics and read very extensively all major works on traditional ethics, ranging from the main classics in pre-Qin, pre-Wei and Jin, and pre-Sui and Tang eras as well as those from the Song, Yuan, Ming, and Qing dynasties. As He Huaihong later recalled, this decade-long "educational make-up" gave him a "more comprehensive understanding of the main elements of Chinese history and culture as well as its origins and ramifications."[51]

In his doctoral dissertation, "Contract Ethics and Social Justice" (1990), He Huaihong explored the philosophical logic among propositions about life preservation, promotion of law, property rights, and equal distribution of profits, all in the name of justice. He also analyzed the contrasting priorities between equality and liberty in light of the debate between John Rawls and Robert Nozick. This discussion had strong relevance for China in the late 1980s and early 1990s, when the private sector reemerged. One year before receiving his Ph.D. degree, He began teaching philosophy and ethics at the China Youth University for Political Sciences in Beijing. He spent one year at Harvard University as a visiting scholar in 1993–94, which he calls the "most pleasant and productive year of learning and reading in my career."[52] During this period of foreign study he learned to recognize the importance of cul-

49. Ibid., p. 346.
50. Ibid., p. 353.
51. Ibid., p. 356.
52. Ibid., p. 348.

tural pluralism and the imperative for diversity and mutual respect in a globalized world.[53] After he returned to China, He taught at the Institute of Chinese Studies of the Chinese Academy of Arts in Beijing from 1995 to 1998.

In 1994 He Huaihong wrote *A Theory of Conscience: The Transformation of Traditional Morality in the New Society*—his most important book on Chinese ethics, as he described in the preface to the 2009 edition.[54] This book has been widely seen as "a groundbreaking work in the study of the Chinese traditional philosophy."[55] Partly because of the book's great contribution to the field of philosophy and ethics, Peking University's Department of Philosophy recruited He Huaihong to its faculty in 1998. He has been a full professor in the department ever since and previously also served as the director of the department's Ethics Program for many years. As He Huaihong points out, Peking University was the cradle of the contemporary Chinese study of ethics.[56] Established in 1912, the Department of Philosophy had many leading scholars serving on its faculty over the century, including Cai Yuanpei, Hu Shi, Jiang Menglin, Xiong Shili, Liang Shuming, Feng Youlan, Zhu Guangqian, Zhang Dainian, and Tang Yijie. The founders of the CCP, Chen Duxiu and Li Dazhao, taught in the department in their early careers. The first contemporary Chinese textbook on ethics was written by Liu Shipei, the first book on the history of Chinese ethics was written by Cai Yuanpei, and the first Chinese book on comparative ethics was written by Huang Jianzhong—all three of whom served as professors of philosophy at Peking University at the time of publication.[57]

In the past two decades, the department has recruited a number of internationally known scholars, including Rainer Schäfer, who previously taught at University of Heidelberg and University of Bonn, and the aforementioned Tu Weiming. Inspired by both the great tradition in the study of philosophy at Peking University and extensive exposure to Western schools of thought

53. Ibid., p. 349.

54. He Huaihong, *Liangxin lun* [A theory of conscience], revised ed. (Beijing: Peking University Press, 2009), p. 1.

55. Shao Zijie, "Zhou Zhixing duihua He Huaihong: Fenlie shidai de zuidi xiandu gongshi" [Zhou Zhixing's dialogue with He Huaihong: minimum consensus at a time of split], Consensus Net, August 13, 2011 (http://21ccom.net/articles/sxwh/shsc/article_2011081343175.html).

56. He Huaihong, *Shengsheng dade* [The great virtue of life-giving] (Beijing: Peking University Press, 2011), p. 134.

57. Ibid.

through professional exchanges, He Huaihong has been remarkably prolific in his intellectual pursuits over the past two decades.

He Huaihong is also one of very few Chinese scholars who incorporate a grasp of Chinese ethical theories with broad expertise in the culture, history, religion, literature, and politics of the country. His study of the circulation of Chinese elites over time, or what he calls the dynamics between "the hereditary society" and "the selection society" (Chinese meritocracy) provides a new perspective on China's 3,000-year history, pointing to the development of a unique sociopolitical structure—a system that holds cultural and intellectual elites in high regard and has promoted social mobility and equal opportunities.[58] While the system was certainly not free from the abuse of power, nepotism, factionalism, and corruption, traditional China did establish a "true selection society in which learning was for the purpose of advancement and the ruling elite was selected from the best scholars" (see chapter 3). As He Huaihong has documented, throughout China's long history the door to membership in the ruling class was often open to those of humble origins. In the Ming dynasty, for example, over 50 percent of officials (*jinshi*) were born into three-generation nonofficial families.[59] This historical fact, He Huaihong argues, shows that China was a part of the global march toward modernity in Tocqueville's terms, as it reflects a shift toward equality (see chapter 3).

In the past decade, He Huaihong has become more conscious of his role as an ethicist in a country searching for cultural and ethical rejuvenation. Hence he has written several nonacademic books for general readership emphasizing the centrality of life in ethical discourse and has been an active participant in the public discourse on ethics in the news media.[60] In the early 2000s, for example, he wrote several dozen essays in his column "Bottom-Line Ethics" in the popular newspaper *New Beijing Daily*, commenting on a wide range of ethical and moral issues such as animal rights, the death penalty, and respect for minority groups (see chapter 13).[61] His most important objectives, as He explicitly asserts, are "to tell stories about our own his-

58. He, *Zixuan ji*, p. 358.

59. He Huaihong, *Xuanju shehui* [The selection society], revised ed. (Beijing: Peking University Press 2011), p. 100.

60. He Huaihong, *Zunzhong shengming* [Respect life] (Guangzhou: Guangdong Jiaoyu Publishing House, 1998).

61. He Huaihong, *Zhongguo de youshang* [The sorrow of China] (Beijing: Law Press, 2011), p. 258.

tory, to resolve the problems confronting our nation, and to build our own research framework."[62]

Minimum Moral Standards and Maximum Ethical Concerns

Arguably the most important contribution that He Huaihong has made to the field of ethics is twofold: his theoretical concept of minimum moral standards, on the one hand, and his broad and multidisciplinary approach to promoting maximum ethical concerns, on the other.

MINIMUM MORAL STANDARDS: UNIVERSAL ETHICS

During the past half-century, if not longer, Chinese society has repeatedly and continually failed to observe minimum moral standards. In He Huaihong's words, that failure "threatens the very foundation of our society" (see chapter 10). In He's view, it is imperative for the Chinese nation to hold the bottom line in ethical codes and social norms. Over the past two decades, the phrase most frequently used in his scholarly writing and public outreach is "minimum moral standards" (*dixian lunli*, 底线伦理). There are a number of English translations of He Huaihong's concept of minimum moral standards, including "bottom-line ethics," "minimalist ethics," and "moral minimalism."[63] The concept can be traced back to the writings of Western philosophers such as Immanuel Kant, William David Ross, and John Rawls, who all sought a consensus on basic moral norms or a primary moral obligation.[64] After World War II, philosopher Theodor W. Adorno, a German exile living in the United States, returned to his homeland and wrote *Minima Moralia: Reflections from Damaged Life*, which further developed the concept of minimum moral standards in the wake of all of the horrible tragedies caused by fascism in the first half of the twentieth century.[65]

He Huaihong has substantially advanced the theory of minimum moral standards, especially by combining it with Chinese traditional philosophy. He divides minimum moral standards into three categories: first, the basic natural and social responsibilities that every person must meet; second, standards associated with laws and social institutions; and third, professional

62. He, *Zixuan ji*, p. 341.

63. For a more detailed discussion of the conceptual development of minimum moral standards, see He, *Shengsheng dade*, p. 193.

64. Ibid., p. 192.

65. Theodor Adorno, *Minima Moralia: Reflections from Damaged Life*, translated by E. F. N. Jephcott (New York: Verso, 2006).

ethics and morality of specific areas of human activity, for example, government and the Internet (see chapter 10).

He Huaihong argues that society and individuals should all fulfill their own responsibilities. For society, these fall in the realm of social justice while for individuals they pertain to basic obligations, the foremost being "respect for human life and liberty."[66] Furthermore, minimum moral standards should be (1) *perpetual* (in the sense of "continuity between traditional society and modern"), honored all the time; (2) *objective*, not subject to changes in different circumstances; and (3) *universal*, beyond cultural and ethnic boundaries.

The first of these traits, He Huaihong believes, has ties to the Chinese traditional concept of conscience (*liangxin*, 良心 or *liangzhi*, 良知), which was thought to guide individuals in the development of basic moral and ethical codes. In *A Theory of Conscience*, He systematically explores traditional culture's great attention to these basic moral standards and its view that conscience is a natural and inherent gift.[67] This is reflected in the remarks of early Chinese philosopher Mencius, for example, who noted that "humans all have the feeling of compassion."[68]

Traditional Chinese ethics also provides rational reasons why a consensus on minimum moral standards is both feasible and desirable. Confucius's motto "Do not do unto others what you would not have done to yourself" speaks loud and clear about the rationality of such a consensus.[69] He Huaihong agrees that a human being's fundamental sense of compassion, sympathy, and responsibility is real, "but it is often weakened by a range of influences to the point that it no longer disciplines us and drives our conduct" (see chapter 1). Therefore he claims that "we need to work on every level of our consciousness: beliefs, emotions, rationality, experience, intuition. We must not reject any idea on any level that could help us in our fight to improve the environment. And we must hope that no matter how minimal it may be, we can find some broad-based consensus and broad-based will to act" (see chapter 15).

---

66. He, *Liangxin lun*, pp. 337, 241; Dao Erdun, "Du He Huaihong Xin gangchang" [On He Huaihong's *New Principles*]. *Nanfang Zhoumu* [Southern Weekly], August 6, 2013. See also http://infzm.com/content/93455; and Yin Zhenqiu, "He Huaihong 'dixian lunli' sixiang chouyi" [Discussion of He Huaihong's "minimum moral standards"], *Daode yu wenming* [Morality and Civilization], No. 2 (2010).

67. He, *Liangzin lun*, p. 7.

68. "Ceyin zhixin, renjieyouzhi" [恻隐之心,人皆有之].

69. "Jisuo buyu, wushi yuren" [己所不欲，勿施于人].

As for the second trait, He Huaihong argues that because minimum moral standards are based on objective criteria, they should not be subject to change and cannot be decreased. Otherwise, these standards would be more like "springboards" (*tanhuang*) rather than a "bottom line" (*dixian*).[70] That is to say, they are basic global norms that aim to ban murder, theft, fraud, and rape and call for a compassionate and humane approach to other people.[71] Because these ethical codes are so basic and minimal, they are able to reach the maximum range of consensus.

This emphasis on objectivity leads to the notion of universal ethics (*pubian lunli*, 普遍伦理), the third trait of He Huaihong's theory of minimum moral standards. In He's view, such standards should apply equally to all individuals, all groups, all classes, and all nations without exception.[72] This does not mean that human values around the world are or should be the same. In He's words, "People's values and ultimate concerns are varied; they may contradict and even clash with each other" (see chapter 2). He Huaihong reasons that an ethical system consists of two main components: normative principles and value-based beliefs, so that "when we consider universal ethics, we must give priority to the norms of moral behavior rather than value systems" (see chapter 2).

At the same time, He Huaihong firmly believes in universal values (*pushi jiazhi*, 普世价值) and argues that universal ethics are achievable for the very reason that some values are shared universally. For He Huaihong, "human nature does not vary much in this world" and "traditional Chinese moral habits bear creditable comparison with those of any culture in the world" (see chapter 8). He also believes that values, like ideas, can be disseminated across national borders. In a recent article on American democracy and constitutionalism, He Huaihong stated that the May Fourth Movement disseminated many Western ideas into China, including not only Marxism, but also so-called Mr. Democracy, Mr. Science, Mr. Law, and Mr. Morality.[73] Some of these concepts have notably stirred intellectual discourse in twentieth-century China. In He's

70. Liu Lu, "Zhengzhi meiyou namonan" [Honesty should not be difficult], *Jiefang ribao* [Liberation Daily], May 9, 2014. See also Chinese Writers Net, http://www.chinawriter.com.cn/2014/2014-05-09/203192.html.

71. Shao, "Zhou Zhixing duihua He Huaihong."

72. Ibid.

73. He Huaihong, "Meiguo shi you yige guannian chansheng de guojia, zhege guannian jiushi 'Duli Xuanyan'" [The United States is a country that was born with a concept, and that concept is called the *Declaration of Independence*] *Fenghuang dushu* [Phoenix Reading], November 26, 2013 (http://chuansong.me/n/240070).

words, "without reference to Western ideas, a modern and contemporary Chinese history would not know where to start. These ideas and values have been deeply assimilated into our daily lives and various institutions."[74]

In a sense, while minimum moral standards are not subject to change, ideological values, cultural norms, and social ethics in a given country do change, sometimes quite profoundly. Cong Riyun, a well-known public intellectual and professor at the China University of Political Science and Law, recently asked an intriguing question: Which "cultural gap" is bigger: the one between present-day China and present-day United States, or that between China today and the China of 200 years ago? Cong's answer was undoubtedly the latter, as he jokingly said that more than half of the women in the country today would probably commit suicide if required to live in nineteenth-century China. This point illustrates the impact of the dissemination of Western values in China over the past couple of centuries.[75]

He Huaihong's concept of minimum moral standards not only provides a realistic paradigm to deal with moral decay in Chinese society, but also aims to reaffirm universal ethics and universal values—notions that have unfortunately been rejected by most Chinese leaders and conservative intellectuals.[76]

MAXIMUM ETHICAL CONCERNS: POLITICAL AND CULTURAL TRANSFORMATION

Some critics argue that He Huaihong's emphasis on ethics may divert public attention from the problems of China's political system. For example, Hou Shuyi, a professor of law at the Shandong Institute of Technology, refers to He's "moral self-discipline" (*daode zilü*) as wishful thinking.[77] Hou states one should not overlook the fact that Confucian ethics were the ideological basis

74. Ibid.

75. Cong Riyun, "Pushi jiazhi yu Zhongguo daolu" [Universal values and China's path], Consensus Net, June 14, 2013 (http://congriyun.blog.21ccom.net/?p=10).

76. One exception in the Chinese leadership is Wen Jiabao, who wrote an important article on the challenges confronting Chinese foreign policy. In it, he argued that things such as democracy, rule of law, freedom, and human rights are not something peculiar to Western countries. Rather, they are common values pursued by mankind and therefore should be seen as universal values, to which China should also adhere. See Wen Jiabao, "Our Historical Tasks at the Primary Stage of Socialism and Several Issues Concerning China's Foreign Policy," Ministry of Foreign Affairs of the People's Republic of China Website, February 26, 2007 (http://www.fmprc.gov.cn/mfa_chn/ziliao_611306/tytj_611312/zcwj_611316/t300993.shtml).

77. Hou Shuyi, "Beida jiaoshou He Huaihong tan daode cai zui budaode" [Peking University Professor Huaihong's view of morality as the most immoral], Hexun Net, October 10, 2007 (http://opinion.hexun.com/2007-10-10/100865161.html).

of autocratic imperial rule and were invoked to maintain the legitimacy and order of the feudal system. Moreover, unless institutional restraint and legal mechanisms are given priority, any discussion of ethics could be highly misleading and certainly would not prevent moral decay. In Hou's view, good governance in a given country is not based on moral self-discipline, but relies on sound and sustainable political institutions.[78]

He Huaihong does recognize both the flaws of traditional Chinese ethics and the political and institutional factors behind moral decay in present-day China. As he observes, "In traditional morality, the most important elements are not attitudes and behaviors among individuals or between an individual and society, but self-knowledge, self-development, and moral self-perfection" (see chapter 2). He Huaihong considers morality "to be mainly the morality of society and social norms." Ethics refers not to individual ethics (*geren daode*) but first and foremost to institutional ethics (*zhidu lunli*), meaning the justice of the institutional system—how it constrains the behaviors of individuals, especially those who are in power.[79] He Huaihong states explicitly that "in today's world, if we wish to protect our safety and our dignity, rule of law is the only option" (see chapter 9). As for individuals, He believes that ethical awakening is actually the "people's awakening" or "individual liberalization," which should involve a transformation in the relationship between the state, society, communities, and individuals.

He Huaihong has been openly critical of excessive interference in societal autonomy and individual liberty by the PRC's political powers (see chapter 14). In his view, this interference has destroyed part of the country's traditional ethical foundation and has caused other remaining parts to lose their constraining power.[80] He finds that even the Chinese leadership's recent efforts to promote ethical reconstruction usually do not take into consideration the need for autonomy in ethical discourse. Just as morality should not operate in place of institutions and law, it should have its own function, for example, in achieving consensus in society on the basis of the aforementioned minimum moral standards.[81] In He's view, the mixing of political

---

78. Ibid.

79. Xu Linling, "He Huaihong: Xunqiu jiduan zhijian de zongdao he houdao" [He Huaihong: Seeking kindness and the middle-way between extremes], Nanfang renwu zhoukan [Southern people weekly], November 10, 2013, and also http://www.nfpeople.com/story_view.php?id=4958.

80. Dao, "Du He Huaihong Xin gangchang."

81. Wang, "He Huaihong."

propaganda and ideological doctrines with ethical discussion does not res-
onate well with the Chinese public.[82]

In 2005, eight years before President Xi Jinping launched his bold political campaign against official corruption, He Huaihong outlined six integrated measures to deal with this rampant problem: (1) make it harder
(*buneng*), (2) make it riskier (*bugan*), (3) make it unnecessary (*bubi*), (4)
make it contemptible (*buxie*), (5) make it shameful (*buren*), and (6) make it
undesirable (*buyu*). Ultimately, He calls for a set of broad-ranging, systemwide efforts to curtail corruption, including "a constitutional set of checks
and balances" (see chapter 12).

Along with this much-needed political transformation, He Huaihong proposes the establishment of new moral principles (*xin gangchang*, 新纲常),
including the following three: "the people set guidelines for the government"
(*minwei zhenggang*, 民为政纲), "rightness sets guidelines for human beings"
(*yiwei rengang*, 义为人纲), and "the living set guidelines for all things"
(*shengwei wugang*, 生为物纲). Next he proposes five new constants borrowed from "virtues identified in the classics": benevolence (*ren*), rightness
(*yi*), ritual (*li*), wisdom (*zhi*), and faithfulness (*xin*)—as well as five redefined
relationships (chapter 5). He calls for a new cultural transformation in a rapidly changing sociopolitical environment in twenty-first century China and
in a new and challenging ecological condition in the world (see chapter 1).
He Huaihong identifies many important differences between the old and
new moral principles. The new ethics represents a move toward equality
between people and requires that those of high status do their duty by those
of low status: that is to say, those who govern should be accountable to the
citizens. The new ethics also highlights the importance of environmental
protection. As some commentators observe, He Huaihong's new principles
reflect his deep ethical concern about governance in modern society.[83]

Although these new principles are directed primarily at the Chinese people, they reflect He Huaihong's profound interest in placing Chinese ethical
discourse in a global perspective and in having "an academic dialogue on an
equal footing with the West and the world."[84] Some of the chapters in this
volume concern ethical duty in international relations, especially since this is
a period in which weapons of mass destruction, environmental and ecological challenges, ethnic cleansing, widespread violence and terrorism, cyber-
security, and other issues constitute serious threats to the survival of

82. Xu, "He Huaihong."
83. Dao, "Du He Huaihong Xin gangchang."
84. He, *Zixuan ji*, p. 359.

humankind (see chapters, 16, 17, and 18). As He points out, "Our material and military power is at an extraordinary peak, but the spiritual and cultural bonds that keep us connected to one another have never been weaker" (chapter 19).

He Huaihong's global perspective and his keen interest in having a Chinese ethical dialogue with the West spring not only from his familiarity with Western ethics but also from the Chinese sentiment that Western ethical theories have a strong sense of exclusivity. In the eyes of many non-Western countries, Western modernity reflects military and economic conquest, colonial rule, and Western centrism in the cultural domain.[85] In a way, the international dialogue on ethical issues that He Huaihong and his like-minded Chinese scholars seek can promote cross-cultural understanding.

While this volume focuses on the intellectual odyssey of one truly extraordinary Chinese ethicist, it is also about the broader experience of China's journey into the twenty-first century—about the country's painful attempt to recover from the severe moral decay caused by the destruction of Chinese ethical principles over the last century. Readers will, of course, arrive at their own opinions on He Huaihong's assessment of China's present-day ethical status and the utility of his proposed new ethical principles. One can safely say, however, that the ongoing Chinese ethical discourse is among the most important factors that will determine the prospects, trajectory, and implications of China's rise on the world stage. The general English-speaking readership and analysts in the China field in particular will be richly rewarded for being well informed about this Chinese ethical discourse—and indeed, the philosophical and political insights thoughtfully presented in the following pages.

---

85. Xu Jia, *Zhongguo jinxiandai lunli qimeng* [Modern Chinese ethics enlightenment] (Beijing: Zhongguo shehui kexue chubanshe, 2014), p. 343.

PART I

RECONSTRUCTING CHINA'S SOCIAL ETHICS

CHAPTER ONE

"NEW PRINCIPLES"

Toward a New Framework of Chinese Social Ethics

China overthrew its monarchy a hundred years ago and is now starting its second century as a republic. There has been much to be proud of over the last century: after decades of war and upheaval, in the last thirty years China has achieved astonishing progress both in its economy and as an international presence. The world has been stunned by China's economic rise. But those achievements do not seem to have generated solidarity and cohesion among China's citizens; they have not built up our confidence in ourselves or each other. We see polluted rivers, contaminated food, violent police, uncaring passers-by, greedy officials, and self-interested citizens. We see people seeming to celebrate violence and abuse; we see millionaires scrambling to leave the country. A startling number of officials seem to have already evacuated their families in anticipation of the day when they will flee abroad with their looted fortunes. Perhaps most shocking is what happens to children in our society: two-year-old Yueyue, run over by a car and ignored by dozens who saw her; whole groups of children killed and injured in kindergarten bus accidents.[1] Such problems and disasters are the shame of our society. They are China's tragedy.

This chapter is an edited version of an article by the same title first published in *Morality and Civilization*, no. 4 (2012).

1. The "Little Yueyue" tragedy (广东小悦悦悲剧) refers to an October 2011 incident in Foshan, Guangdong Province, in which a two-year-old girl, Yueyue, was hit and run over by two separate vehicles on the street yet ignored by passers-by. She died a few days later. This incident aroused collective anguish among the Chinese public over the cold-

But I do not think that they represent China's "moral collapse," as some have argued. I still believe in humanity and in particular the humanity of the Chinese people. I believe what Mencius said: "Humans all have the feeling of compassion." Our fundamental sense of sympathy and community is real, but it is often weakened by a range of influences to the point that it no longer disciplines us and drives our conduct.

We need to discuss each specific problem, then work out its direct causes and find ways to neutralize them. But I am not advocating a stopgap approach alone: in the face of so many problems, that would likely have no effect. We need not just a patch to help us muddle through but also a permanent cure. So on the one hand, we have the urgent task of forestalling disaster and social disintegration; on the other hand, we have the more fundamental goal of searching for the keys to lasting peace and security in our society. Most of the past century was a transitional period, marked by extreme turbulence. An old society was completely destroyed in those convulsions. But today we still have not yet properly established new social and conceptual systems that offer us unity, confidence, and lasting stability. We have only just emerged from our convulsive transitional period, and though things seem peaceful now, we may still be in a transformational phase. We have not yet created a new society with mechanisms for long-term stability; we have to be constantly on guard against the return of turmoil. So there is an urgent need to work out and build a new type of society, and the first step in that process is to lay firm moral foundations, from ethical fundamentals to political justice. In other words, we need to explore and construct a full ethics for a republic, covering everything from institutional justice to individual duty.

But this is precisely the area where the soft power that we have to work with is far from up to the task. Old political ideologies have completely failed to keep up with changing social reality, with the result that people find themselves stuck with a public morality that does not reflect the way that they live. Empty rhetoric is everywhere, starkly divorced from real conduct. Our old ideology was born from a theory of conquest (in this case, revolution), not a theory of governance. It started as a foreign import, and in its early incarna-

---

bloodedness of those who hit and ignored her and the absence of public ethics in society. The kindergarten school bus tragedies (幼儿园校车惨祸) refer to a continuing series of traffic accidents and deaths involving unregulated kindergarten school buses and operators in rural China. In these accidents, the school buses often were overloaded, poorly maintained, and operated by irresponsible drivers hired by private kindergartens. These tragedies ignited people's anger over the country's underfunded public education system and the greediness of the private kindergarten owners.

tions was much concerned with attacking China's cultural traditions. It never gave us the tools to build a lasting polity. Recent political ideals are an improvement: the "eight honors and eight disgraces," "harmonious society," and "scientific outlook on development" attempt to draw on the resources of ancient Chinese thought and combine them with a modern sensibility.[2] But slogans like "eight honors and eight disgraces" are hardly a complete, free-standing moral theory. And the phrase "harmonious society" is so vacuous and so obviously at odds with the reality of Chinese life that it has become little more than a punch line. Moreover, the interpretation of these slogans is always excessively ideological and fails to properly embrace China's millennia of distinctive cultural traditions. I believe that we should be embarking on many parallel projects to explore and exploit the rich seam of ethical resources that runs through China's history and culture and apply those resources to the modern world. Such projects could generate an ethical framework to underpin a new social morality.

At the beginning of the twentieth century, in *New People* and other writings, Liang Qichao made an attempt to set out an ethic for a new society.[3] During Taiwan's "economic miracle" years, a debate erupted in Taiwan over

---

2. "The eight honors and eight disgraces" (八荣八耻), also known as the socialist core value system, are a set of moral concepts developed by Hu Jintao, the former Chinese president, during the Sixth Plenum Meeting of the 16th Chinese Communist Party Central Committee in late 2011. Extolling virtues such as patriotism, unity, hard work, and honesty, the concepts endeavor to promote Chinese social morality; they are integrated into the national education curriculum. The "harmonious society" (和谐社会) refers to a political doctrine laid out by Hu Jintao after the Sixth Plenum Meeting that calls for the creation of a "socialist harmonious society," further signaling a shift in the party's focus from promoting all-out economic growth to solving the resulting social tensions. "Scientific outlook on development" (科学发展观) refers to new theoretical guidance for the Chinese Communist Party that advocates comprehensive, coordinated, and sustainable development. It is one of former president Hu Jintao's signature theoretical innovations and political legacies, and it was written into the party's constitution after the 17th Party Congress in 2007.

3. Liang Qichao (梁启超, 1873–1929), a native of Xinhui, Guangdong Province, was a Chinese scholar, journalist, philosopher, and reformist during the late Qing Dynasty. Advocating constitutional monarchy, he played an active role, together with Kang Youwei, in the famous Hundred Days' Reform. *New People* (新民说) is a collection of articles that Liang Qichao published from 1902 to the end of 1903 in his biweekly journal *New Citizen* (新民丛报). Introducing Western political thought and comparing it with traditional Chinese thinking, Liang argued that China's traditional value system might have to be torn down to make way for a new system.

adding a new, sixth relationship to the five relationships recognized as ethically important in traditional Confucianism.[4] While the Confucian relationships are mainly between those who know each other well, the sixth relationship, citizenship, would link strangers. In 1940, during the war against Japan, He Lin published an article in the third issue of *Strategies of a Warring State* entitled "A New Discussion of the Five Relationships," in which he wrote:

> For thousands of years, the five Confucian relationships have endured as one of the most powerful traditional concepts shaping the moral lives of Chinese people. These relationships lie at the core of our ethical code; they constitute the regulatory framework for the Chinese ethnicity. It is our goal to discover the most current spirit of modernity through an interrogation of these old traditions. This approach, of finding the new within the old, exemplifies our adaptive acceptance of our heritage.[5]

Near the end of the article, he repeats the point: "The question today is: how do we locate a permanent, indestructible foundation among the broken shards of the old ethical code? And, on this foundation, how do we assemble ideals and standards of behavior for modern lives and modern society?" Other writers, such as Ch'ien Mu in his *Outline of Chinese History* and Feng Youlan in *Six Books of Continuity and Renewal*, have also tried to revive our traditions and restore respect to them through a process of renewal and adaptation.[6] Of course, the "enlightenment" represented by the May Fourth Movement has had an enormous impact, but it also has its blind spots and

---

4. "The five constant relationships" (五伦) refers to the five fundamental relationships in Confucian philosophy: those between ruler and subject, father and son, elder brother and younger brother, husband and wife, and friend and friend. The five relationships constitute the basic hierarchical structure of Confucian society.

5. He Lin (贺麟, 1902–92), a native of Jintang, Sichuan Province, was a Chinese scholar and philosopher who was regarded as the leader in "neo-idealism." He studied Western philosophy in the United States and Germany and taught in the philosophy departments of leading Chinese universities, including Peking University. He was a fellow at the Chinese Academy of Social Sciences in 1955–92, specializing in Western philosophy.

6. Ch'ien Mu (Qian Mu) (钱穆, 1895–1990), a native of Wuxi, Jiangsu Province, was a preeminent Chinese historian, educator, and philosopher in the twentieth century. During the 1930s, Ch'ien taught at top Chinese universities, including Peking University and Tsinghua University. He left mainland China for Hong Kong in 1949 and later moved to Taiwan in 1966. Unlike other scholars influenced by the New Culture Movement during this era, Ch'ien was a defender of traditional Confucian values. Feng Youlan (冯友兰,

abuses.[7] It is perhaps time to shine a light on enlightenment itself—that is, to locate the abuses inherent within it.

The most important task is to develop a set of fundamental moral principles—*gangchang* (纲常), or "three guidelines and five constants" (*san gang wu chang*, 三纲五常)—to anchor our ethical system. For many, "moral principles" means nothing more than prescriptions and restrictions, but we do not have to see them in that way. The old principles of Confucianism are the "three guidelines and five constants." The "three guidelines" are those that the ruler sets for the subject; the husband sets for the wife; and the father sets for the son. The "five constants" can mean either the "five constant relationships" or "the five constant virtues." The relationships are those between ruler and subject; father and son; husband and wife; elder brother and younger brother; and friend and friend. With the exception of the last, they are all obedience relationships. The five constant virtues are benevolence, rightness, ritual, wisdom, and faithfulness. The three guidelines and five constants have been given a bad name for nearly a century. They have been seen as an enemy to overcome, so much so that today many Chinese people think of the guidelines and constants as the biggest obstacle to progress. It has become commonplace to say "The old rules kill the human spirit" or "Prescriptive labels eat our humanity." But that view is wrong. Chinese civilization exists only because Confucian guidelines and constants maintained it over so many centuries. And if we are today attempting to construct a new, more rational system of social ethics, then our purpose is the same as that of Confucius: to build a space for people to live in freedom.

Aside from this misunderstanding of our own history, another objection to fixed moral principles comes from the modern world. In modern societies, relativism—and sometimes nihilism—are commonplace. Relativism disputes and rejects universal moral principles. But if we take a hard look at our own

---

1895–1990), was an influential and leading Chinese philosopher in the modern era. A native of Nanyang, Henan Province, Feng graduated from Columbia University with a Ph.D. in philosophy in 1923 and went on to teach at leading Chinese universities such as Tsinghua University. Throughout his life, he worked on reconciling traditional Chinese thought with the methods and concerns of modern Western philosophy.

7. The May Fourth Movement (五四运动) was an anti-imperialist demonstration initiated by students in Beijing on May 4, 1919, as a direct result of China's diplomatic failure at the Paris Peace Conference to prevent Japan from taking over Shandong. The movement soon ignited national anger against imperialism and marked the upsurge of Chinese nationalism. Due to its dynamic intellectual and cultural discourse, this "Chinese Renaissance" was seen as the first enlightenment movement in China's modern history.

psychology and the realities of history, we do indeed find certain natural moral principles. We find that there are certain acts—the indiscriminate harming of members of our own species or the killing of innocents—that can never be justified and against which our very psychology rebels. Take another example: there is a fairly universal intuition that humanity must have a basic social order, because without it we have no way to reduce our exposure to danger. In every civilization, every religion, and every legal code we find these shared intuitions and rules. Of course, they represent very limited, very primitive principles—and that is precisely what we need for our ethical foundations.

I believe that what we now need to locate is precisely this kind of eternal, solid moral foundation. We need the moral principles behind the old moral principles—their distilled moral principles. Once we find them, we can give new meaning to these distilled principles by applying them to modern times, expanding and interpreting them for our changed society. In fact, beneath the rules of the old moral code we do see more basic, more eternal elements. For example, lying within the old code is an endorsement of a basic political and social order that helps to protect human life. It is this element that preserves human society and the existence of the group. This seems to have been what Zhu Xi meant when he wrote, "The guidelines and constants will not be destroyed in a million years."[8] Preservation of the species and socialization: these have been always intuitively recognized as natural principles.

Of course, depending on our subjective attitudes and our moral efforts, those principles can be more or less fully realized; they go through periods of flourishing and decay. But our core moral principles have never changed, never in the history of China's countless dynasties. Even under the "tyrannical Qin"—the object of severe criticism by Zhu Xi—our foundational moral principles were not lost. That is why we identify morality as independent of politics to some extent and more permanent than any specific political system or ideology. And if we turn from Chinese historical comparisons to comparisons across the world, we find that all religions, cultures, and nations share certain fundamental moral prescriptions, though their details and forms vary with respect to historical and ethnic particulars.

8. Zhu Xi (朱熹, 1130–1200), a native of Wuyuan, Jiangxi Province, was a preeminent scholar and philosopher during the Song Dynasty (960–1628). Zhu created "neo-Confucianism" by selecting and recompiling Confucian classics with his own commentary. His commentary restored Confucianism's original focus on moral cultivation after the more bureaucratic stance of the preceding dynasties, and neo-Confucianism was regarded as the orthodoxy of Confucianism for the imperial exams until they were abolished in 1905.

In Chinese history, the Confucians who have dominated our politics have of course given much attention to the moral foundations of our polity. But that concern is not unique to the Confucians. The *Guanzi*, a compilation of philosophical writings often seen as the ancestor of the legalist school, includes an essay on "the four cardinal virtues," which it defines as ritual, rightness, integrity, and the sense of shame.[9] "The state has four cardinal virtues," it states. "If one is eliminated, the state will totter. If two, it will be in danger. If three, it will be overthrown. If all four are eliminated, it will be totally destroyed." Of course, if one cardinal virtue totters, it can be set straight. A state can pull itself out of danger. Even a state that has been "overthrown" can "rise" again. But if all four virtues are destroyed—if ritual, rightness, good faith, and the sense of shame are all lost—then the state will be destroyed, and "what has been totally destroyed can never be restored."

The last century has rained blow after blow on those virtues. Many times, all four have been weakened to the point of near collapse. China's glorious millennia of history are also a burden, and onto the weight of those centuries has been added humiliation and turmoil, followed by a century of violence and war. Now, suddenly, we are returning from the margins to a position in the spotlight on world affairs. Responsibilities are piling up; we face many questions. China has seen a massive resurgence in its economy and its strength as a state, but its culture and ethics seem to have lagged behind and in some aspects even to have regressed. As a result, social and moral reconstruction seem ever more vital and urgent. In the face of so many questions, we must start to triage and focus on the most important. However limited our time is, quick fixes will not do; we must try to find a model that will stand the test of time. Here I attempt to describe one conception of a new Chinese social ethics for a modern society.

The New Chinese Social Ethics

The reason for calling my proposal a "new" ethics (*xin gangchang*, 新纲常) is that we are marking a shift from the traditional to the modern. Though I call them "Chinese," it is important to specify which China is referred to: in this case, my focus is the cultural tradition, not the present polity of mainland

9. *Guanzi* (《管子》) is a collection of philosophical essays by Guan Zhong (管仲, 725–645 BC), an ancient Chinese philosopher and counselor to Duke Huan of Qi during the Spring and Autumn period (770–476 BC). These essays are about effective government and superior statecraft, combining both Confucian ritual and legalist order.

China. We must, for example, consider "greater China": the lives and experiences of other ethnic Chinese, though the primary point of reference will, of course, be mainland China. If we want mainland China to be a leader in the future development of Chinese culture—and certainly if we wish to bring closer the day of Chinese unification—then we must not be limited by simplistic divisions of state or political entities. In particular, we must not be bound in our discussion by an overly narrow political ideology.

Commentators on Confucius have observed that in the *Spring and Autumn Annals*, he already treats as Chinese those barbarians who have been assimilated into Chinese culture and as barbarian those ethnic Chinese who have become barbarians. Confucius himself says in the *Analects*, "If the rituals are lost, then seek them among the people" and "The *dao* does not prevail! I shall set out over the sea on a raft." These words express his inclusiveness, his interest in the populace, in culture, and in the universal values that culture expresses. It would befit us to learn from his example. Morality draws its lifeblood from the community. Morality must grow naturally, but it also needs institutional protection and support from society.

An ethical system can be understood as having two parts: normative principles and value-based beliefs. Of those, the principles are more important. The Chinese word for ethics can be deconstructed into "human relations" and "reasoning," so we should proceed as with all reasoning: by proposing and arguing for principles that will underpin the ethical system. In modern society, in particular, we must first give our attention to principles governing conduct, institutions, and policies. So we must start with a set of basic moral or ethical principles, and I shall frame them using the traditional language: I shall propose a set of new guidelines and constants. In Chinese, *gang*, the term for "guideline," signals to us that these rules will be in the form of moral principles and that they are deep, fundamental principles. *Chang*, the term for "constant," has a dual meaning: that these rules are both eternal and in continual operation.

THE THREE NEW GUIDELINES

First are the three new guidelines. The three old guidelines state that "the ruler sets guidelines for the subject; the husband sets guidelines for the wife; the father sets guidelines for the son." While retaining the framework of control and subordination, we can abandon the hierarchical relationships that these rules establish between individuals and avoid conflating familial relations with social and political institutions. So I tentatively propose three new principles: "The people set guidelines for the government; rightness sets guidelines for human beings; the living set guidelines for all things."

THE PEOPLE SET GUIDELINES FOR THE GOVERNMENT (民为政纲). "Government" here refers to all aspects of the administration of our polity. "The people" refers not simply to a collection of individuals; the term's meaning can be extended to express the fundamental value that government must respect and the primary moral principle that government must obey: that the people are the source, owner, and subject of government.

"The people" should include every person, so government should in principle serve all people. But we know that government is fundamentally unlike other institutions, or ungoverned systems, in that it must involve power—specifically the power to compel. There is a necessary relationship of command and compliance. So in the theory of government we can—and must—draw a distinction between rulers, enforcers, political leaders, officials, and other holders of power and those people who do not hold that kind of authority. The latter are citizens, in the sense of "John Q. Citizen"; they have no government authority, and they, the governed, vastly outnumber the governors. This distinction is of vital importance, because it prevents us from mistaking rule by the few (or even the one) for rule by "the people" or "the nation." It precludes the claim *"L'État, c'est moi"*—"The state, it is me."

When this rule is properly applied, the interests and opinions of citizens should be the primary point of reference for those who govern. Naturally, the identities of the two groups are not set in stone. There can be traffic between them and vertical mobility: officials can become citizens; citizens can become officials. When designing political systems, we should make all efforts to promote vertical mobility between the two groups, and we should counter both open and covert heredity of social status. Also, to a certain extent, those in the official group are still citizens. Whatever position they hold, they must still retain their identities as citizens. In this sense, citizenship is a universal value, not just a status. Citizenship encompasses every person. So when we say "The people are the source of government" or "The people set guidelines for the government," it means that power does not serve the few who are in government, nor in fact does it serve the majority. It serves the entire citizenry, every member of society.

But as we just noted, to prevent excessive concentration and abuse of power in the name of "the people," we must still clearly distinguish between those who wield power as a part of their day-to-day duties and those who do not. Looking at present-day and historical evidence, we find that every society seems to include these two groups of people: there is always a group of those who govern, and they are always relatively few in number. We do not need an overly romantic conception of democracy—one that imagines that the entire populace can engage directly in every aspect of daily governance. That would easily give a few ambitious individuals the excuse to create a tyranny in the name of "the people." It is better to honestly admit that the power to govern is always assigned to some group and that doing so is necessary for the efficient administration of government. However, we must rigorously monitor and limit this power. Therefore, given this necessary division, we still need to affirm that the people set guidelines for the government or the rulers. Those in power must accept the rule of the governed, of the citizenry, and must answer to them.

Of course, this relationship can be worked out at basic or higher levels. The basic level simply affirms that the people are fundamental: "The people are the root of a country; if the root is firm, the country is tranquil." Those who govern should concern themselves with standards of living and should be responsive to the will of the people. To put it in more modern terms, we should have "government for the people," or, in the words of Hu Jintao, "we must exercise power for the people, identify ourselves with them, and work for their interests." (These formulations also assume a distinction between those who govern and the people.) This defines the basic level of the governed-governor relationship. In recognition of the dominant trend in modern society, we should also reduce the distance felt between the people and the governors. If we fully commit to a structure in which power is wielded for the people and recognize that the ultimate foundation for political legitimacy lies in public consent, then we will move toward democracy— rule-of-law democracy, constitutional democracy. This kind of democracy is the higher-level realization of the principle that the people set guidelines for the government. In a rule-of-law, constitutional democracy, the people can fully exercise their political rights, effectively monitor and check those who govern, and peacefully select and replace them. Of course, even in a democratic system, the "demos" (the people) and the "kratia" (the power) are never completely merged. There will always be a distinct group that governs, day to day; there will always be differences in power and status. So even in a democracy, the principle that the people set guidelines for the government, that the people govern the governors, must be upheld and reinforced.

RIGHTNESS SETS GUIDELINES FOR HUMAN BEINGS (义为人纲). The principle that the people set guidelines for the government imposes duties on those who hold power by virtue of their roles in government. It applies primarily to institutional justice and the ethical responsibilities of the minority with power. Institutional justice can, of course, be seen as one part of a broader set of ethical responsibilities applying to all people. So we also need to suggest a universal system of duty that applies equally to every person and at the same time includes the specific duties of the political ethic discussed above. Specific duties arise as a result of one's occupation; universal duties arise simply as a function of being a person. And if we look at these duties as arising simply from being a person, simply from being a member of society, then we find that they must have certain other features, which are worth discussing separately.

We noted that there will always be differences in political power, so the relationships between people and agents of government are never relationships of total equality. Everyone cannot be treated the same. But fair mechanisms of vertical mobility and participation allow us to say that there is equality of political opportunity and participation. The requirement that government be subject to the guidelines of the people is a way of generating another sort of equality. Government agents therefore should concede that their authority comes from the people and should accept more duties and responsibilities. But when we talk about duties that should be accepted by everyone, by every member of society, these are universal, equal duties that allow no distinction between persons and no ordering or ranking. This equality is constituted in persons, and its referent is persons. That means that the basic requirement of "what is right" is equal treatment, in at least a few fundamental aspects. The ethical "golden rule"—and the Confucian formulation of it—is ultimately about equality in the way you treat yourself and others. From this, we can derive the directive to treat people as people and from that the most common ethical strictures: do not kill, do not steal, do not lie, do no sexual violence.

So all people should follow the basic strictures of what is right; what is right should determine the fundamental rules of conduct for all people. That is not to say that there are no differences between people or that there should be no differences between people. Rather, it is to say that there are some basic rules of behavior that should be equally observed by and demanded of all persons. If we want to say that this duty arises from a kind of difference, the relevant difference is not among persons but rather between people and other animals. In ancient China, it was held that the difference between men and beasts lay in virtue—in a sense of right and wrong, a sense of morality. As Mencius says, if a man has no virtue in his heart and his conduct is not right, then "what is there to choose between him and a brute?" In the modern

West, philosophers from Kant to Rawls tell us that the distinctive features of humans are our reason and our sense of justice. Reason allows us to order our own lives; our sense of what is right allows us to order a society in which we can live together.

When the thinkers of ancient China spoke of what is right, it included a right to life that was equal and fully developed for all. But it did not require absolute equality in terms of institutional authority or even equality before the law. But our modern conception of what is right is an autonomous, equal, and independent form of justice. This modern conception brooks no distinctions between persons in their fundamental rights, though it may still allow inequality in the distribution of power, money, and status. All people are absolutely equal before the law, and all people have an equal right to political participation. They also must accept the duties that are concomitant with their rights. In addition to their duties as citizens, people should also accept their natural duties and professional ethical duties. The ethics of government can be seen as one specific kind of professional ethics, but it is worth discussing separately, as above, because of the unique importance of government, which impinges on the life of every person.

THE LIVING SET GUIDELINES FOR ALL THINGS (生为物纲). If "The people set guidelines for the government" is the moral principle for the realm of government, and "Rightness sets guidelines for human beings" is the moral principle for the broader realm of society, then "The living set guidelines for all things" is the principle with the very broadest scope: it applies to everything in the natural universe. Within their respective principles, the terms "government" and "people" define both the scope of application and the ethical subjects on whom those principles are binding. In this last principle, the term "all things" is different: it represents a scope of application that encompasses all physical things, all of existence. But the ethical subject that is bound by this principle is humanity. Of course, humans are a part of the world. But we are different from every other animal and thing, because only humankind has consciousness and reason. Therefore humans must accept the role of moral agents. So only humans, the "paragon of animals," are the ethical subjects of this moral duty; only we are obliged to steward all other "things."

So what is this duty? What is the fundamental moral principle governing what we do with the things around us? It can be expressed as "survival" or perhaps "coexistence." This principle seems to have been well understood in the ancient literature on The Way (Dao). The *Book of Changes* says "Production and reproduction is what is called change. . . . The great attribute of heaven and earth is the giving and maintaining of life." Laozi wrote, "The

Way conforms to its own nature."[10] There were also specific rules of conduct: "Fine nets are not allowed to enter the pools and ponds . . . the axes and bills enter the hills and forests only at the proper time." Today we have more than fifty years of experience of systematic environmental ethics and experiments in ecological practice to draw on. But there has been no change in the prime directive or governing framework: now, as then, it is "coexistence."

The Five New Constants

This section is in two parts. The first part discusses the five constant relationships—five social relations that we frequently have to navigate. The second part discusses the five constant virtues—five eternal virtues that we should possess.

THE FIVE CONSTANT RELATIONSHIPS. The five relationships in classical philosophy are between ruler and subject, father and son, husband and wife, older and younger brothers, and friends. Those were the relationships that ancient society regarded as vital. But enormous changes have occurred, both within Chinese society and around it, so from the perspective of modern social ethics, I believe that the following five key relationships can be discerned:

1. Humankind and nature: the relationship between people and the natural world.

2. Group relationships: the relationships between people in groups. On the international level, these occur primarily as relations between nation-states. Within one country, they are primarily the relationships between ethnic groups, though of course other examples exist: relations between regions or between social groups and so forth.

---

10. The *Book of Changes* (《周易》), also known as *Zhouyi, I-Ching,* or the *Classic of Changes,* is an ancient Chinese text on the dynamic balance of opposites, often used for divination. The *Book of Changes* is believed to have been written by the mythical prehistoric emperor of China, Fu Xi (伏羲, 3000–2000 BC) and perfected by King Wen of Zhou (周文王, 1152–1056 BC) during the Western Zhou Dynasty (1046–771 BC). Both Confucianism and Taoism take their philosophical roots from the *Book of Changes,* making it still politically and philosophically influential in modern China as well as other Confucian societies in East Asia. Laozi (老子, ca. 571–471 BC) was an ancient Chinese thinker and philosopher during the Spring and Autumn period (770–476 BC) of Chinese history. As the author of *Daodejing* (*Tao-te Ching*) and the founder of Taoism, Laozi promulgated the virtues of "naturalness" (自然, *ziran*) and "nonaction" (无为, *wuwei*). Laozi has also been transformed into a religious figure as the founder of Taoism (also romanized as "Daoism").

3. Social relationships (narrowly understood): the institutional relationship of individuals with the state: relations between individuals and institutions and between individuals and the national government.

4. Individual relationships: relationships between individuals and specific other individuals, in particular, relationships between strangers.

5. Personal relationships: relationships including parental, spousal, fraternal, and all other family relationships and relationships between friends.

Corresponding to each of these five relationships are five virtues or ethical expectations, which I summarize as harmony with nature; peace between groups; fairness in society; individuals doing right by each other; and closeness in personal relationships.

1. Harmony with nature: This ethical expectation means that the relationship between humankind and nature should be one of harmony and coexistence, not of victory and defeat, conqueror and conquered. Nor should it be purely the relationship of exploiter to exploited. Here, harmony with nature is not the individual, spiritual experience of oneness with nature (though that spiritual experience is a precious resource for our treatment of the natural world); rather, harmony with nature is a rule for societies. It states that human beings should see themselves and nature as part of an indivisible whole and, accordingly, should pursue harmony in their relationship with nature. While the natural world can exist without humanity, humanity cannot exist without nature. It is therefore incumbent on us to make harmony and coexistence our goal and to make great efforts to achieve it. Nature is not going to bend to accommodate humankind; humankind must accommodate itself to nature. Thus a reasonable relationship between humankind and nature is not for humanity to try to conquer and defeat nature; it is to hold nature close and treat it kindly. Only by doing so can we maintain any form of sustainable development. If humanity only exploits and abuses nature, then nature will inevitably punish us; humanity will ultimately find itself abandoned by nature.

2. Peace between groups: First, this expectation means that relations between nation-states should be calm and peaceful. States must make great efforts to avoid the use of force, to avoid war, and to pursue cooperation for mutual gain. Second, ethnic groups within a state must pursue peaceful and harmonious relations so that they can unite and cooperate.

3. Fairness in society: This expectation means that humanity must follow the ancient principle "all under heaven for the public good": a society's institutional arrangements and policies should embody the principle of justice and should treat every person equally. Society and government should protect the rights of every citizen, and individuals should carry out their duties as citizens.

4. *Individuals doing right by each other:* This expectation means that in their relations with other individuals, people should follow general principles of morality and courtesy and should perform their natural duties. These include the golden rule, formulated in the classical literature as "do not do to others what you would not have done to yourself" and interpreted in modern times as "tolerance." In a modern society, we must take special care when interacting with strangers to treat them as equals and to act reasonably and do right by them.

5. *Closeness in personal relationships:* This expectation is slightly different from "doing right": it is a closer and friendlier relationship. Through marriage and friendship, certain people who were once strangers enter into a personal relationship. Compared with the total number of people in our community, only very few people are included in any one individual's personal relationships—necessarily, otherwise they could not be so close. Personal relationships form a fundamental social cell, and though these cells are small, they are extremely important to the happiness of their members. There are rich philosophical resources in the ancient literature concerning these relationships. The "five relationships" appear in some of China's very earliest books, the *Book of Documents* and the *Historical Records* ("Annals of the Five Emperors"): "Fathers became just, mothers loving, elder brothers sociable, younger ones respectful, and children filial."[11] Mencius adds: "between friends, fidelity." Family love and friendship are still highly prized among Chinese people, though they have changed: the ideas of rank and obedience are much criticized today, and a clearer distinction is drawn between family and nonfamily relationships. But there is certainly good reason to keep them on our list of fundamental social "moral principles."

THE FIVE CONSTANT VIRTUES. Here I borrow the five virtues that were identified in the ancient classics: benevolence (仁, *ren*), rightness (义, *yi*), rit-

---

11. The *Book of Documents* (《尚书》), also known as *Shujing*, refers to one of the Five Classics of Confucianism. It comprises fifty-eight chapters describing the sages of ancient China, including the legendary kings Yao and Shun. The *Book of Documents* is often considered the first narrative history of ancient China. "Annals of the Five Emperors"(《五帝本纪》) is the first chapter of the 130-chapter *Historical Records* (《史记》), written by Sima Qian (135–86 BC) during the Western Han Dynasty (202 BC–AD 9). It lists the records of five prehistoric legendary Chinese emperors: Huang Di (the Yellow Emperor), Emperor Zhuan Xu, Emperor Di Ku, Emperor Rao, and Emperor Shun.

ual (礼, *li*), wisdom (智, *zhi*) and faithfulness (信, *xin*). These five concepts, with all their connotations, still have great force today, though we can and should apply new meanings and new interpretations to them. The five virtues can be understood as institutional virtues, but here I am looking at them primarily as personal qualities. I interpret them using the formulation of Mencius, who identifies each of the first four as having its origin in one of four affective attitudes. Mencius, who uses these founts of morality to start his discussion of the virtues, believes that all people possess these four "sources of goodness." They provide the motivation for morality and give us reason to believe that morality will prevail. At the same time, bearing in mind the performative nature of virtues, I also reference the cardinal virtues of ancient Greece: temperance, courage, prudence, and justice.

1.Benevolence: Mencius says: "The feeling of compassion is the origin of benevolence." Compassion is a softness of heart, sympathy, or pity. In ancient China, benevolence was believed to be the "master virtue," so compassion is not just the origin of benevolence; it is the most important of the four attitudes, and it can be seen as the source of all morality. Looked at in performative terms, "benevolence is the characteristic element of humanity"; it is "treating people as people," or acting toward other people with humanity.

2. Rightness: Mencius says: "The feeling of shame and dislike is the origin of rightness." In this tenet, Mencius highlights both the fundamental nature of this sense—that is, the sense of what is right is first and foremost a prohibition on evil; it is a sense of shame and distaste for evil. If compassion is a positive motivator for virtuous conduct, then shame and dislike are negative motivators, and for some people, negative motivations may even outweigh positive spurs to action. Among the Greek virtues, it is not only justice that corresponds to Mencian rightness; courage also fits in this category. For Mencius, courage is not physical bravado but a determination to do one's duty, whatever the obstacles: "I will go forward against thousands and tens of thousands."

3. Ritual: Ritual is both a social institution and a personal commitment to courtesy. Here we address ritual mainly as a personal virtue: courtesy and propriety. Mencius says: "The feeling of modesty and the desire to accommodate is the origin of ritual. . . . Ritual is an attitude of honor and respect." Accommodating others implies controlling and restricting ourselves: self-restraint is a prerequisite for proper ritual. And self-restraint means limiting our desires, particularly our material desires. The virtue of ritual can therefore be viewed as closest to the ancient Greek virtue of temperance. Combining ritual and temperance, we get manners. From the etiquette of public spaces to the urbane warmth of the cultured individual, good manners maintain a kind of balance with the courageous impulse to do one's duty as described in the preceding paragraph.

4. Wisdom: Mencius says: "A heart that distinguishes right from wrong is the origin of wisdom." Right and wrong here refers to moral rightness, to what is proper and what is improper. Mencius has attributed the first three virtues to moral feelings or will; here what we see is the rational capacity to make moral judgments. Wisdom is the ability to recognize what is right, but it is not simply the knowledge of moral rules. It includes the ability to weigh and consider: the will and the wisdom to make moral judgments or choices, including the wisdom to find a balance and to seek a middle way. This understanding of wisdom is compatible with the ancient Greek concept, though the Mencian version is more narrowly focused on moral reasoning and moral choice.

5. Faithfulness (also called sincerity or trustworthiness): Good faith should suffuse all of the virtues listed above: all the virtues require both subjective honesty and objective reliability. Each person should demonstrate sincerity in his or her words and actions in order to generate trust between persons and good faith in the public sphere. Within our own society, we can see this lesson very clearly: for government action to be effective, there must be basic public credibility. And to launch a harmonious society, there must be a basic level of trust between people. So good faith can be seen as pervasive; it can also be seen as an objective. It is both a personal virtue and a social condition to which we aspire.

The First and the Ultimate (Beliefs and First Steps)

The moral principles discussed in the previous section are moral rules and principles. For the value-based beliefs that should inform our new Chinese social ethics, we can adapt and update the set of five characters often found on display in traditional homes: *tian, di, jun, qin, shi*: heaven, earth, ruler, family, teacher. Hung on the walls of living rooms or next to the household shrine, these words were objects of reverence in the popular Chinese tradition, particularly during the long centuries of stability during the Ming and Qing Dynasties. Even after the republic replaced the Qing Empire, many people kept the five; the only change was to substitute "country" for "ruler." With the correct interpretation, I believe that these five—heaven, earth, country, family, teacher—still represent a system of beliefs that can command widespread acceptance. Here I attempt to give a new interpretation for each of them.

1. Heaven: Though the same character in Chinese can represent both "nature" and "heaven," the two concepts are distinct. Here we speak of heaven as a spiritual concept. Reverence for heaven refers to a spiritual belief in what is highest, most transcendental. This reverence may take many forms. It may be a particular, highly elaborated religion, or it may be a simple, primitive faith. But without exception, it must include an element of the transcendental and an element of piety or awe.

2. Earth: Traditionally, "heaven and earth" have often been yoked together as an inseparable pair. Here we split them up. I take "earth" to refer to nature, in particular to the Earth that supports us: the land upon which we crawl; this broad plain across which we and our families scurry in such numbers; the home where we grew up. Our home is a specific, immediate presence, and we cannot but feel a sense of closeness to and appreciation of it.

3. Country: This is, of course, our state, the polity into which we are born and which we generally leave only on our death. But a country is not just a system of institutions. It is also our nation, in the sense of being the home of our culture. It is our motherland, because our families have been here for many generations. We might leave it and travel all over the world, but it is a permanent part of our psyche. We want the best for it; we want to make a contribution to it ourselves. And the further away we are, the more we seem to yearn for it.

4. Family: Family can in theory refer to any relative. But as a belief, "family" concerns the love, respect, and duty that we feel toward those higher up the family tree than ourselves, particularly our direct ancestors. This is one of China's most persistent and potent traditions. Our duty toward those who came before us does not end with their death; knowing our roots means respecting and loving our origins.

5. Teacher: This is another characteristic feature of the Chinese tradition: the high status accorded to culture and education and the respect for those who do its work. But as Confucius said, "If three people walk past, one of them will be a teacher for me." The respect for teachers can be extended to anyone who can teach us or who sets us an example. It can be extended to a respect for knowledge and for practical wisdom and to appreciation and esteem for artists and scientists.

These five values can be summarized as follows: "Revere Heaven; embrace the Earth; cherish one's country; honor one's family; respect teachers." These value-based beliefs vary from person to person in their expression and in the ways that they combine. Their status or rank varies; in some people, not all of these beliefs are present. But I think that these five elements, while being highly flexible, encapsulate the key features of the Chinese cultural tradition. They are a blend of the emotional, the rational, experience, and beliefs. They do not tell us specifically what we should or should not do; they do not give direct instructions or proscriptions concerning our conduct. But they can serve us as a foundation. They can provide belief to back up our social ethics and thereby supplement our sense of ethical duty with stronger support, authority, and sanctions.

In discussing the first steps to be taken to promote these new Chinese social ethics, I again adapt language from the classics. When Confucius's student Zilu asks where governments should start, the master replies: "They must rectify names!" Zilu thinks that this is rather roundabout, but Confucius reprimands him: "If names are not correct, then language will not make sense; if language does not make sense then plans will not succeed." If names are not correct, then "the people will not know what to do. . . . So when a good ruler names a thing, it must be a name he can use in discussion; when he discusses a thing, he must be able to act on it."

However, in our society today, we can see many obvious examples of names that seem divorced from reality and conduct that fails to live up to our rhetoric. There is a disconnect between our ideology and social practice; between the superstructure above and its economic foundations; between the government and the private sphere. These disconnects are interfering with social trust, particularly with trust between the top and bottom, between the authorities and the public. They have provoked a credibility crisis. Because of these disconnects, we are constantly faced with insincerity; we are habituated to it. This sincerity gap is the underlying obstacle to building trust in our society. When there is no good faith in the language of our most fundamental social practices, when they are filled with empty rhetoric, how can we expect to find sincerity anywhere else?

If we want to be sure that our words match our deeds, that names match reality, then we need to make adjustments. Those adjustments will take time and may perhaps flow in both directions. On the one hand, we need to eliminate unjustifiable names and create more realistic ones; on the other hand, when a name has been validated by history, we should also adapt our reality to conform to that name. So which of these processes will dominate? Adapting language to match reality, or adapting reality to fit our language? If we maintain the principle of "seeking truth from facts," then it is likely to be the former. We still have many unrealistic names, much specious phrasing, particularly in formal settings. Often, even those speaking do not believe the rhetoric that they use. But I will not discuss specific examples here. Rather I want to paraphrase what Confucius said on the "rectification of names." I would like to propose a new rectification of names, adapted to the needs of modern life: "Let officials be officials, let citizens be citizens, let people be people, and let things be things."

Let officials be officials. First of all, officials should be like officials. It is no good to simply redesignate officials as "public servants." The term "public servant" is itself an example of disconnection between name and reality, a distortion that generates more confusion. In order to fulfill their political functions, officials must be granted a certain level of power. The problem is that this power must be strictly defined and balanced with concomitant responsibilities. As has been said, to rule a country, one must first control its functionaries; to improve the citizenry, one must first improve the officials. China has always been blighted by officials using their authority as the ultimate currency, but the modern incarnation of the problem seems especially severe. Officials are lionized everywhere, but that is coupled with unprecedented public anger and hatred toward the same officials. That indicates two things: that officials have control over vast resources of power, money, and fame and that there is a huge gap between the expectations of the public and the ethical conduct of officials. So the most urgent need today is to establish standards of accountability and ethics for officials and to foster proper political commitment among them. Of course, doing so will require corresponding changes in our state structures. Ultimately, a full solution to the problem will probably emerge only from greater rule of law and democracy: unbundling the precious commodities of political power, economic resources, and public fame and allowing broader access to all of them.

Let citizens be citizens. Second, the people need to act like citizens, specifically citizens of a modern state. Unlike the hazy concept of "the people," citizenship entails a distinct set of rights and duties that inheres in each individual. So the populace needs to build its capacity to act as a citizenry. Every citizen must uphold his or her own rights boldly and effectively; at the same time, citizens must also actively accept the obligations that come with citizenship. All people must accept their responsibilities as members of society and improve themselves and their capacity for citizenship. That improvement will require more than the introduction of new ideas. It requires a long process of habituation to a world in which citizens organize themselves spontaneously and on a voluntary basis.

Let people be people. People must be treated as persons: every individual must be treated in a human and humane way. No person is to be subject to discrimination or humiliation. All people are to be enabled to live a life of dignity as befits their status as a person. To achieve this, there must, of course, be special concern for the disadvantaged, but we must also encourage excellence, achievement, and innovation, so that each person uses his or her capacities to the fullest.

Let things be things. Things must be treated as the objects that they are, neither exaggerated nor diminished. Zhuangzi wrote: "Treat things as things, and do not be enslaved to them."[12] This means that people should temper their interactions with material things; they should properly handle their material desires. No one should become a servant to things or allow his or her desire for things to escalate. Uncontrolled escalation of material desires inevitably damages the ecosystem, deranging the existing material order. To allow things to exist in their natural form, we need to control human material desires, make efficient use of the things that we need, and stop wasting natural resources, damaging the environment, and polluting our ecosystem.

Of course, there are many other names in need of rectification. The ethics of various professions offer many examples: whatever occupation a person has, that person should properly carry out all of the duties associated with that occupation. A society should do its best to provide a good job for each person, and each person should contribute as much as his or her abilities allow.

Comparison of the Old and New Ethics

Table 1-1, which provides a summary of the preceding sections, reveals four notable differences between the old ethics and my new Chinese social ethics.

—The new ethics sharpens the distinction between government and the people, between the public and the private spheres. There is less prescription in the private sphere: family relations have been removed from the three guidelines, and while private connections occupy four of the old five relationships, they occupy only one of the new.

—In contrast, the environment figures much more prominently in the new ethics. There are many more principles governing the relationship between humanity and nature. This is in line with modern practice, and it is also part of our duty to the world. It is an expansion of elements already present in traditional Chinese thought, and it seeks a path of sustainable development for China as the country completes its dramatic economic ascent.

12. Zhuangzi (庄子, ca. 369–286 BC) was a representative of Taoism during the Warring States period (403–221 BC). Zhuangzi further developed Taoism after Laozi in the eponymous book *Zhuangzi*, which described Dao (The Way) as universal and the origin of everything in the universe.

—The new ethics represents a move toward equality between people, particularly in relationships within the private sphere. However, the belief system retains the element of "respect."

—The primary axis of state institutions has been turned. The emphasis is no longer on those of low status meeting their obligations to those of high status—on subjects doing their duty to the ruler. Now those of high status must do their duty to those of low status: those who govern are answerable to the citizens. In fact, "citizen" has been raised to the level of a universal value, and citizens now represent much broader principles than rulers. But at the same time, the new ethics accepts the numerical realities: that there will always be a few who do the work of government and who thus have power. However, those who are politicians or who take part in governance must accept the people as their fundamental and ultimate master.

That shift is perhaps the largest difference between the old and new ethics. It reflects the biggest institutional change of the last century: from a monarchy to a century of republicanism. But the path from our current state to a republic that embodies democracy and rule of law will be long and hard. "The ruler sets guidelines for the subjects" was the most important rule in all of the old ethics. That rule effectively excluded the people from participation in government, however much ancient thinkers might have written of the people being the "root of the country." Ancient China had no other models with which to compare its state institutions, and we can see in the traditional ethics how specific institutional arrangements are mistaken for fundamental principles. The division between "ruler" and "subject" is presented as a fundamental, eternal distinction, but in reality it was just a reflection of the ancient writers' belief in what they considered fundamental principles of government. The Confucian writers supported this system because their moral principles demanded peace, continuity, and the protection of life above all else.

Of course, the guidelines and constants set out above are just the beginning of a moral theory. The details of the theory remain to be worked out, and there is a need for much more interpretation. But this is true of any set of ethical principles. To a certain extent, any set of moral principles can only be a framework. It is precisely their incompleteness that gives them their universality and allows for flexibility in interpretation and judgment. In addition to the guidelines and constants, I have sketched out values, beliefs, and practical first steps. Beliefs are the ultimate ideals; the guidelines and constants are the inviolable core; and rectifying names is our urgent duty.

Table 1-1. *Comparison of the Old and New Ethics*

Teachings	Old ethics	New ethics
Guidelines	Ruler sets guidelines for subjects. Husband sets guidelines for wife. Father sets guidelines for son.	People set guidelines for government. Rightness sets guidelines for human beings. The living set guidelines for all things.
Five constant relationships	Ruler–subject Father–son Husband–wife Older brother–younger brother Friend–friend	Humankind and nature Group relationships Social relationships Individual relationships Personal relationships
Five constant virtues	Benevolence Rightness Ritual Wisdom Faithfulness	Same five, with new interpretations
Beliefs	Heaven Earth Ruler Family Teacher	Heaven Earth Country Family Teacher
Rectification of names	Let rulers be rulers. Let subjects be subjects. Let fathers be fathers. Let sons be sons.	Let officials be officials. Let citizens be citizens. Let people be people. Let things be things.

These questions have been turning over in my mind for many years, but only recently have certain events prompted me to commit them to writing. Naturally, this is a very preliminary exploration of these issues. I have only proposed an outline; I could not possibly flesh it out or offer full arguments here. I only hope that those who have thought more deeply than I will offer their criticisms and comments and that we can labor together to build anew our shared morality. The last century brought many changes; the passage of a century demands that we rebuild. The last century brought much destruction; in the new century, we rise again. That is what we hope for.

CHAPTER TWO

A CHINESE THEORY OF CONSCIENCE

The Contemporary Transformation of Traditional Morality

This chapter presents a brief introduction to a theory of conscience that I have been developing. This theory of conscience attempts, with sympathy and respect, to re-explain Chinese traditional morality and re-examine historical resources in order to restore the broken connection between the past and the present. However, it also tries to face the consequences of the enormous and rapid changes that China underwent at the end of the twentieth century and to respond to the various spiritual and moral challenges originating within modern society.

Thus my new theory of conscience has a hereditary relationship with traditional theories of conscience, yet there are some quite important differences between the two. A fundamental difference is that of the moral point of view: the new theory of conscience has to make the shift from an egoist point of view to a social point of view; from a specific point of view to a universal point of view. This exploration aims to form a kind of universal moral minimum, or an ethics of basic consensus that draws on Chinese resources and Chinese discourse.

This chapter is an edited version of "A Theory of Conscience," in He Huaihong, *A Theory of Conscience* (Shanghai: SDX Publishing House, 1994).

Chinese Traditional Society and Traditional Morality

I consider ethics to be mainly social ethics, so my inquiry into morality in recent years has been focused on changes in social structure in ancient China. In light of de Tocqueville's generalization that the main current in modern European and American society is continued movement toward equality, I describe a tendency toward political equality in Chinese history after the disintegration of the feudal hereditary system in the Spring and Autumn period (春秋, 770–476 BC). In analyzing the social implications of the development of the system for selecting scholar-officials in ancient China via the transformation from *chaju* (察举, recommendation-based selection) to *keju* (科举, examination-based selection), I also illustrate a corresponding movement toward political equality in terms of optimal political opportunity embedded in a socially mobile hierarchy. However, such equality of opportunity remained within the sphere of hierarchical minority rule, and its contradiction with the rational intent for social equity often left Chinese society in a predicament.

My basic conclusion from the study of Chinese social history is that Chinese society before the Warring States period (475–221 BC), especially in the Western Zhou Dynasty (1027–770 BC) and the Spring and Autumn period, was a "hereditary society"—on the whole, a closed hierarchical society. In the more than 2,000 years since the Qin Dynasty (221–207 BC) established a united and centralized empire and an ordered bureaucratic system, Chinese society gradually became a "selection society"—an open or mobile hierarchical society (discussed in more detail in chapter 3). The selection of officials depended on universal and strict institutions that evaluated a person's cultural level and moral orientation.

The morality of traditional society is seen in the hierarchical society in which officials and the common people were divided under a monarchy. Generally speaking, the masses were not concerned with political power. Although all persons theoretically had the opportunity to become an official through examination, they did not have the opportunity of universal political participation. In other words, there was no democracy.

Therefore, at that time the governing morality of traditional society was an elite morality, a gentleman's morality, a minority morality. For the majority of people, the question of morality was a question of custom to be adopted and improved under the influence of the elite morality. Once a commoner ascended to the status of scholar-official through the strict examination process, he was no longer a common person. Certainly, only a minority succeeded. In this hierarchical society, the life philosophy and value system held by the elite minority could function as a sufficient social ethic. While this morality most prominently fostered the objective of becoming a scholar on one's own, it also functioned in correcting the mind of the monarch and improving the customs of the common people. However, the elitism of this morality is undeniable. The elite morality supported and maintained the hierarchical society, and the hierarchical society stimulated and strengthened the development of the elite morality. From the Song Dynasty (960–1279) to the Ming Dynasty (1368–1644), Confucianism had developed and greatly elevated the position of abstract thinking in traditional philosophy. Traditional conscience theory—Wang Yangming is generally regarded as its main proponent—was carried forward in the course of that development.[1]

According to traditional conscience theory, the ultimate goal of a person is self-cultivation. Conscience enables a person to become a wise or noble individual. Moreover, conscience is the simplest and most trustworthy way of reaching this end. For human beings, conscience has the deepest and the most fundamental ontological significance, because the pursuit of wisdom is regarded as the most important and highest stage of one's life. The main objective of traditional conscience theory was not only to guide the general masses in the development of ordinary virtues but also to help certain persons, a minority, approach as closely as possible the ideal model of a wise sage. It pursued moral perfectionism and tried to establish an ultimate condition whereby individuals could live quietly and happily. In other words, traditional conscience theory was not only applied as social ethics but was also regarded as a comprehensive life philosophy, even a religious belief.

In conclusion, traditional morality, especially the traditional conscience theory that developed rapidly over the last several centuries, was primarily a morality of gentlemen—of the upper stratum, the ruling class and cultural elite. In this sense, it was also a minority morality. Its requirements were noble and strict. We can summarize the two basic features of traditional conscience theory. First, it was a gentleman's pursuit of wisdom and devotion of oneself to moral nobility. Second, it focused on the ego as a moral subject and aimed at self-perfection. We perhaps may call it "noble egoism."

1. Wang Yangming (王阳明, 1472–1529), a native of Yuyao, Zhejiang Province, was a politician and military official as well as an influential Confucian philosopher during the Ming Dynasty (1368–1644). Having studied the thought of Zhu Xi during his early years, Wang contributed to the development of Zhu's "neo-Confucianism" by emphasizing the impact of personal morality on social well-being and the unity of knowing and acting.

Significant Change in Contemporary China

A huge and radical change in social structure took place in China in the twentieth century. The Chinese in the beginning and at the end of the century seemed to exist in two quite different worlds. The abolition of the examination system in 1905 was the first important event of the century and the basic symbol of China's dramatic transformation (see chapter 4 for a detailed discussion of this topic). In my opinion, the abolition consisted of more than the destruction of a dynasty. It not only meant the disappearance of an institution that had lasted over 1,300 years, but also the end of a social structure (the selection society) that originated more than 2,000 ago. Moreover, it meant the end of a social system (the hierarchical society) that had an even longer history. After a series of stormy revolutions, hierarchy was no longer an acceptable form of social organization. The idea of equality had already spread widely within the social system and taken root in the hearts of the people. Today, with an awareness of social equality, the quest for different values and life ideals has become more and more evident.

With this sea change in Chinese society, contemporary "new Confucianism," represented by Xiong Shili and Mou Zongsan, led the traditional theory of conscience to a more internal and exquisite stage of ontological development.[2] It called itself "moral metaphysics"—a philosophical foundation of ethics. Today, it is more suitable to call it "a noble philosophy of human life." I think that ethics must first answer questions such as which social institutions are just; which human behaviors are right; and which obligations members of society need to meet. Modern ethics must be universal, open to the whole society and its members. Today, Chinese society has already changed radically, realizing a sort of social and economic equality. Morality must now be considered binding for all people.

---

2. Xiong Shili (熊十力, 1885–1968), a native of Huanggang, Hubei Province, was a modern Chinese neo-Confucian philosopher. His most notable work is the controversial eight-volume *New Treaties of Consciousness Only* (新唯识论, Xin Weishi lun), published in 1944. According to Xiong, reality is in perpetual transformation, consisting of unceasing "closing" and "opening" movements that give rise to all. Mou Zongsan (牟宗三, 1909–1995), a native of Xixia, Shandong Province, also was a modern neo-Confucian philosopher. Mou's study sought to reinterpret and reconstruct Chinese traditional philosophy as an alternative to the dominant Western philosophy. As a Chinese nationalist, Mou strived to restore Chinese traditional philosophy including Confucianism, Taoism, and Buddhism to a position of prestige in the world.

The Key Question of Moral Transformation

The traditional theory of conscience has been fruitful for the philosophy of human life, and it has had a great influence on the morality of traditional society. If it is to exert the same influence on the morality of modern society, it must undergo a fundamental transformation and achieve a new level of transcendence. The test of transcendence is universality—whether the theory can turn from the point of view of the self to the point of view of society, from the specific point of view to the universal point of view.

Can a new universal ethics for modern society be deduced from the noble egoism of the traditional theory of conscience? In my opinion, that is logically untenable because it is not suitable for society as a whole to have self-cultivation (*xiu shen*, 修身) as the central focus and wisdom as the ultimate goal. In traditional morality, the most important elements are not attitudes and behaviors among individuals or between an individual and society, but self-knowledge, self-development, and moral self-perfection.

In the view of traditional conscience theory it even can be said, in some sense, that how society or others treat me or any other individual is not important. They in principle do not affect my self-cultivation, although they are necessary means for my self-improvement. I am most concerned with performing my duty and perfecting my personality. My duty is not affected by the attitudes of others or by whether they perform equally. I stress only my own duty, because it is what I do that matters most for my life's purpose, not what others do. It is what I do, rather than what others do, that really decides what kind of person I can become and whether I can reach the highest exemplification of virtuous wisdom. Noble egoism is thus a one-sided duty, an unconditioned duty, and an infinite duty, because it places demands only on me. I have the rights to myself; furthermore, perhaps my deepest thirst is to become a sage.

Noble egoism served a meaningful and productive role in Chinese history. But we cannot deduce from it a system of equal obligations and moderate duties suitable for modern society. Although self-discipline is very important, we should ascertain the rules and duties of discipline first. In ascertaining those duties, the point of view that regards the moral ego as the center of all morality cannot exist in tandem with an attitude that places an individual in an equal position with all others. In noble egoism the self is always the subject—the observing subject, the acting subject, and the subject of doing his duty to others; it is not allowed that the self is also the object—an observed object, an object acted upon, and the object of other subjects in doing their own duties. Therefore, it is impossible to derive a modern system of equal and moderate duties from a self-centered point of view, regardless if it is that of a utilitarian egoism or a "noble egoism." A modern system needs to transcend the self and take a point of view that does not regard the self as the metaphysical center, that even excludes and suspends the self.

It is evident that modern society does not and cannot require the morality of traditional wisdom, which demands that everyone first be concerned with the world's troubles and last seek their own happiness. According to Kant's "universalizability principle," that demand cannot be universalized. We may take the example of a line to purchase a ticket. There are three possible rules for lining up: whoever arrives first buys first; whenever I arrive, I will buy after the others (the traditional noble egoism or moral egoism); whenever I arrive, I will buy before the others (the selfish or self-interested egoism). Obviously, only the first rule can be universalized and demanded of all members of a society as a universal rule.

Toward a Universal and Moral Minimum

My theory of conscience attempts to explore a kind of moral minimum concerning all peoples living in modern society. In some sense, it endeavors to explain duties rather than conscience. Everyone must accept these duties in order to become a qualified member of society. Conscience to me simply means a respect for another person's feelings and an understanding of the reasons behind these duties—that is, it is a kind of moral consciousness of duty and a moral sense of responsibility.

THE UNIVERSAL ETHICS AND THE MORAL MINIMUM. The conscience interpreted as the highest spiritual stage reached by individuals through long self-discipline or instant intuition, or the conscience that implies the ultimate concern for humanity, is beyond the scope of this work. I want to explore the social direction of conscience rather than its self-direction. The former points at the righteous rather than the wise or saintly. Just as a bishop said in Victor Hugo's *Les Miserables*, "To be a saint is the exception; to be a just person is the rule."

First, the moral minimum is relative to traditional morality. In both East and West, traditional societies were hierarchical societies, where morality was related to nobility and often concerned only the ruling minority. For example, Confucius describes "noblesse oblige" and expressed the nature of traditional morality in his saying that "the virtue of a gentleman is like wind and that of the people is like grass. The grass must bend when the wind blows across it."[3] However, in the modern era, morality must be a morality for all

3. *The Analects of Confucius* 12:19.

peoples, treating all peoples equally. Accordingly, its requirements and demands must be reduced.

Second, the moral minimum is relative to the various ideals of human life, beliefs, and ultimate values. It emphasizes the basic nature of modern morality. That means that ideas about what constitutes a true good life and final values do not determine the distinction between right and wrong. No longer does the former serve as the grounds of the latter. People living in modern society must first satisfy the requirements of the moral minimum; then they may look after their life ideal. Morality is not all there is to human life. One may seek one's own life ideal and follow one's own life plan as long as one is not violating the basic moral requirements. One may climb one's own life summit and may live either a noble life, a saintly life, or a materially comfortable and satisfied life as long as no others are harmed.

Although the moral minimum represents only basic duties, it has a logical priority—after all, to build a house, you must first lay the foundation. The foundation provided by the moral minimum must be shared universally by all people, who have their own reasonable life plan. Today it is impossible to deduce the moral norms for all people from a particular system of values and beliefs, just as a foundation suited for all houses cannot be determined by the design of one house.

This relates to my understanding of the concepts of morality. I consider morality to be mainly the morality of society and social norms. Various religions and life philosophies may address the question of the ultimate meaning of human life in rather different ways. The moral minimum should nonetheless be a universal ethic. It should be binding for all and equally demanding of all. In Chinese traditional society, there was a kind of moral maximum, but it was not universal. It was demanded only of those who had the highest social status or the best cultural training. During Mao Zedong's time, especially during the Cultural Revolution, another kind of moral maximum (a revolutionary morality) almost became a universal ethic binding all people with a very "high" and strict standard of behavior. But it failed.

THE MORAL MINIMUM AND THE SUPPORTING SPIRIT. Universal ethics insists on the objective universality of certain basic moral norms and duties, but the grounds that support the norms have changed since the world entered the modern era. The moral minimum tends to have the joint support of various rational systems of values and beliefs, not only the isolated support of one of them.

The principle of universal ethics also insists that there is continuity between traditional society and modern society and that some basic elements central to traditional morality have remained unchanged. With the governing moral systems in traditional societies, the scopes of concern and fundamental life values are very different; their moral concepts and methods of argument also are different. But the contents of their core are roughly the same. The morality of modern society tends to separate its understanding of what is good from that of traditional society by emphasizing the individual, and since the ethics of modern society focuses on the rightness of behavior, its scope is smaller. A consensus of scope, therefore, must be established.

The principle of universal ethics tries to expound and justify the contents, scope, and basis of the basic duties that all members of modern society must perform. It elaborates neither the entirety nor the highest ideal of human life. It only makes a statement about the moral basis for human life. But that basis is very important and precedes the ideal value. Not all human behaviors are moral behaviors; in fact, most human behaviors under most conditions are not moral behaviors. But there is a kind of moral minimum to human behaviors. No one can ever have absolute freedom to do what he or she wants. There is always something that no one should ever do. The basic morals should be followed by all people who have reasonable life plans. We should not deduce moral norms that prescribe a particular value system for all people. On the contrary, we should try to establish a system of basic moral norms that does not express any partiality to any specific value system and life plan.

Therefore, when we consider universal ethics, we must give priority to the norms of moral behavior rather than value systems. We must distinguish between basic ethical norms and various religious beliefs and value systems. The former requires that we reach a consensus, while the latter allows various reasonable differences to exist. In other words, we should first seek common ground in a set of basic norms and only afterward search for higher values. Before we can have truly inclusive dialogue and integrity of discourse, all of us must first agree that dialogue, not war, is the path to resolving our differences. We must first establish the willingness for dialogue and the ethical norms to guide it.

On the other hand, the moral minimum and life ideals or religious beliefs may be interrelated and even mutually conditioned. While the genuine and lasting realization of any life ideals must be bounded by the moral minimum, universal compliance with the moral minimum requires the support of life ideals or religion as well. But the two spheres are quite different. While the standards for ultimate or religious values are relative to individuals, the standard of the moral minimum is singular, that is, there is only one standard to measure all people's behaviors. There are no standards that differ for different people. The moral minimum applies to the whole of society and is equally demanding of all people. It often requires enforcement by law. By contrast, the life ideals of people are plural. People's values and ultimate concerns are varied; they may contradict and even clash with each other, yet an individual is free to choose any of them.

Now the question is whether the norms of a universal moral minimum need to be so rudimentary that they can be supported jointly by all reasonable life ideals or various particular value systems of different civilizations and cultural traditions. In my opinion, "universal ethics" means first an ethics that applies equally to all individuals, all peoples, and all nations without exception. Second, it is an ethics that seeks as wide an agreement and consensus as possible. However, if it aims to reach such objectives, it has to limit itself to a moral minimum only.

Basic duties need a kind of spiritual support that highly respects norms, though the spirit may be expressed in different ways by different people and nations. One who is able to obey social duties is to be regarded as a good person in the sense that the person can at least be considered righteous no matter his or her religion. However, not only does the universal morality mean the universal fulfillment of norms, it also entails a kind of understanding of, concern for, and sympathy toward people. Without such a moral "'enlivening," the morality of norms alone may harden or wither due to the lack of moral "lifeblood." A kind sympathy for other human beings and a concern for all life will remind us of the deepest meaning and true source of morality. It also will remind us to ponder the relationship between morality and life and the possibility of social morality—including the universal ethics of modern society—transforming itself anew.

PART II

HISTORICAL AND SOCIOLOGICAL ORIGINS OF CHINESE CULTURAL NORMS

CHAPTER THREE

The Selection Society

The concept of a "selection society" emerged in contrast to the "hereditary society," which existed during the Western Zhou Dynasty and the Spring and Autumn period.[1] My goal in this chapter is to provide an explanation for the main social trends within the predominant Chinese cultural sphere during the dynastic period from the Qin-Han Dynasties to the late Qing Dynasty and to explain how China's unique social structures eventually emerged from those trends.

Clearly, the concept of a selection society is going to be more controversial than the hereditary society concept, which I have used to explain Zhou and Spring and Autumn history. So I should first explain that though the Chinese terms for "selection" and "election" are the same, the "selection" referred to here is completely different from the modern concept of "election." Unlike modern elections, selection in ancient China was a top-down process in which the ruler chose those who would govern. It was the minority selecting the minority. But selection was not merely an expression of the will and whims of individuals: it was highly systematized and objective.[2]

This chapter is an edited version of "Introduction," in He Huaihong, *The Selection Society and Its Fate* (Shanghai: SDX Joint Publishing Company, 1998).

1. See He Huaihong, *The Hereditary Society and Its Collapse* (Shanghai: SDX Joint Publishing Company, 1996).

2. For example, it is completely different from Mao Zedong's selection of a successor, a one-off event dependent on the will of one individual.

In theory, almost no one was excluded from the selection process. In practice, only very few ever participated and even fewer worked the system well enough to eventually be chosen. The participants in the system were not selectors: they were aiming to be selected; they were nominating themselves. Ultimately, they were selected on the basis of either the recommendation of others or their measurable performance on the examinations. Of course, the selected were a group, not a single person, and they did not themselves immediately become senior policymakers. Rather, they formed the monarch's body of officials, or pool of potential officials. The qualities that were examined in the selection process were the individual's virtue; ability; personal renown and family background; and cultural refinement. Each cohort selected was not a uniform group but a collection of disparate personalities. Selection did not bring an instant change in national policy, just an injection of new blood into the class of officials. So it was an elite process: in terms of both its form and its participants, it was an activity of the few. Selection was determined by a particular set of criteria. The selection process never spoke directly to the fundamental legitimacy of the state or the government, but it lent stability to Chinese society and allowed for the formation of reasonable expectations. It was a major factor in the distribution of resources, social stratification, and the possibility of status changes among individuals.

I first review the theory of Chinese society and history, which I am aiming to replace, then describe the selection society from a new perspective, with the necessary theoretical explanation and some initial historical evidence.

Two Interpretations of Chinese History

In ancient China, there were many functional analyses and descriptions of social and political arrangements. There were even theoretical accounts of the origins of human society. Before the Qin Dynasty, Xunzi, Mozi, Mencius and others had produced highly elaborate social theories.[3] So ancient China possessed a well-developed diachronic sense of history, but there was a rela-

3. Xunzi (荀子, 313–238 BC) was a Confucian philosopher during the Warring States period (403–221 BC). Contrary to the belief of Mencius (孟子, 372–289 BC) that human beings are innately good, Xunzi believed that human nature needed to be rectified through education and ritual. Mozi (墨子, dates unknown) was a philosopher during the Warring States period. Few details of his life are known, but as the one who introduced philosophical argumentation and debate, as Socrates did in ancient Greece, he was arguably the first true philosopher in Chinese history. Mozi and his school of thought advocated impartial concern for all and opposition to military aggression.

tive lack of theory concerning social change and advancement. There was also little sense of geographical space, as there were no suitable contemporary candidates for comparison. Thus ancient thinkers found it difficult to develop a comparative, synchronic concept of social structure.

But when China collided with the West in modern times, it discovered an utterly novel form of social organization that had far surpassed Chinese civilization in terms of wealth and power. China's one-dimensional, cyclic vision of society and history was instantly bankrupted. We fairly quickly accepted in its place a linear conception of history as an irreversible, one-directional, unbroken train of progress. There was a brief period when a range of Western historical theories competed for acceptance in China. But one theory—specifically the Russian interpretation of one theory—quickly achieved dominance and became China's standard view of history. This was Stalin's simplified "five-stage model."[4] It was quickly applied to the history of China (though where exactly the boundaries between different stages lay was a source of much controversy). This theory drove Chinese thinkers for the first time to look at their own history through the lens of social structure, and that approach was extremely fruitful, producing many new insights.

Today we are well accustomed to explaining China's last two millennia of history with the shorthand phrase "feudal society." We apply the term "feudal" to the very core and essence of our cultural tradition. We unthinkingly toss around terms like "feudal autocracy" and "feudal unification" without pausing to realize that these phrases are contradictions in terms. The feudal model has become the dominant model for interpreting China's history. Over the last decade, some mainland authors have started to use the term with some caution or have avoided using it at all; some have even attempted to propose new explanatory frameworks. But the feudal model is still repeated and shared in many contexts: in the news, on radio and television, and in schools. It still provides common ground among cultural scholars who in other areas differ sharply and even contradict each other. Though its grip is weakening in mainland China, the "feudal" model is still dominant.

But the point I want to make is that this concept, "feudal," is a very recent addition to Chinese historiography. Its arguments, in their current form, have been made for no more than fifty or sixty years. To be blunt, it is a very

4. The five-stage model ("五阶段模式") refers to the historical development theory originating from Marxism and developed by Soviet historians during the 1920s. The theory dictates that all human societies progress in sequence along five stages: primitive communism–slavery–feudalism–capitalism–communism. Chinese scholars are now highly skeptical of the compatibility of this model with the reality of Chinese history.

"modern" concept, and it is at odds with the interpretation of the people who were actually a part of traditional Chinese society; in fact, it contradicts them. The historians of dynastic China would have recognized "feudalism" as the ancient *fengjian* enfeoffment system of the Zhou Dynasty. They believed that it had been replaced by the time of the Qin unification with a centralized bureaucracy of commanderies and counties. In contrast, the modern view, espoused by Guo Moruo and allied scholars, sees the Spring and Autumn period as the slave society phase in Marxist historiography and the Warring States period and Qin Dynasty as the beginning of China's feudal phase.[5] There have been variations, placing the beginning of the feudal phase as early as the Western Zhou or as late as the Wei-Jin Dynasties, but all agree that approximately the last 2,000 years of Chinese history, up to the late Qing Dynasty, were feudal in nature.

This claim is in fact a theoretical necessity: capitalist society (which in China appeared as the variant "semi-colonial, semi-feudal") must be preceded by feudal society, otherwise Chinese history would have violated the necessary and objective historical rule of progress from feudal to capitalist. And if that historical rule was voided, it would have been impossible to explain China's revolutions as democratic, class revolutions. The logical train of thought with which we have all become familiar is this: how could anything but a feudal society come before a capitalist society? If so, would that not mean that the Marxist theory of history was invalid? Maybe even all of historical materialism? If so, then how would we know how the revolution should develop? Who should be rising up, overthrowing whom, taking whose power? This logic gradually became ingrained, universally recognized as the background to our understanding of history. Often it was unspoken, because it was so completely undisputed.

The feudal model of Chinese dynastic history was proposed during the twentieth century, China's century of popular revolution. What is becoming increasingly apparent is that the twentieth century was just another historic transition period from one social formation to another. The Chinese term that came to mean "feudal" was originally a system of enfeoffment, through

5. Guo Moruo (郭沫若, 1892–1978), a native of Leshan, Sichuan Province, was a modern Chinese historian, archaeologist, and poet. Guo joined the Communist Party in August 1927 during the Nanchang Revolution and held important government positions after 1949, including president of the Chinese Academy of Sciences and vice chairman of the Chinese People's Political Consultative Conference (CPPCC). Guo was famous for his poetry and academic achievements during his early career, but he became controversial after 1949 and during the Cultural Revolution.

which the ruler would assign territories to members of his clan. During the warlord era, when revolutionary zeal targeted primarily the feudal warlords, opposition to feudalism meant, more than anything, opposition to warlords. Feudalism was at this time understood mainly as an elite power system, not significantly different from enfeoffment feudalism. Warlord feudalism was not identical to enfeoffment: it was no longer a matter of the family relationships of the royal clan. But it was very comparable to the autonomous military colonies of the Tang Dynasty borderlands, for example. When the Kuomintang leadership launched the Northern Expedition against the warlords, their primary objective was to unify the national territory.[6] They were basically uninterested in mobilizing the lower orders; they did not reform rural land ownership. Defeating the warlords was obviously not going to bring about a broad-based social revolution. That required drawing in landlords and rich farmers as local targets to be overthrown.

This change in target, from feudal warlords to feudal landlords, meant a shift in focus from the political to the economic and from the elite to the entire population. The concept of feudal landlords presaged the emergence of a full theory of feudal society. In his 1930 *Studies in Ancient Chinese Society*, Guo Moruo explicitly rejects the old understanding of "feudal" as enfeoffment and proposes a new theory of a feudal society based on class conflict and the economic relationship between landowners and farmers. This new theory was elevated to the status of fact by Mao Zedong in *The Chinese Revolution and the Chinese Communist Party* and other writings. It was one of the Chinese Communist Party's major calls to action as it marshalled mass engagement in its land reforms and revolutionary war. The new reading of feudalism remained a vivid and persistent presence after 1949, in the "permanent revolution" that cemented the complete break with the old traditions.

So the political weight of the feudal society model was enormous. But in terms of historical research, its significance lay mainly in directing the attention of Chinese historians to areas that traditional academics had often ignored: the economy and the lower orders of society, the governed. In this sense, it did have a positive effect. It made Chinese historians look at the forgotten history of the lower orders and research a history outside of elite politics. But this historical research project was inevitably scarred by its

6. The Northern Expedition Period (北伐时期, 1926–28) refers to efforts led by the Kuomintang (Nationalist Party) based in Guangdong against warlords in northern China. Its main objective was to unify China under the Nationalist banner by ending the rule of local warlords. It led to the demise of the Beiyang government and to the Chinese reunification of 1928.

overriding political motivation and its utility as a call to arms. It was always functionalist and reactive. The Communists called on the people to overturn the "three great mountains" (imperialism, feudalism, and bureaucratic capitalism) and tarred China's thousands of years of history a uniform black—or at least cast those millennia as a long dark age. Now, though, we have left the turbulence and revolt of the mid-century behind and entered a calmer period of reconstruction. It is inevitable that we should begin correcting the wilder excesses of that moralistic antagonism to our own history. And it is not just the specific condemnations that we need to correct: the whole conceptual basis is flawed.

For a Chinese scholar, another important issue is suspicion of the origins of the model. The social theories that are currently standard in China are modern, Western creations, the result of analyzing modern capitalist societies. We cannot but wonder: Do they really have sufficient explanatory power? Do they really fit the facts of Chinese history? In the spirit of respect for history and the search for historical truth, it seems that we must at least try to find a new explanatory social model. It should be one that meshes better with both historical fact and with the understanding of dynastic history that was prevalent during dynastic times.

There is another explanatory model, which also originated overseas but has gained increasing traction within China: Weber's model of bureaucracy. Roughly speaking, this model defines China as a feudal aristocracy up to the Spring and Autumn period and as a bureaucratic empire in the Warring States and dynastic periods. These labels derive from changes in the form of the state and government. This model is popular among some overseas historians and Chinese historians who do not accept the slavery-feudalism narrative. Histories that invoke "autocracy" or "empire" are generally versions of this theory.

The concept of a bureaucratic society does capture one of the key changes during the Spring and Autumn and Warring States periods. It grasps the uniquely political and bureaucratic character of the Chinese system, which lasted for thousands of years: how the system drew into itself all social resources of authority, wealth, status, and fame. China after the Qin-Han unification was indeed a bureaucratic empire in which the monarch held absolute power, and over time it developed into an ever more dense, more perfect bureaucracy.

But bureaucracy is less a concept from sociology than it is from political science; it is not so much a social structure as an institutional model.[7] This

---

7. Perhaps because Weberian bureaucracy does not provide a full sociological framework, it combines easily with other explanatory models, including the feudal society model. It can also, of course, combine with the selection society model.

model is little concerned with the relationship between the bureaucracy and the lower orders, with class structure, or with the constitution of the ruling upper class and mechanisms for entry. Rather, it concentrates on the relationships between bureaucrats and ruler, on the administrative function of the bureaucrats themselves, on the legitimacy and rationality of the bureaucratic state, and so on. Moreover, while the Weberian concept of bureaucracy captures well the political developments over the centuries of the Spring and Autumn and Warring States periods, it does not straightforwardly explain the important social changes in the subsequent 2,000 years of Chinese history. In particular, it fails to pick out some of the unique features of China as a civilization. For these reasons, it would be useful for us to shift our gaze downward, to look away from the emperor and his bureaucrats to the base of traditional Chinese society and how it relates to the upper strata.

A New Perspective

The dominance of the feudal model of Chinese history has meant that since 1949, mainland historians have given little attention to the selection mechanisms of dynastic China. The subject has become an orphan of historical research. There has been a steady stream of work on the subject from Taiwan and Hong Kong, but they have generally been institutional histories, as have the few books that have appeared in mainland China over the last few years. Overseas, some scholars working in the tradition of Western social sciences have studied the imperial examination system as a mechanism of social mobility. The most notable of these is Ping-ti Ho's *The Ladder of Success in Imperial China: Aspects of Social Mobility, 1638–1911*.[8] Performing a quantitative and statistical analysis of extant data on those who won status and renown in the examinations, Ho finds levels of vertical mobility that even modern Western states cannot easily match. This is a sociological approach, but Ho's concern is primarily social mobility rather than class structure. The social form in which I am interested is an account of the fundamental structure of society.

Of course, the biggest factor affecting social mobility is social structure; however, many studies of mobility go no further than quantification. They make no effort to link mobility to structure—a criticism also voiced by the

8. Ping-ti Ho: *The Ladder of Success in Imperial China: Aspects of Social Mobility, 1638–1911* (Columbia University Press, 1962). See also Chang Chung-li, *The Chinese Gentry: Studies on Their Role in Nineteenth-Century Chinese Society* (University of Washington Press, 1955); Robert Marsh, *The Mandarin* (New York: Free Press of Glencoe, 1961).

Polish sociologist Wlodzimierz Wesolowski.[9] But I am not interested in social structure merely for its impact on social mobility. I want to examine a phenomenon that may be unique to China: institutionalized upward mobility. This means not just persistent *structural mobility* but a social system with an inherently *mobile structure*. Mobility was a permanent structural element in dynastic Chinese society. Simply looking at mobility itself is in my view insufficient to capture the depth and breadth of the social changes that occurred over the 2,000 years between the Qin-Han and the late Qing Dynasties. In particular, it fails to capture the features that distinguish Chinese society from its Western counterparts. Over those two millennia, Chinese society gradually transformed from a closed, rigid, stratified society into an open, mobile, stratified society: the selection society.

The approach I am describing here could be described as a broad-based, whole-society perspective on social class. However, the object of this analysis is not the loose, subtle, fluid, and diverse stratification of modern societies; it is an extreme, rigid, unipolar division into the many and the few. And the analysis focuses on the class mobility of individuals. Class structure and social mobility are the explanatory tools that I use to comprehend the traditional society of dynastic China.

Are the core issues that I address in my research on social structures a good basis for this kind of sociological history? Those issues are on two levels. On the level of society, the issue is the ongoing redistribution of social resources in the broadest sense (including political authority, economic benefits, and social status—simply put, power, money, and fame) and the continual reconstitution of the governing class. On the level of the individual, the issue is the reasonable expectations that persons could have in their society and the various paths to upward mobility open to them. To borrow a phrase coined by the political scientist Harold Lasswell, my central question is "Who gets what, when, and how?" The things that individuals desired were, of course, universally valued social resources. They were scarce, and they could motivate individuals to strive for the extraordinary. But who actually succeeded in obtaining them? How did they obtain them and what criteria decided their success? These questions define the basic axis of social stratification.

I believe that the question of distribution of resources, the question of to whom they should belong, is one of the basic distinguishing marks of differ-

9. See Bogdan W. Mach and W. Wesolowski, *Social Mobility and Social Structure* (Routledge and Kegan Paul, 1986). The authors attempt to bridge Marx and Weber: starting with features shared by both thinkers, they combine a Marxist theory of class structure with research on social mobility.

ent social structures. That is true whatever definition is given to social resources. For any given historical period, we may choose to focus on means of production, or political power, or legal status, and so on. Examining the changes in distribution of one of these specific social resources can help us to understand a single historical phase, but to distinguish properly between the different social structures of different historical phases, no single criterion will suffice. Multiple indices are needed. As Daniel Bell says, "The distributions of wealth, power and status . . . are central to any society."[10] Fernand Braudel also believes in applying Pierre Bourdieu's radical sociological theories to the past, admitting from the beginning that the basic task of any society is to reproduce its ruling elite—those with political power.[11]

However, in the modern world, many have understood a society's resources only in a narrow, economic sense. As I have written before, in the foreword to *The Hereditary Society*, definitions of social structures by those who live in modern societies tend to share a common feature: they give extreme prominence to the function of economic factors, seeing economics as the most decisive factor in a social order. But we must apply this principle to historical societies only with caution and careful reflection, particularly when looking at non-Western societies. China's civilization has some features that are strikingly different from those of Western cultures. While Western feudal societies were fairly martial in character, China's feudal society, even as far back as the Spring and Autumn period, showed signs of strong "cultural" regulation through the arts and ritual. And traditional policymakers did not seem to consciously pursue economic development. They did not see large, sustained increases in wealth as a major factor in human happiness. In dynastic China, cultural and moral factors seem to have played an increasingly important and prominent role in social stratification.

This brings us back to the question of why we need the concepts of "hereditary society" and "selection society." They imply a certain way of looking at history. In this approach, my understanding of social structure is realist: it is a society's class structure. The focus is on the relationship between class structure and individual advancement.

Over the course of the millennia, the three primary sources of social value—power, wealth, and fame—were bound tightly together, with institutional power in the most prominent position. Becoming a functionary of the

10. Daniel Bell, *The Coming of Post-Industrial Society: A Venture in Social Forecasting* (Commercial Press, 1986), p. 54.

11. Fernand Braudel, *Civilization and Capitalism, 15th–18th Centuries*, vol. 2, trans. Gu Liang, Shi Kangqiang (Beijing: SDX Joint Publishing Company, 1993), p. 523.

state was the main road upward, and the cultural obsession with being an official has persisted for thousands of years. Just as modern society emphasizes the economic, throughout China's long history we see a sustained emphasis on power. But looked at in terms of social stratification, the first and more important question is this: How did one become an official? What were the conditions for entry into this class? Starting in the Qin-Han Dynasties, China gradually developed an answer to that question that is unique among world civilizations. It demands an interpretation to match its uniqueness.

Support for the Selection Society

The purpose of my research is to propose a new theoretical framework for the interpretation of the historical structures of Chinese society and their changes, a framework different from those currently popular. This interpretive framework is not only an empirical result; it is also an attempt at a conceptual model that can be used to approach Chinese social history. It is a hypothesis, similar to Weber's "ideal type" or "pure type."

But any hypothesis that claims to have historical explanatory power, however tentative it may be, must provide answers to two types of challenge. The first is theoretical: Is this concept theoretically sound? Is it logically consistent? Is the distribution of social goods a reasonable approach to investigating Chinese social structure and its historical changes? The second type of challenge is evidential: we must find historical evidence to support the explanatory concepts. In fact, while theoretical soundness is important, I believe that empirical tests against history are more important. We must test whether the concept of the selection society has sufficient explanatory power when we apply it to a specific period in history, whether it really gives us a new tool in our historical toolkit. My empirical test of the explanatory power of the concept is not, of course, confined to this introduction. This entire book can be read as an attempt to test its power.

But in this section, I want first of all to point out a precondition for the existence of a selection society and then look at the status and impact of the selection process in traditional Chinese society. First, let us look at the general form of traditional Chinese society as we understand it. This basic form is the traditional social order that lasted from the Qin-Han Dynasties through to the demise of the Qing Dynasty. Though it went through many changes, some fundamental features never changed. Those fundamental features include

—*an absolute monarch.* The monarch commanded the utmost deference. He was to some extent constrained by the "mandate of Heaven," the rules of his ancestors, and certain laws, but in practice he was the highest authority and the source of all power and law.

—*a bureaucratic administration.* Under the monarch, there were bureaucratic systems staffed with scholar-officials.

—*a stratified society.* Two major classes were always present: a class of officials, who governed with the monarch; and a class of farmers, laborers, and merchants, who were governed.

—*a close congruence between social order and ethical order.* The ethical order referred to here is the family hierarchy—that is, the traditional Confucian understanding of ethics as relations between persons. Up until the Spring and Autumn period, the congruence of social and ethical order was built into the institutions of the state, with the enfeoffment system being the most obvious example. From the Qin-Han Dynasties onward, this congruence was conceptual and attitudinal, manifested in the patriarchal organization of society.

The administrative bureaucracy and social stratification played vital roles in establishing the selection society. There had to be a well-defined, non-hereditary corps of officials, with a constant supply to make up for natural turnover. And because of the wide chasm between the classes, "selection" in this traditional system actually meant elevation, moving the individuals from the lower class who met the requirements into the upper class. Without a class system, there would be no upper and lower classes and no elevation.

When we look at the status of the selection system in traditional Chinese society, first we must appreciate the political importance of the officials who came through the selection process. Even during the earliest phase, the Han *chaju* examinations period, and certainly during the later *keju* examinations period, those who passed the exams were the backbone of the ruling elite. They were regarded as the most legitimate candidates for administrative office, and they were granted enormous respect. Second, when we look at the positions to which they could rise, we see that they were not consigned to lower posts. They became senior officials, policymakers rather than mere functionaries. Often they entered the civil service at a very senior level: a first-rank county official, where a county might have hundreds of thousands of residents. And the very highest position in government—that of *zaixiang*, or chancellor—was virtually monopolized by those who had come through the examination system.[12] For example, of the seventy-one prime ministers

---

12. Chancellor, or *zaixiang* (宰相), refers to the highest-ranking official in the ancient Chinese bureaucracy, similar to the modern day prime minister. Although the chancellor was established as the head of government, the chancellor's power (相权) was constantly

during the Northern Song Dynasty, sixty-four were products of the examination system. Several of the others were appointed in exceptional circumstances; only three times was someone who was not a degree-holder appointed prime minister in the usual way. During the Ming and Qing Dynasties, the most senior members of government were not only selected from among the "presented scholars"—those who had passed the highest-level examinations—they were generally those who had achieved the best results in the exams and so had been inducted into the Hanlin Academy.[13] Of the more than 170 prime ministers of the Ming Dynasty, 90 percent were Hanlin academicians. In the Qing Dynasty, 119 Han Chinese officials were admitted into the Grand Secretariat, all of them graduates of the examinations. And of the 119, all but one were the first presented scholars in their families; the one exception was Zuo Zongtang, who did come from a family of officials.[14]

Now let us look at the status and importance of the examination system in Chinese society. A traditional Chinese saying, "If that road opens, then all roads are open," acknowledged that political power, wealth, and status were deeply intertwined. And the result of giving power to the best scholars was that learning was strongly encouraged throughout society. The Song Emperor Zhenzong wrote in his poem "Encouraging Learning": "To be

---

at odds with the emperor's power (王权) throughout Chinese history. The *zaixiang* position was first instituted in the Qin Dynasty (221–206 BC) and terminated in the Ming Dynasty, with power increasingly centralized in the hands of the emperor.

13. *Jinshi*, or presented scholar (进士), was the most advanced degree conferred by the Chinese imperial examination system, which was administered at the local, provincial, and national levels. *Jinshi* degrees were awarded to graduates who passed the national-level exams administered in the capital by the emperor himself and were likely to become high-level officials in the imperial government. The Hanlin Academy (翰林院) served as a prestigious official academic institution in the Chinese political establishment from the Tang Dynasty in the eighth century to the end of the Qing Dynasty in 1911. The members of the Hanlin Academy were top graduates of the imperial examination system, and the academy also served as a reservoir for talented individuals who passed the imperial examinations prior to their assignment to key government positions.

14. Zuo Zongtang (左宗棠, 1812–85), a native of Xiangyin, Hunan Province, was an important official and military leader in the late Qing Dynasty. As a top graduate of the imperial examination system, Zuo was later promoted to the position of governor of various provinces and regions. He was one of the major leaders of China's self-strengthening Westernization movement, and he led the military campaign to claim Xinjiang from the Ottoman Empire in 1876.

wealthy you need not purchase fertile fields,/ Thousands of tons of corn are to be found in the books./ To build a house you need not set up high beams,/ Golden mansions are to be found in the books./ To travel you need not worry about not having servants and attendants,/ Large entourages of horses and carriages are to be found in the books./ To find a wife you need not worry about not having good matchmakers,/ Maidens as beautiful as jade are to be found in the books./ When a man wishes to fulfill the ambition of his life,/ He needs only to diligently study the six classics by the window!"[15] Wang Anshi also wrote a poem with the same title: "Reading takes no great effort,/ Reading brings rewards 10,000 times greater. . . . Read the classics by your window,/ Seek the meaning of books by a lamp,/ The poor are rich because of books,/ The rich are noble because of books."[16] Over time, upward and downward mobility meant that learning permeated the entire country, making the Chinese the most bookish culture in world history. Even those who could not read themselves understood that ink on paper was precious, and there was a universal reverence for literature and the written word.

One possible objection is that the examination system only ever involved a minority of people and that the number of those ultimately "selected" was even smaller. Why then claim that this system constituted a social structure? There are two responses. One is that every traditional society has a small ruling elite (and that may be a hidden truth about modern societies as well). The other response is that we should understand the performative nature of the examination system and its impact on the whole culture. The various examination rituals had a startling impact on the nonparticipating majority. There were multiple levels to the system, and most people would directly encounter only graduates of the lowest level. But even the lowest level had a notable social impact. In *Degree Titles of the Chinese Imperial Examinations*, Qi Rushan explores the social significance of each degree awarded. As he explains, *tong sheng*, the term for candidates for the initial, local examina-

15. Song emperor Zhenzong (宋真宗, 968–1022), real name Zhao Heng, was the third emperor of the Northern Song Dynasty (960–1127). He was known for his high literary achievements but mediocre statecraft and weak diplomacy. During the reign of Song Zhenzong, the Northern Song Dynasty succumbed to the Northern Liao Dynasty (907–1125) with the signing of the Chanyuan Treaty in 1004.

16. Wang Anshi (王安石, 1021–1086), a native of Fuzhou, Jiangxi Province, was an economist, chancellor, and poet during the Northern Song Dynasty (960–1127). During his tenure as chancellor, Wang was famous for promulgating audacious reform policies. However, his reform policies were bitterly opposed by the conservative faction and were largely abolished after he was removed from the position.

tions, refers not to a degree but a class.[17] Someone who sat the county examinations would be known within the local government offices. The names of ordinary subjects were not recorded; they were just a number, a statistic. But a man who signed up for the examinations would be entered into the rolls of the national academies, and he would be treated with a little more respect than the average member of the public.

Thus the titles awarded in the examinations were not just decorations for those who wished to stand out. They were the only way to enhance one's identity or status and a foundation for further advancement. Degree titles therefore took on remarkable importance, becoming an object of public desire, envy, respect, and awe. In his memoirs, Chen Duxiu writes that though he did not share his mother's reverence for the imperial examinations, he did understand it:

> Because in the society of the time, the imperial examinations were not just an empty title. They controlled the lives of ordinary people everywhere. You had to have a degree to become a senior official. . . . Polite expressions of good wishes were all wishes for success in the examinations: may you study well, may you come top in the exams. A husband with a degree would be a direct source of pride and status for a woman; if a household did not have a degree, then the servants would see their mistress as no better than them. If the son of a poor farmer . . . was allowed to go with his teacher to the town and attend the examinations, then he would return home with a new status. It didn't matter if he'd scribbled complete rubbish and failed even to place in the results, he was now someone. The most heartless and cruel of landlords would now look at this tenant farmer household with new eyes. In the villages it was summed up in this pithy observation: "Even a fart in examination hall brings honor to your ancestors."[18]

17. Qi Rushan (齐如山, 1875–1962), a native of Gaoyang, Hebei Province, was a playwright, opera scholar, and historian in modern China. Qi received a traditional Chinese education yet also managed to master English, French, German, and Russian. After several trips to France, he began writing plays in the 1910s. His new plays revived people's interest in traditional Chinese drama, both in China and the West. *Tong sheng* (童生) was the "child student" level in China's imperial examination system, which applied to examinees waiting to pass the entry-level examinations. There was no actual age limit for this group of examinees, who could maintain their *tong sheng* status even in their senior years.

18. Chen Duxiu, *Selected Essays*, vol. 2 (Beijing: SDX Joint Publishing Company, 1984), pp. 556–57. Chen Duxiu (陈独秀, 1879–1942), a native of Anqing, Anhui Province, was one of the founding members of the Chinese Communist Party in 1921.

In Weber's terms, Chinese scholar-officials had "charisma." We can see examples of this in the novel *The Scholars*, when Butcher Hu acts completely differently toward his son-in-law Fan Jin after Fan finally obtains his provincial-level degree.[19] When Fan loses his mind out of pure elation at his academic success, Butcher Hu slaps him, but his hand immediately starts to "dully ache."

Over the 2,000 years from the Qin-Han to the late Qing Dynasties, the general trend was the growing importance of the selection process, both in its place in Chinese government and in its influence on Chinese society. This trend ultimately resulted in a true selection society in which learning was for the purpose of advancement and the ruling elite was selected from the best scholars. I believe that this conception of history is correct in its broad outline and is well supported by historical evidence.

However, the very introductory sketch presented in this chapter is just a beginning. There are three questions to explore if we are to give the selection society concept a more systematic treatment. The first is "How did the selection process affect social structure? How did it create a society that allocated its resources primarily through this selection process?" The second is "What were the fundamental principles and standards of selection? How effective were they? Did those standards enable the system to achieve its objectives and perform its social function?" The third is "What were the internal tensions in this society, and how did it resolve them? And how did external factors force an end to the system in modern times?"

The Selection Society is therefore divided into three parts. The first part revolves around an exploration of the forms of the selection system in dynastic China and the social impact of the shift from the *chaju* system to the much more comprehensive *keju* examination system. Borrowing from de Tocqueville's analysis of the trends and features of modern American and European societies, I describe how Chinese traditional society developed as the selection system was refined; how it shifted toward a single path to great

---

Chen was an activist during the May Fourth Movement and later became the first chairman and general secretary of the Chinese Communist Party. However, he was later sidelined and purged due to his criticism of Stalin.

19. *Rulin Waishi*, or *The Scholars* (《儒林外史》), is a Qing Dynasty (1644–1911) novel written by Wu Jingzi (1701–1754). Set in the Ming Dynasty (1368–1644), the novel was a reflection of the reality of the imperial examination system in the Qing Dynasty. Through satiric stories, the novel ridiculed ambitious yet didactic Confucian scholars in the imperial examination system.

political power, with great equality of opportunity; and how that reinforced a stratified social structure with built-in mobility.

The second part focuses on the conditions for selection into the ruling elite. In particular, it examines the "eight-legged" essay, the highly specified writing format that became the core of the examinations. I look at the processes, the specific requirements, the function, and the social meaning and impact of the selection system and at how it selected its recruits and how its recruits gained selection. I also attempt to restore some of the reputation of the "eight-legged" essay, which has taken such a battering since the early twentieth century. The deeper purpose of this part is to discuss in detail the social structures that the examination system helped form over the course of millennia.

The third part analyzes some of the inherent tensions within China's selection society, the problems that it faced and the traditional solutions. It then describes how, as a result of China's collision with the West, the imperial examinations were abandoned in the late Qing Dynasty. It examines the reasons for this change, the processes by which it happened, and its far-reaching social impact. The end of the examinations signaled not just the end of 2,000 years of China's selection society but the end of a social class system that had persisted for thousands of years.

This volume, which is a sequel to *The Hereditary Society*, traces a path from the transitional Warring States period into the two millennia of Chinese history that ended with the Qing Dynasty. It proposes a new sociological interpretation, unlike the current widely accepted frameworks, to explain Liang Shuming's "riddle of history": why China's history from the Qin-Han Dynasties to the Qing Dynasty followed such a unique path, so unlike that of European history.[20] It is my hope that together, *The Hereditary Society* and *The Selection Society* will form a structurally coherent and fairly comprehensive sociological framework for Chinese history.

However, it is not my aim to merely stress the uniqueness of Chinese civilization. We should also notice some universals in the transitions between traditional and modern societies. China's traditional society had in fact many modern elements, and it was moving in the direction of "modernity," albeit

---

20. Liang Shuming (梁漱溟, 1893–1988), a native of Guilin, Guangxi Province, was a philosopher, teacher, and leader in the rural development movement in the late Qing Dynasty and early Republican eras of Chinese history. In 1917, Liang was recruited to Peking University's department of philosophy. Liang was a Confucian scholar and believed that Western civilizations were doomed to failure and thus advocated against the complete adoption of Western institutions in China.

in a way that was rather different from the way of the West. The development over 2,000 years of China's selection mechanisms—from the recommendation system (*chaju*) to the examination system (*keju*)—represents a move toward equality of opportunity by means of narrowing the paths of advancement to a single route. This trend toward equality is in some ways similar to the equality movement that followed the collapse of Western feudal systems, though it has some obvious unique features. China was indeed a part of the global march to modernity that de Tocqueville described as a shift toward equality. We could even say that dynastic China faced the burdens and difficulties of modernity earlier than the West. The selection society interpretation can thus also be seen as an attempt to explore the relationship between China's past and the modern era from within China and to start to reflect on and criticize the concept of modernity from our own perspective.

CHAPTER FOUR

1905: The End of Traditional Chinese Society

In my beginning is my end. . . . In my end is my beginning.
—T. S. Eliot, "East Coker"

Of all the momentous years at the end of the nineteenth and the start of the twentieth century, 1905 does not immediately seize our attention. Compared with the drama of 1898 (Hundred Days' Reform), 1900 (Boxer Rebellion), and 1911 (end of the Qing dynasty), it seems somewhat uneventful. But to me, 1905 symbolizes the end of traditional Chinese society. The event that marks this decisive break is the abolition of the imperial examination system. On September 2, 1905, a petition was submitted to the emperor by Yuan Shikai, viceroy of Zhili.[1] It was signed by five others: Zhao Erzhuan, the military commander of Shengjing; Zhang Zhidong, viceroy of Huguang; Zhou Fu, viceroy of Liangjiang; Cen Chunxuan, viceroy of Liangguang; and Duanfang, the governor of Hunan.[2] It requested an immediate end to the *keju*

This chapter is an edited version of an article by the same title first published in *Twenty-First Century* [Hong Kong], vol. 89 (June 2005).

1. Yuan Shikai (袁世凯, 1859–1916), a native of Dingcheng, Henan Province, was a powerful Chinese general and politician famous for his role in events leading up to the abdication of the last Qing emperor; his autocratic rule as the second president of the Republic of China, after Sun Yat-sen; and his short-lived attempt to revive the Chinese monarchy.

2. Zhao Erzhuan (赵尔巽, 1844–1927), a native of Tieling, Liaoning Province, was a politician and military leader in the late Qing Dynasty. During the final years of the Qing Dynasty, Zhao was appointed governor of Hunan and general of Shengjing. After the collapse of the dynasty, Zhao compiled the dynasty's official history. He also served briefly as

system—the imperial examinations. The emperor approved the petition, and from the year *bingwu* (1906), all local, provincial, and national examinations were canceled.

The abolition of the imperial examinations was, of course, the result of multiple factors and ongoing pressures, but it was in 1905 that those pressures came to a head. When it came, the abolition of the examinations had an enormous impact, marking as it did a fundamental break with Chinese history. Thus 1905 is a key link in the chain of transformations that modern Chinese society has undergone: it marks the end of a millennium of dynastic history and the beginning of a century of turmoil. In 1905, ancient practices crumbled or faced fundamental reform and new institutions and ideas sprang into being. The events of that year would shape the entire twentieth century.

The abolition of the imperial examination system was one of the earliest and most far-reaching of the many profound changes brought by the twentieth century. It was much more than just the end of a dynasty.[3] This chapter discusses the meaning of this event in the light of some preliminary historical research.[4]

---

interim chairman of the political council of the Duan Qirui government in 1925. Zhang Zhidong (张之洞, 1837–1909), a native of Nanpi, Hebei Province, was a prominent politician during the late Qing Dynasty. Zhang was one of the major advocates of the Self-Strengthening Movement. During his career, Zhang was appointed to a number of high-level positions, including as governor of Shanxi and viceroy of Huguang. Zhou Fu (周馥, 1837–1921), a native of Jiande, Anhui Province, was a politician in the late Qing Dynasty. As an advocate of the Self-Strengthening Movement, Zhou served as governor in multiple areas. Cen Chunxuan (岑春煊, 1861–1933), a native of Xilin, Guangxi Province, was a politician in the late Qing Dynasty. Cen served as governor in multiple areas and was known for his effort to rescue Empress Dowager Cixi and the Emperor Guangxu when they fled Beijing in 1900. Duanfang (端方 1861–1911), a Manchu, was a politician, educator, and antiques collector during the late Qing Dynasty. Duanfang served both as governor and viceroy in multiple provinces and regions. He was also known for his engagement with the West and his effort to promote overseas education.

3. American historians such as Rozman believe that the abolition of the imperial examinations was a more important historical break than the Xinhai Revolution. The integration of the old society had been maintained by the examination system. Now it was lost, and China thus lost the necessary foundation for modernization. I agree with Rozman on the importance of the abolition but for rather different reasons. See Gilbert Rozman, *The Modernization of China*, trans. Duan Xiaoguang and others (Jiangsu People's Publishing House, 1988).

4. For more information, see my work on the changes in Chinese society from the Spring and Autumn period to the late Qing Dynasty: *The Hereditary Society and Its Col-*

The End of the Traditional Selection Mechanism

The abolition of the imperial examinations meant the disappearance of a way of government that had lasted for more than 1,300 years since its introduction during the Tang Dynasty. But it was more than that. It was the end of dynastic China's selection system, a social institution that had been in existence for over 2,000 years. This point is often forgotten, so I want to dwell on it here: what took place in 1905 marked the abolition of the traditional Chinese selection society. The examination system operated from the Tang to the Qing Dynasty, but it had a predecessor in the recommendation system used from the Han to the Tang Dynasty. The two systems cannot be understood separately. The examination system developed directly out of the recommendation system, as a corrective to some of its problems. Together, the recommendation and examination systems constituted dynastic China's mechanisms of selection of scholar-officials. Plenty of information is available on these systems in the sections on civil service recruitment in the official dynastic histories. The state-sponsored encyclopedias on law and institutions also give very clear accounts.

When the Qin Dynasty unified China, it instituted a bureaucratic model of empire in which power was highly centralized. This model gave the selection system a purpose by creating a real demand for officials to fill civil service positions. The Han Dynasty conquered the Qin Dynasty and took over its institutions wholesale, but initially the Han Dynasty favored a different approach to recruiting its officials. It was only sixty or seventy years after the Han took power that it made the crucial change in the way that the ruling class reproduced itself. The emperors Wen (180–157 BC) and Jing (157–141 BC) had conducted occasional searches for "capable and straight-talking" men. But it was only under Emperor Wu (141–87 BC) that prime minister Dong Zhongshu spoke out against allowing positions to be passed from father to son and against selling official posts: "Let all the marquises, county governors, and officials with a stipend of two thousand *dan* each recommend virtuous men from among their staff or the residents of their counties. They should recommend two men each year, to be employed as palace guards."[5]

---

lapse (1996), and *The Selection Society and Its Fate* (1998), both published by SDX Joint Publishing Company as part of the SDX and HYI Academic Series.

5. Dong Zhongshu (董仲舒, 179–04 BC), a leading Confucian thinker during the Han Dynasty (202 BC–AD 220), was known for the promotion of Confucianism as the official ideology of the Chinese state.

Finally, in 134 BC, the emperor "ordered that each county and territory should recommend one filial, honest man." That decree does not sound especially dramatic, but as Lao Gan has written, it "laid the foundation for selection mechanisms that would last for millennia."[6] In 128 BC, another decree demanded that officials must make recommendations: "Any failure to recommend the filial when called upon to do so shall be seen as a failure to follow orders. Failure to find honest men is a failure to carry out one's duty, and will lead to removal from office." With this, the emperor achieved full compliance with his recommendation system. Reading through the *Book of Han*, we do indeed find records of officials dismissed from office for failing to make honest recommendations. In 106 BC, Emperor Wu created permanent governorships in the thirteen prefectures of his empire and ordered each of the governors to "find men of outstanding ability and virtue among the officials and people, who could in future be ministers or ambassadors." This was the first time that the state had specified both "virtue and ability." Those qualities became a standard requirement during the Eastern Han Dynasty (AD 25–220), and thereafter became the two key criteria in the recommendation process.

In AD 92–94, Emperor He ruled that "counties and territories with over 200,000 people must recommend one person per year," thereby fixing the ratio between recommendations and population, helping to further regularize the ongoing search for honest, filial men. There were a number of other categories in which officials were to make recommendations—for example, "astute and honest men" and "simple, honest, courteous, and frugal" men. At the same time, the state university system was beginning, and it would grow during the Han Dynasty until there were tens of thousands of students at university. This system prefigured the later deep links between schools and the examination system.

What exactly did "recommendation" mean? Even harsh critics of American democracy have to admit that in the 200-plus years of U.S. history, one thing has remained unshakeable: the presidential election is held every four years. That is something that no sitting president can change. Similarly, China's selection mechanisms generated stability and continuity, particularly

6. Lao Gan (劳干, 1907–2003), a native of Changsha, Hunan Province, was a historian in modern China. Lao graduated from Peking University in 1930 and later conducted research at Harvard University. As an expert on Han Dynasty history, Lao later taught history at major Taiwanese universities and at the University of California. Quote from Lao Gan, "Han dai chaju zhidu kao [An Investigation of the Recommendation System in the Han Dynasty]," *Bulletin of the Institute of History and Philology Academia Sinica* 17 (1945), reprinted in 1987, Zhonghua Book Company, p. 83.

with the later examination system. After a certain point, even the emperor would not have been able to end the examinations. Even in times of war or natural disaster, the examinations had to go ahead, postponed or in another venue. And the emperor could not possibly grant a degree title to anyone who had not earned it in the examinations.[7]

The recommendation system was different because it emphasized personal connections. Those making the recommendations knew every aspect of the candidate, not just his ability to write or his academic prowess but his character and wit. And candidates could not rely on an exceptional performance on one particular day. They had to be worthy of recommendation day in and day out; even their family background might come under scrutiny.

However, in the absence of external controls, this system of personal connections also created the possibility of abuse, factionalism, and corruption. There were two options for addressing those problems. One was to partially close the door that the recommendation system had opened, further segregating the ruling class from the rest of the population and minimizing opportunities for commoners to rise and gain entry. That would effectively suppress their ambition and desire for status. The other option was to fling the door completely open, to make the ruling class open to all but force everyone to gain entry through a series of strict and scrupulously fair examinations.

In the centuries from the Eastern Han Dynasty (25–220) to the Wei and Jin Dynasties (220-420) and the Northern and Southern Dynasties (420–589), it can be argued that the main strategy used was the first: restriction of opportunity. But beginning in the Tang Dynasty (618–907) and lasting to the Qing Dynasty, the second strategy finally won out. During the Tang, the examination system was formally established, open to anyone, and degrees were awarded solely on the strength of a candidate's writing.

During the Song Dynasty (960–1279), a number of innovations were introduced to end any contact between examiners and candidates: the examination venue was locked for the duration of the exam; scripts were submitted without names; finally, even handwriting was disguised by having a copyist write out all scripts before submission. All factors other than a person's writing were gradually filtered out of the process. Examiners did not know who submitted a particular script, still less what his family background might be. Many of the changes and procedures surrounding the examinations focused on ensuring anonymity for candidates. The result was that by the Song

7. For more on the continuity and independence of the selection mechanisms, see Têng Ssu-yü, *Zhongguo kaoshi zhidu shi* [A History of the Chinese Examination System] (Taiwan Student Book Company, 1982), p. 337.

Dynasty, the principle that family background should not be a factor in appointments to officialdom was well established. In the examination hall, a candidate's only weapon was his own intelligence. Over time, the progressive elimination of personal factors, the closing off of other routes to official appointment, and the fixing of a single examination syllabus all contributed to giving the state an objective, neutral, and egalitarian mechanism whereby it could assess candidates and decide appointments.

During the Ming Dynasty (1368–1644), the examination system reached a state of perfection. Detailed rules were formalized for each round of the examinations, with every procedure strictly regulated. Schools by this time had fully adapted and were virtually a part of the examination system. The Qing Dynasty (1644–1911) strictly adhered to the practices that it inherited from the Ming, making only marginal adjustments to the regulations.

Today, the strictest examinations in China are the university entrance exams. The comparison is instructive: the university exams today simply cannot compare with the imperial examinations—in their significance for social status, the strictness of their requirements, or the objectivity of their assessment of a candidate—not to mention the relative lengths of the traditions that they represent. In fact, the examination system was strikingly modern in its features: it was objective, fair, individualist, and instrumentalist. It seems to be one of the cruel jokes of history that it was this system that was scrapped first as China launched itself into Western-dominated "modernity." But perhaps the end was inevitable. After all, China was dealing with enormous changes in both its external environment and its own value system.

The End of the Selection Society

While the examination system played an important role in the Chinese dynastic state, it also affected the structure of Chinese society. Its abolition therefore had far-reaching effects. The 2,000 years of Chinese dynastic history, bookended by the massive upheavals of the Warring States period and the twentieth century, saw the emergence of a distinctive social structure. I believe that over those 2,000 years, the traditional selection mechanisms gradually molded a new society, characterized by a form of vertical social mobility. It was more than just sustained structural mobility: dynastic society developed an inherently mobile social structure. Mobility was itself a permanent and fundamental feature of the social landscape. Over this period Chinese society evolved from the closed, rigid, hierarchical society of the Warring States period—what I call the hereditary society—to a mobile hierarchical society: the selection society.

This is only a tentative hypothesis, a potential historical perspective on the broad sweep of Chinese history. But I propose this hypothesis confident that it does have some explanatory power. It seems to accurately reflect the realities of history; at the very least, it matches the understanding of those who actually lived in the periods under discussion (though of course they would not have used the terminology of the social sciences). And it is consistent with the theories of leading historians and sociologists. Fernand Braudel has argued that over the long term, "structure" is the most important question in social theory.[8] Peter Blau proposed that social structure is defined by social positions, the number of people who occupy those positions, and the effect of the distribution of social positions on social relations.[9] And Kenichi Tominaga agrees that the key concept in defining social classes is "social capital."

I cannot give a full account of the evidence for my perspective here. But I can point out what sort of questions this explanatory framework must address. One set of questions concerns the importance of the selection mechanism in traditional Chinese society: Did it become the primary means by which the ruling class reproduced itself? Did it become the primary lever for the distribution of social capital? Did it become the normal and legitimate channel for social advancement? Did it have a halo effect on other classes, including the farmers who made up the vast majority of the population? Another set of questions concerns the status of those selected: Did they achieve real power? What positions did they reach? What types of family and social background did they come from?

Ping-ti Ho has conducted research on social mobility during the Ming and Qing Dynasties. He examined the records of 12,226 men who obtained the highest degree, the "presented scholar" degree, over forty-eight examination cycles during the Ming and Qing Dynasties. Ho finds that during the Ming, 47.5 percent of degree winners fell into category A, which includes winners whose family had no degree holders of any kind within the preceding three generations, and 2.5 percent fell into category B, which includes winners whose family had a low degree holder within the preceding three generations but no one with an official position. Those two categories total 50 percent, meaning that half of all people awarded the presented scholar degree came from families of commoners who had been nothing but com-

8. Fernand Braudel, *Ecrits sur l'histoire* (Paris: 1969), pp. 104, 108.

9. Peter M. Blau, *Inequality and Heterogeneity: A Primitive Theory of Social Structure* (New York: Free Press, 1977).

moners for generations. During the Qing Dynasty, 19.1 percent of presented scholars were from category A and 18.1 percent were from category B, for a total of 37.2 percent. The averages over the two dynasties are 30.2 percent for category A and 12.1 percent for category B; the two categories combined average 42.3 percent. Ho considers finding this rate of mobility among the elites of Western societies unlikely.[10]

Of course, China goes through continuous internal change, and the course of change is not always linear. Sometimes change is cyclical, sometimes it meanders, and there are imbalances between different regions. But many scholars seem to agree on this point: the most significant upheavals in China's society came during the Warring States period and the twentieth century.[11] There were many changes in the two millennia between those two periods, but in terms of structure, Chinese society was relatively stable.[12] So how should we characterize this structure, which remained so constant for so long? Can we develop a general explanation for the entire period? Historians using the concepts of Max Weber describe dynastic China as a "bureaucratic empire." Marxist-influenced historians have labeled this period "feudal," and that remains the dominant characterization of the period.[13] In an attempt to

10. See Ping-ti Ho: *The Ladder of Success in Imperial China* (New York: Columbia University Press,1962). For more information on this topic, see Pan Guangdan and Fei Xiaotong, "Keju yu shehui liudong [The Examination System and Social Mobility]," reprinted in *Shehui kexue* [Social Science], vol. 1, no. 4 (1947) [Tsinghua University]; Sun Guodong, "Tang Song zhi ji shehui mendi zhi xiaorong [Mixing of Families of Different Backgrounds between the Tang and Song]," *Xin Ya Xuebao* [New Asia Journal], vol. 4 (1959); Kracke, "Region, Family, and Individual in the Chinese Examination System," reprinted in *Zhongguo sixiang yu zhidu lunji* [Chinese Thought and Systems] (Taipei: Linking Publishing Company, 1976); Yan Buke, *Chaju zhidu bianqian shigao* [Outline of the Evolution of the Recommendation System] (Shenyang: Liaoning University Press, 1991); Huang Liuzhu, *Qin Han shijin zhidu* [Civil Service Recruitment Systems in the Qin and Han] (Xian: Northwest University Press, 1985).

11. Wang Guowei has suggested that a similar change occurred at the end of the Shang Dynasty, but there is little historical evidence from that period.

12. Jin Guantao and Liu Qingfeng did some of the earliest research into the "hyperstable structure" of traditional Chinese society. See *Xingshuai yu weiji* [Rise and Fall and Crisis] (Hunan People's Press, 1984).

13. Even historians who work in the evidence-oriented style of traditional Qing scholars, avoiding grand theories where possible, often take recourse to this framework without even realizing it when they discuss issues beyond the scope of their own primary research. Historians who criticize Marxism are not free of this problem. They oppose Marx's accounts of the present and future but still accept his explanation of China's history.

retrospectively describe a long process of evolution toward a hierarchical society with inherent mobility, I propose to replace those terms by naming the social structure found during the dynastic period the "selection society."

But the abolition of the examination system put an end to that mobility. The path into this class had disappeared; the pool of prospective candidates soon dried up. The class of official scholars who had ruled the empire with the monarch very quickly disappeared.

The End of the Traditional Hierarchical Society

As I see it, 1905 did not just signal the end of the selection society, it also marked the end of an even longer standing social arrangement: the hierarchical class system. Perhaps it is that fact that made the upheavals of the twentieth century even more important than the equally large changes during the Warring States period, which saw a shift from a closed, static class hierarchy to a hierarchical system with built-in mobility. Abolishing the imperial examinations started the political project of moving away from any kind of hierarchy toward an equal society. Officials who had been promoted through the examination track and their students now absorbed an entirely new ideology. They became the instigators working to mobilize and radicalize the population; scholars who had always believed Mencius's law that "those who work with their minds govern others" suddenly became cheerleaders for labor. The students of the new schools went down into the coal mines to tell miners "Workers are the law." In the last chapter of my book *The Selection Society and Its Fate*, I describe the impact that the abolition of imperial examinations had on twentieth century history:

> The end of the imperial examination system was part of a movement to kick-start science and education in this country, and to create a new, educated citizenry. In the last few years of the Qing Dynasty, the new education movement scored considerable successes. However, the new schools only ever managed to serve part of the function of the old examination system. They generated a pool of potential candidates for assimilation into the ruling class, but the process of selection and promotion never got started. To a certain extent, the new schools took on the role of preparing future administrators for government positions, but the Qing government ended before the new system could fully evolve. The class of old officials lost their influence; their last acts of importance were in the Xinhai Revolution that finally overthrew the

Qing monarchy. Meanwhile, the army of current or prospective students, who had been learning for the examinations, lost their motivation. They were driven to protest, and they became the leaders who spurred the masses on to revolution. Scholar-officials lost their roots; scholar-students lost their prospects.

After the monarch was deposed in the Xinhai Revolution, the scholar-officials were replaced by new forms of power that they were not equipped to resist. The overthrow of the Qing Dynasty was not the end of the revolution. It was just the opening volley in a series of revolutions over the twentieth century, and it was during those revolutions that China's old officials, as a class, were finally buried. The scholar-officials passed into history. They took their books and left the villages that they had governed. They flocked to the cities to find jobs with the new government, to learn more, or to do business. Of course, the brightest and best of them moved fastest. The officials who stayed behind in their districts were often the oldest or the least able. A new breed of "peasant officials" emerged, without the learning and cultivation of previous generations of officials, and they often became local leaders. Rural China was abandoned by the educated elites, and the rule of law and clan morality began to break down. Clashes between landowners and poor tenant farmers escalated, and rural China became a hotbed of revolution.

The ruling elite of traditional China had begun its self-destruction as a class in 1905, with the abolition of the imperial examinations. In 1919, with the launch of the May Fourth Movement, the students that they had taught hammered the last nails into the coffin of their value system. All of that can be seen as a natural process. One could even say that if a traditional culture wants to rise again, phoenix-like, such destruction is a necessary step. In fact, the twentieth-century revolutions of 1911 and 1919 can be seen as just an extension of the abolition of the examinations, though the abolition was not the only necessary and sufficient condition. After the Xinhai Revolution, there was a brief period of experimentation with parliamentary government and strongman dictatorship. None of those rational institutions or military governments lasted, each undermined by a range of factors. Finally, power was seized by a political and military organization built on ideological belief.

In all the effects of the abolition of the imperial examinations, the changes in the educated class were the most direct, and they have attracted the most comment over the last century. Under the old system, the best students were selected to be officials. The educated class and the ruling class were virtually synonymous. But after the Xinhai Revolution, with the scholar-officials no longer a force, society's central heights were occupied first by the military, then by political parties supported by force of arms. As Yu Ying-shih has documented, this was a period of "marginalization" of the educated class. (In fact, marginalization is not a broad enough concept to describe the complete transformation of the educated class over the past century. In particular, it does not tell us anything about the changes in the composition of this class.) But it was change in the class system that had a deeper, more far-reaching impact. If we take a wider perspective, we can identify the salient change more precisely: not the marginalization of the educated, but a shift toward equality.

There has been a global trend, extending far beyond China, to remove class distinctions from legal regulations. The concept of equality has achieved universal dissemination, and it is widely accepted as a principle for organizing society. Equality is an ideal that has led to huge social change; it is a check on government power in times of peace. Equality is now often taken to be a measure of the legitimacy of a government. It is applied in the assessment of all public policy, and sometimes it is even usurped as a justification for efforts in the private sphere. Though the concept of equality is often confused, its emotional appeal remains powerful.[14]

I will not repeat the whole process here but will restrict myself to suggesting that in China, the twentieth century was a completely new type of transitional period. We can perhaps call it the age of "mass participation." It began with the efforts of the educated—and the political parties of the educated—to enlighten the masses and call them to action: to make the masses the agents of history. But ultimately, the leaders still controlled events, and they used violence to achieve their ends.

Whatever the truth of that period, Chinese society today has entered a period of calm. The series of political movements and military campaigns that occurred from 1919 to 1989, from the May Fourth Movement to Tiananmen Square, were part of a transition from which we have now emerged. The state administration still monopolizes most status and power. Today it allies with markets and possesses more material resources—and is

14. *The Selection Society and Its Fate*, pp. 416–23.

more motivated by material resources—than before. Its officials identify strongly with the institution, to which they belong. It is a highly mature contemporary bureaucracy.

From the beginning of the modern age, we can perceive a global trend, discovered and described by many researchers, from inequality toward equality. To a certain extent, we can say that the social arrangements of almost all pre-modern civilizations were hierarchical class systems. Different social classes had differing levels of power and responsibility, which were publicly accepted and often enshrined in law. The nineteenth-century French philosopher Pierre Leroux saw that reality when he said, "We are today between two worlds, between one [the unequal world of slavery,] which is coming to an end, and another world [of equality,] which is just beginning."[15]

I mentioned before that the selection society ultimately generated very significant vertical mobility and equality of political opportunity. However, that equality of opportunity did not mean that all people were able to achieve positions of power or that all people enjoyed equal rights. The people who made up the ruling class came from among the ordinary people, but that does not necessarily imply that the society was more equal. Bringing ordinary people into the ruling class is different from making all of society more equal. In traditional China, the ruling class was open to ordinary people, but it was always structurally removed from them: it loomed far above them in status. There was always a strictly hierarchical structure, with a wide gulf between officials and ordinary people, between those who worked with their minds and those who labored with their hands. That gap meant differences in the level of respect, wealth, and fame that they were accorded. The end of the imperial examinations effectively ended this traditional hierarchical society.

Officials Continue as a Social Nexus

Many traditional elements of society were swept away. Soon after 1905, the monarchy came to an end. But one thing did not end and has not ended to this day: the dominance of the state. The state occupies the prime position of social power, it is the key decisive factor in any enterprise, and agents of the state remain nexuses of social resources. China has from the very beginning been motivated by and oriented toward political power. Throughout China's history, politics has always played a decisive role.

15. Pierre Leroux, *De L'égalité* (Commercial Press, 1988), p. 246.

Over the millennia, the three primary sources of social value—political power, wealth, and social status—were bound tightly together, with political power being the most decisive. Becoming a political player was the primary road upward, and the cultural obsession with being an "official" has persisted throughout the 5,000 years of China's civilization. One common view of the Warring States period is that it was a transition from selecting rulers by birth to selecting rulers by learning. But however rulers were picked, both models included a class of rulers, who were the most important elements of both systems.

Political power was the most important route to all of Weber's three social resources: wealth, social status, and reputation. A person with political power, with a position as a state official, was virtually assured of plentiful access to other social resources. But possession of other resources would not necessarily enable a person to obtain political power; in fact, that person might find his political power limited by those resources. All values and resources were concentrated in political power. Those with ambition in any field were generally constrained to seek success first in the political field; all other routes to success were mere offshoots of the political process. Just as the economy is emphasized in modern society, politics and the state were emphasized throughout the long history of China.

Of course, the state had a particular form in dynastic China. Though it was refined to a level of near perfection, it was never cold or impersonal; it had an inherent courtliness and warmth. We can consider the writers and poets who also served as officials, people like Su Dongpo or Ouyang Xiu.[16] The imperial examination system forced all Chinese officials to begin their careers with poetry. And the model of a tolerant state advocated in the Confucian classics often allowed them to achieve success in their official duties through a relaxed, low-key approach.

But economic factors were never as important as political factors in Chinese history. In fact, it may be the defining characteristic of China that eco-

---

16. Su Dongpo (苏东坡, 1037–1101), a native of Meishan, Sichuan Province, was a statesman, poet, painter, and calligrapher of the Song Dynasty (960–1026). Politically, Su aligned himself with Sima Guang and the conservative faction in court against the "New Policies" promoted by Wang Anshi. Su also had many literary achievements, and his essays and poems remain highly influential in China to this day. Ouyang Xiu (欧阳修, 1007–1072), a native of Jishui, Jiangxi Province, was a historian, essayist, and poet of the Song Dynasty. Ouyang was one of the major players in the Qingli Reforms of the 1040s and was in charge of writing the *New History of the Tang Dynasty*. He also was regarded as one of the great prose masters of the Tang and Song era.

nomics was secondary. So when the California School attempts to define Chinese "exceptionalism" in economic terms, it is in reality taking a eurocentric approach.[17] The Great Divergence was not able to explain why the economy of China's Yangtze Delta was so advanced but then slipped so far behind over the course of a century. To do so, we need to pay more attention to properly categorizing Chinese culture as a whole. In particular, we need to recognize that it is a culture dominated by politics. A political analysis is more useful than any economic analysis for locating the essence of Chinese society. Despite similarities between China and the West on many economic factors, despite similar levels of development, differences in state institutions and the value systems that underlay them meant that China could not independently develop a market economy (capitalism) incorporating the rule of law, freedom, and democracy.

Throughout its history, China has never escaped its concentration on the political or the concentration of values and resources in the state and its officials: not during the hereditary hierarchical society before the Spring and Autumn period or the hierarchical selection society that came after it; not during the "wandering masters" period of the Warring States period; not during the violent upheavals of the twentieth century. But there have been changes in the criteria by which the ruling classes have been selected: sometimes by birth, sometimes by level of education, sometimes by some special ability or virtue, sometimes by loyalty to an institution or even an individual. Sometimes it was no more than Machiavellian politics. To some extent these fundamental changes determined the nature and outward form of the ruling class and the government, and they had an impact on popular perceptions of the quality of government and the levels of popular acceptance and respect that it commanded.

Whatever their form, the selection mechanisms of traditional China did not reduce the political orientation of our civilization. If anything, they strengthened the emphasis on the political and the role of officials as nexuses of resources. The selection mechanism, which began to function from the Han Dynasty, gradually began to apply severe pressure to those who had gained status, reputation, and influence through other channels (economic, military) during the Warring States period. From that point, China began to construct a monolithic social structure in which political office was the key

17. The California School (加州学派) refers to a school of thought in comparative economic history originating at Harvard University and Cambridge University. Since the 1980s, a group of economic historians at the University of California at Irvine have reexamined Chinese economic history and rejected the notion of "Western centralism."

to everything. A situation like the Warring States "hundred schools" could never emerge again.[18] In some ways, this system was like a return to the early Spring and Autumn period, when hereditary offices were the most important social factor. It also made politics pervasive and led to the gradual refinement of the bureaucratic system to a level of high perfection.

These features—pervasive politics and officials as nexuses of resources—are the key characteristics running through the history of China, through the different societies before and after the Spring and Autumn period and even through the transitional periods of the Warring States and the twentieth century. They have had—and continue to have—a far-reaching impact on Chinese society and life. They may even be the only essentially "Chinese" features that we have not managed to eliminate from our culture. Can we now gradually weaken them in order to improve our political culture, in particular our bureaucracy? Or would any such attempt require the use of the state as an instrument—would it in fact require that we first strengthen the political state?

How Should We Understand Politics?

We often describe contemporary society as an "equal society," but the equality that we have achieved thus far extends only to a few popular issues: socioeconomic benefits and fundamental citizens' rights. The values of our institutions and our policies have become more responsive to the will of the people—or the will of the majority—resulting in greater equality of opportunity, realized to varying degrees, and "equal rights." But political power and political authority still exist, and their social function implies that they must entail a complex spectrum of differences and inequalities, some of them very large. If the officials who decide and execute policy are inevitably a small minority, no matter how they are selected, and if during their time in office they must have greater power than other people in order to fulfill the function for which they were selected, then who they are and how they are selected, managed, constrained, removed, and replaced is indeed a vital issue.

What can we learn from China's traditional selection mechanisms and from a comparison of those mechanisms and the modern (democratic) system of elections? We could say that modern election systems seem to be more concerned with egress, with replacing officeholders. They are very successful

18. The Contention of a Hundred Schools of Thought during the Warring States period (百家争鸣) refers to the free exchange of thought and discussion that characterized the period between the sixth century BC and AD 221, also referred to as the Golden Age of Chinese philosophy.

in arranging peaceful transitions of power, but not as successful in selecting capable people to hold office. China's traditional selection mechanism focused mainly on ingress: the selection of capable individuals. In fact, it was highly successful in selecting people but not so successful in replacing them. So consider this: since democratic systems have found a solution to the problem of how to peacefully replace ineffective members of the ruling elite, can we take some inspiration from the traditional selection system to aid us in selecting more suitable rulers? Can the traditional selection system be combined with a modern election system? Can we combine democracy with a requirement for personal excellence? Can a small ruling group be compatible with decisionmaking by the majority? Can we combine numerical quantity with quality? Can wisdom be combined with politics? If the answer to these questions is yes, then can our new melded system solve the problem of congestion in the Chinese system, with incumbents blocking entry and major policy changes being difficult to engineer? Can it solve the problem of the divergence between knowledge and power and the short-termism that elections and vote seeking can create in democratic nations? Can China's highly developed equality of opportunity to be selected fit with the modern West's highly developed equality of opportunity to participate? Can we transition smoothly from equality of selection to equality of participation? And can the attitudes toward rule of law and the spirit of rationality derived from the traditional selection mechanism become a philosophical and institutional resource for progress today? Do those attitudes have anything to teach our contemporary constitutional order and social-legal constructs?[19]

This discussion focuses primarily on the institutions of state. If we turn our attention to the broader community, then it may be that the best solution for a society is to unbundle the social resources of power, wealth, and status. That would reduce the intense focus on the political and reduce the concentration of social value in government agents. Citizens would be free and able to use their abilities and receive their just deserts under fairer conditions. The best measure of the legitimacy and quality of state institutions is their ability to create and protect this kind of more egalitarian social structure.

---

19. Some researchers believe so. In Pan Wei's discussion of "disinterested officials" for his proposed "consultative justice system," he looks to the imperial examination system as an inspiration. Xiao Han has proposed a constitutional system including an examination system. I have also read conference papers on using the institutional resources of an examination system from Zhang Xiangping and Daniel Bell of Hong Kong University.

A New Beginning

China's traditional selection mechanism survived for an extraordinarily long stretch of history. But along the way it faced many challenges, of which I have previously written a systematic account.[20] Like anything in this world, the examination system was fated to come to an end; it contained the seeds of its own destruction from the very beginning. However, it is fair to say that its longevity and vitality remain a source of wonder. The course of its emergence, development, and end covers over 2,000 years. This vast length poses a challenge: would we dare claim that any of our modern institutions will last for millennia? This is an age of fast change.[21]

At the beginning of the twenty-first century, we face what may be another new start. Economically, China is set to become a giant; perhaps it is one already. But our beliefs, our concepts, and our institutions are not distinctive enough or well developed enough to attract global interest. China is largely cut off from its own traditions, but imported ideologies have not rooted themselves sufficiently to become eternal "beliefs" with a broad base of subscribers. The death of Zhao Ziyang in early 2005 had huge symbolic importance for many people precisely because he was a symbol of the failure of top-down reform in our political institutions.[22] Police torture was abolished a century ago, but Sun Zhigang was still beaten to death; the imperial exami-

20. He Huaihong, "The Dilemma of History," in *The Selection Society* (Peking University Press, 2011).

21. When I arrived in Shanghai in early 1967, hanging on the frontage of the Bund was a huge banner: "May the People's Commune of Shanghai last 10,000 years!" In fact, the name of the people's commune was changed after just a month. Its successor institution, the Revolutionary Committee, lasted longer: it was disbanded after ten years. On June 1, some of the members of the faculty of philosophy and administrators at my institution, Peking University, wrote the posters and banners that are sometimes credited with starting the Cultural Revolution. They were in effect the "proclamation" of the Beijing Commune, an institution that was the equal of the Paris Commune in revolutionary fervor. But very quickly, those posters were repudiated and torn down. What all of these events tell us is that history cannot be created easily. Crafting something eternal is very tough.

22. Zhao Ziyang (赵紫阳, 1919–2005), a native of Huaxian, Henan Province, was a high-ranking politician in the People's Republic of China. Zhao was the third premier and later general secretary of the Chinese Communist Party from 1987 until 1989. He was famous for his leniency toward student protests leading up to the Tiananmen Square demonstrations on June 4, 1989. He was stripped of all official titles after the Tiananmen Square protests and held under house arrest until his quiet death in 2005.

nations were abolished over a century ago, but the education system in this country remains disappointing; the selection of officials is still not a properly codified process; throughout the length and breadth of this country, corruption and abuse of power continue unchecked; a real constitutional order remains a distant dream; equality exists on paper only; rural living standards are still an unresolved problem.[23] And as divisions grow between regions and between the rich and the poor, given the twentieth century's heritage of revolution, is another storm brewing? If we include issues like Taiwan, might we then in fact see dark clouds of war gathering? Whatever the answers to those questions, we have no choice but to move forward. There is an aphorism of Bertolt Brecht's that it would serve us well to remember: "Don't start with the good old things but the bad new ones."

23. Sun Zhigang (孙志刚, 1976–2003) was a twenty-seven-year-old migrant worker who was beaten to death by repatriation workers in Guangzhou in 2003. Sun was stopped by police in Guangzhou; lacking the proper residence papers and identification, he was sent to the Custody and Repatriation Service as a vagrant. His brutal death triggered great anger among the Chinese public, which ultimately led to the end of the flawed Custody and Repatriation Service that year.

CHAPTER FIVE

THREE SOURCES OF CHINESE TRADITION AND THE IMPETUS FOR CULTURAL RENAISSANCE

In April 2004, when the website *La Jeunesse* was launched at Peking University, I wrote a question-and-answer article discussing three different types of tradition that exist in contemporary China. The first is the "thousand-year tradition": traditional Chinese historical culture, which still shapes us in many subtle ways. The second is the "hundred-year tradition": the tradition of the enlightenment, followed by revolution. The third is the "ten-year tradition": if indeed it can be called a tradition, this refers to the impact of the market economy from the 1990s onward. Thus there are three main historical heritages shaping our present "reality" and our future. We could say that they are the three fundamental limiting circumstances that currently define how we make history.

The first tradition is a tradition measured in millennia. This is the tradition that developed over China's 3,000 years of civilization in the time before it confronted the West and a world different from itself. We could also call this tradition a "millenarian" tradition: the Chinese people of this period believed in an ideal world, though their ideal was in fact just a variation on their fundamental historical framework. They were simply unaware of any other options, and throughout China's long history, beliefs were stable—or, perhaps, stagnant. To put it another way, their dreams or ideals were often expressed as a "reverse utopianism": they dreamed of the "Three Dynasty Restoration," restoring the "golden age" of the Xia, Shang, and

This chapter is an edited version of an article by the same title first published in the *Beijing News*, July 3, 2005.

Zhou Dynasties.[1] In this tradition the basic unit of time is long and the rhythm is slow. The underlying view of history from this time is cyclical.

The second tradition is the tradition measured in centuries, the tradition of modernity, particularly since the May Fourth Movement. It covers a period of enlightenment and new thought, followed by a period of constant revolution. This tradition brought wave after wave of disruption and massive change to China's social structure and beliefs. In this tradition, the ideal society lay in the future. Its fundamental unit of time is shorter, and its rhythm faster. This tradition absorbed with alacrity a linear, progressive view of history.

The third tradition is the tradition measured in decades, the period since reform and opening up, particularly since the 1990s. The changes in this period have been as fast as the flickering of a zoetrope. This tradition (if the word applies) has been most clearly marked by the dramatic growth of the economy, the rise of China, and the stunning improvements in material standards of living. This tradition has been characterized by a breakneck pace. Whether this tradition possesses any long-term view of history or ideals is still an open question.

In terms of Hegel's historical dialectic, these three traditions form a cycle of thesis, antithesis, and synthesis. (Note that this is neither the earlier dialectic of the Socratic method, wherein questioning drives individual reasoning, nor the familiar dialectic of class struggle, in which one group destroys another.) The synthesis phase has just started, and we do not yet know whether the ten-year tradition can develop into a new hundred-year or even thousand-year tradition.

The thousand-year tradition is what we conventionally call "traditional" Chinese culture; we could say that it represents tradition in the strict, narrow definition. Its 2,000 years have formed a normative cultural mainstream. The hundred-year tradition is in fact a "tradition" of violent rejection of tradition. It represents a fracture, maybe even a complete break with history. The ten-year tradition is a direct rebound from the hundred-year tradition. As the ten-year tradition began, its reactive nature was made explicit in the political slogan "End chaos and return to order." In some ways it has attempted to return to the thousand-year tradition. At the very least, the ten-year tradition adopts a calmer, more pragmatic view of China and the world—past, present and future.

1. The "Three Dynasty Restoration" (复三代) refers to a belief in restoration of values held by Confucian scholars during the Song Dynasty, which were based on their idealization of the political and social order of the first three Chinese dynasties (Xia, Shang, and Zhou, from 3000 BC to 221 BC).

Of course, both the hundred-year tradition and the ten-year tradition fall within the larger category of "modernity." They both involve attempts to seek universal equality of conditions and equal rights. In this sense, they both stand opposed to China's thousand-year tradition of a hierarchical society. However, the thousand-year tradition and the hundred-year tradition both also subscribe to millenarian beliefs in an ideal society. The difference is that the beliefs of the thousand-year tradition were longer term and less violent, while the hundred-year tradition demanded speed and faded quickly. By contrast, the ten-year tradition is more exploratory—it "crosses the river by feeling the stones." This approach can be shortsighted and so can lead to crisis, but it also has a vitality that can create new opportunities.

Where I differ from Hegel and other readers of history (such as Ray Huang) is this: I do not believe that the course of China's history through these three traditions was in any way inevitable or that it was in retrospect the most likely or best course.[2] China's modernization could just as well have been like that of India or Turkey or of some other kind altogether. I also do not agree that this historical process has arrived at what Alexandre Kojève, interpreting Hegel, called "the end of history."

But we must accept that our present does indeed blend these three traditions. Whether we perceive them or not, these three collide and engage with each other within a single present. The thousand-year tradition affects us primarily on the level of subconscious, through enduring cultural values and beliefs. The hundred-year tradition works on the level of state institutions and political beliefs. The ten-year tradition is changing the texture of our lives in too many ways to enumerate.

The stormy hundred-year tradition has just ended, and though it was shorter than the thousand-year tradition, it leveraged political and social forces far greater than any seen before. Its heritage and its impact have been enormous. The ten-year tradition has brought the tidal wave of globalization. It is not just our present; it seems that it will also be the primary force shaping our future. To call it a tradition is in fact to speak in the future perfect tense: because of certain differences with China's existing culture, we can be sure that at some point in the future it *will have become* a tradition.

---

2. Ray Huang (黄仁宇, 1918–2000), a native of Changsha, Hunan Province, was a Chinese-American historian and philosopher. In his early years, Huang joined the Nationalist army and fought in the Burma campaigns. He graduated from the University of Michigan in 1964 with a Ph.D. in history and taught at a number of U.S. universities, including Harvard. He was known for his idea of macro-history.

For another way of looking at the three traditions, we can borrow an idea first put forward by the New Text Confucians in the Han Dynasty. Dong Zhongshu, a leader of the New Text Movement, divided Confucius's *Spring and Autumn Annals* into three periods on the basis of whether the events were "witnessed" by Confucius, "told" to him, or known to him "from the tradition." Today, we can perhaps divide our history the same way. The history that we are "witnessing" is the play of the ten-year tradition. We see this history unfolding around us, even as we are independent and active participants in it. The history that is "told" to us is the hundred-year tradition. We learn about this history primarily by hearing about it from others; it is the experience of our fathers and grandfathers, who have processed its lessons. The history that comes to us "from the tradition" is, of course, the thousand-year tradition, which we learn about from books. This tradition was rejected and discarded, and only now is it once more gradually emerging into the light. Our memories—and readers of history today—often follow the pattern of intellectual behavior that Dong Zhongshu identified in the *Spring and Autumn Annals*: "[Confucius] spoke cautiously of the things he witnessed himself, bitterly lamented the disasters about which he heard, and spoke only mildly of what came to him from the tradition."

The thousand-year tradition covers a long period, but it is rather distant from us; the ten-year tradition is the shortest but the closest to us; the hundred-year tradition is in between. It is hard to say which tradition has had the greatest impact on our present or which will ultimately have the greatest impact on our future. But we can be sure that China today is not characterized by a simple, single tradition. However, before we talk about the product of the three traditions or about their commonalities, we must carefully identify and carefully distinguish among the three. We must locate their differences and their fault lines.

Rather than rushing to any synthesis, we need to carefully sort and reflect on the three traditions, giving each one due consideration. The time for synthesis is not yet upon us. In fact, it is not yet clear whether there ever will be—or can be—a synthesis. Some believe that our task is not just to know these traditions but to choose among them. If that is the case, then the task will require not a single choice but an ongoing process. Our choices are unlikely to be simple ones—of returning to or enforcing one tradition or another. They will be complex tasks of reassessment and reconstitution. There is much to be done to improve our market economy; our political institutions have much to learn. And in order to use the thousand-year tradition, once the bedrock for generations but suspended now for over a century, we shall have to refresh our memories and learn how to understand and criticize this tradition in new historical circumstances. The future is always opaque to us, and yet it is up to us, as agents, to create it.

The ten-year tradition, closest to us and characterized by the global economy, is often dismissed as merely a culture of the commercial. But we should not underestimate its vast power or its imperious economic success. This success is truly extraordinary. Even if we ignore the massive development of China's coastal cities, we can see it in the "backward" agricultural regions. Thirty years ago, I lived for over six years in a farming and herding region of Inner Mongolia. I saw people engaged in an almost constant battle to maintain just the barest subsistence. During the latter part of the Cultural Revolution, when students were assigned there, they were desperate. "Surely we are not going to spend our lives here with hoes and frozen soil, letting our knowledge and our potential slip away?" Productivity was desperately low, and there were no alternative ways to make a living there. You could work yourself to death, and it would do little to improve the lot of those around you. Today, even most agricultural workers are assured of a basic subsistence. I see old men sitting together playing Chinese chess in the evenings and then wandering unworriedly home. For me, the contrast with the 1970s brings feelings of pleasure and thankfulness. Within such a short time, China has produced such enormous economic progress that the importance of the change cannot be overstated. If there are those who use the growing gap between rich and poor as a reason to criticize Deng Xiaoping and to feel nostalgia for the old days, then I think they have forgotten some basic facts: first of all, people need to eat. Economic sufficiency is a necessary precondition of all cultural and political progress.

But our advances to date have been limited mainly to the economic sphere. Our success in these last thirty years shows, on the one hand, that when we are working in the right direction, together we can create enormous potential. China stumbled for over a hundred years, but finally, in the last three decades it has seized its opportunity—perhaps the last opportunity that the world will give it. But on the other hand, our success is limited; one might say that it is partial and unbalanced. The lack of balance means that our objectives have lost their anchors and that ultimately the imbalances may become a drag on our economic momentum. The most important contrast here is between our fast-developing economy and our lagging and forsaken political culture and cultural spirit. While our hard power has advanced, our "soft power" has not been able to serve its purpose either internally or externally: it has not rallied China's citizens, nor is it attractive to the world.

So how can we build our soft power? First, we must follow some basic, universal principles, and we must develop appropriate theories and practices for a society of citizens. But in addition to those fundamentals, the most important task is to develop our core cultural spirit. In this task, surely we should first consider drawing inspiration from China's history and traditional culture. Ignoring the resources right under our noses and starting from scratch cannot be the best way to go about it. After all, we are Chinese, and this is our tradition. But there is more reason than that: we need to revive and develop our own historical memories anyway, to recover the thousand-year tradition after a century of rejection and thirty years of heavy erosion by the market economy.

So for the sake of our cultural heritage and our task in constructing the present, we should first work not on synthesizing the three traditions, but on bringing together the "30 years" and the "3,000 years." The last 30 years have been the best years of the modern age for this country. They have been a period of synthesis, following the thesis of traditional culture and its violent antithesis. This period has not been long; it has been just 30 years since the 3rd Plenary Session of the 11th Central Committee, at which the decision was made to start the "reforms and opening up." By contrast, it is about 3,000 years since our forebears began to write and we advanced into the glories of China's historic civilization. Bringing together the 30 years and the 3,000 years would mean a confluence of the ancient and modern, of the old and new, of hard economics and soft culture. What we should do is look for sources of cultural strength among the rich historical and cultural deposits of 3,000 years of brilliant civilization. Simply transplanting old culture into the present could not possibly be effective in this fast-changing, globalized world. So there will also have to be creativity, but that creativity should fully absorb and exploit the resources of our tradition.

Of course, between the 3,000 years and the 30 years are the 100 years of turmoil. The twentieth century has also left a powerful heritage, but that heritage is suspect. It requires careful sifting. For example, extremist theories of class warfare and the philosophy of zero-sum conflict are not the inheritance that we should accept. But we do need to listen carefully to and engage with some elements in the hundred-year tradition: its call for equality and the strong emotions that underlay that call. We have to patiently uncover and sever the artificial links that the hundred-year tradition asserted between those emotions and certain untenable theories. It is fairly clear that the 30 years has already adopted some of the most precious essentials from the enlightenment that was a part of the hundred-year tradition.

So, given these three cultural traditions, I believe that our current task is not to unite them but to chart a course between the two extremes, between the 30 years and the 3,000 years. While we build a framework for a public political space, we also need to explore deeper solutions for our distinctive cultural spirit, our Chinese spirit, and for individual ethical needs.

For the renaissance of cultural China, we can hold high expectations, middling expectations, or low expectations. High expectations means aiming to become what Hegel called a "World-Historical people"—to lead the world, to become a world center. That is probably a pipe dream: perhaps not impossible, but unlikely in a world that is growing more pluralistic by the day. More realistic are the middling hopes: that we develop a distinctive Chinese spirit with characteristic beliefs and values that can command the respect and interest of many peoples outside China. Low expectations do not require such creativity or distinctiveness. They aim only at providing a stable environment in China, with sufficient cohesion in its standards and moral quality.

I believe that no matter what our hopes or our prospects, any attempt at a renaissance of Chinese culture must include efforts to renew our spirit. What we need is not just a cultural renewal, not merely a political movement or a social movement: we need first of all to animate our spirit. Or rather, the whole movement should be undergirded by a spirit that has been strengthened and renewed. Our objectives should not be just sociopolitical or cultural. We should have goals for our spirit, and we should devote significant resources to supporting it. When Gandhi led his campaign for India's independence and when Martin Luther King Jr. led the U.S. civil rights movement, they were leading movements of the spirit. The power of those movements and their capacity to create change came from their spiritual roots. Movements that aim only to acquire greater material wealth will never have spiritual power; simple nationalism will never have the spiritual power to draw in other nations. If every people pursues merely the interests of its own state, then we might have a universal value, but it will be a value of exclusion and conflict.

The efforts to build China's cultural spirit will not begin with a stirring call to arms and mass engagement. We first must place the task in the hands of a small group, perhaps just a few individuals. But these few must have roots among the many. A child who grew up in the fields of a small village, a child who walked out of the valleys—perhaps one day, such a child will spark the fire of cultural spirit once again for our ancient race. As Weber wrote: "today [it is] only within the smallest and intimate circles, in personal human situations, in pianissimo, that something is pulsating that corresponds to the prophetic *pneuma*, which in former times swept through the great communities like a firebrand, welding them together."

That is what we need to create. I have written much of heritage. We must not just accept our heritage but go beyond it. Sometimes we must even create something from nothing. The renaissance of Chinese culture will go nowhere without immense creativity. Certainly, we can guarantee nothing. We cannot put our hopes in any historical inevitability. We cannot say for sure that China's cultural renaissance will happen or that it will produce anything of great value, nor can we predict the form in which it may come about. But we can set goals for ourselves and struggle toward those goals stubbornly and diligently. At least when the seed of a new cultural spirit appears, we can furnish the conditions that it needs to grow.

PART III

THE TRANSFORMATION OF ETHICS AND MORALITY IN THE PRC

CHAPTER SIX

THE RED GUARD GENERATION: MANIPULATED REBELLION AND YOUTH VIOLENCE

Everything that exists leaves its mark; the only question is what kind of mark. It is now forty-four years since the rise of the Red Guards, but the impact on both Chinese society and individual members has not yet died.[1] I am interested in particular in the historical fate of that generation. Of that generation, the laboring majority are now mostly retired. But some of the minority—those who never did physical labor—now hold the reins of political power in this country.[2] Others are in key positions in business and academia. In this chapter, I sketch out some of the philosophy and characteristic behaviors of the Red Guards. Have we really left them behind, a relic of history, as is so often thought? Some of the history and stories that I recount here emerged only long after the end of the Cultural Revolution, when I read documents that had later become available. But I have also included some of my own direct observations, from my perspective as a low-ranking Red

This chapter is an edited version of an article first published in the *Beijing Cultural Review*, vol.1 (2011).

1. The Red Guard Movement (红卫兵运动) was a mass movement of young people mobilized by Mao Zedong's Cultural Revolution in 1966 and 1967. The movement was made up of high school and college students, rallied under Mao's instructions to revolt against the incumbent bureaucracy; they played an extremely destructive role in the Cultural Revolution period.

2. The two most powerful men in China today, President Xi Jinping and Premier Li Keqiang, are part of this generation. It is sometimes referred to as the "educated youth generation."

Guard. I was one of the many students in Beijing who joined the movement but were outside the inner circle because they were not born in Beijing.

The Red Guard generation can be defined as all children and students who were between the ages of twelve (the first year of middle school) and twenty-two (the final year of university) in 1966, the year that the Cultural Revolution started—that is, everyone born between 1944 and 1954. For the most part, the real era of the Red Guards was limited to the first two years of the Cultural Revolution. That was when they seized the stage of history and for a moment seemed to be unstoppable. After 1968 the Red Guards were little more than a shadow of their former selves.

By this definition, I was one of the very last of the Red Guard generation. In 1966, when the Cultural Revolution started, I was twelve years old. I had just completed my elementary schooling in the county town of Nanchang, Jiangxi, and had been assigned to Liantang Middle School. I was just beginning to have an adult understanding of the world around me, but I was not yet of an age to be a direct participant in the movement. I was on its fringes, primarily an observer. In 1970–71 I also attended the only high school still operating in Nanchang—then a city of 1 million people. There I did experience some of the "educational revolution" that was a part of the Red Guard mission to "struggle, criticize, and reform."[3] Still later I worked as a freight handler and spent time in the army. Thus I was able to witness the entire range of the Cultural Revolution experience.

The Red Guard generation grew up "under the red flag." The oldest of them were only just starting elementary school in 1949, when the People's Republic was founded. They received a "revolutionary education" from the start. In his song "Balls under the Red Flag," the rock musician Cui Jian has referred to this generation as "eggs laid by the red flag."[4] (All of the phrases in italics below are from the lyrics to this song.)

3. "Struggle, Criticize, and Reform" (斗批改) refers to the initial goals of the Cultural Revolution, articulated by Mao Zedong during the early years of the movement. This slogan attempted to rationalize the movement by setting clear goals: struggling against intraparty capitalists, criticizing capitalist reactionary academic authorities, and reforming any antisocialist superstructure in the cultural and educational arenas.

4. Cui Jian (崔健, 1961–), a native of Beijing, is a Chinese singer-songwriter and guitarist. He is considered to be a pioneer in Chinese rock music and was one of the first Chinese artists to write rock songs. Accordingly, he is often called the father of Chinese rock music. *Balls under the Red Flag* (红旗下的蛋) is a rock album released by Cui Jian in 1994. The album was controversial because it expressed the awakening and confusion of the generation that grew up during the Cultural Revolution and later faced the tide of reform and opening up during the 1990s.

The Red Guard generation's fathers were *flag poles*: they hoisted the red flag over China. The members of the Red Guard generation themselves were *eggs laid by the red flag. The red flag's still aflutter, But there's no fixed direction, The revolution still continues, The old men have even more power.* The Red Guard generation believed that they were in charge, but that was not the case. The lines that they loved to chant more than any others were written by the young Mao Zedong: "The world is ours! The nation is ours!" The response to "I ask, on this boundless land, who rules over man's destiny?" was always a fervent, "We do! We do!" But in fact, they very soon fell out of favor. After a brief period as the anointed sons, they were tossed out like foundlings. Back at the bottom of the social heap, they found that *reality is like a stone, spirit is like an egg.* But, *although stones are hard, eggs are life.* Life, especially young life, is irrepressible, exuberant. It will always find a way to express itself. But today, *money flutters in the air. . . . We are no longer pawns in a chess game, Following lines drawn by others, We try standing up ourselves, Get moving and take a look at everything.* The most outstanding of the Red Guard generation became the key players in today's society, and because of their age, they will dominate China over the next ten to twenty years.

How were the members of the Red Guard generation able to mobilize so quickly? How did they behave once mobilized? On examination, we find that their behavior was deeply conditioned by the social environment in which they lived. The cult of personality around one revolutionary leader, Mao, had begun in the 1940s. By the eve of the Cultural Revolution, it had reached a fever pitch. The Red Guard generation had grown up in an environment of class struggle, an environment that respected violence or at the very least had no hesitation about using violence. Red was the color of respect, the color of revolution, and it was also the color of blood. As the constitution of the Young Pioneers of China tells us: "The red scarf [worn by children who join the Young Pioneers] is a corner of the red flag; it is red with the blood of the revolutionary martyrs." In one of the idealistic epic poems written for the Red Guards, the collective heroes believe in and fervently pray for a third world war that will finally bury the last shreds of the old world order; in the war, the Red Guards conquer Europe and America and finally raise the red flag over the White House.

We can also see some striking characteristics when we look at the Red Guards themselves. The first feature, of course, is their tendency to rebel. The very first Red Guard group, formed at Tsinghua University Middle School, announced itself with three posters inscribed "Long live the revolutionary rebel spirit of the proletariat!" The posters continued, "Revolution is rebellion;

the spirit of Mao Zedong thought is rebellion. . . . Rebel! If not now, then when?" This logic was inculcated in them by Mao Zedong himself, who had written, "In the final analysis, all the truths of Marxism can be summed up in one sentence: To rebel is justified." So, who had the right to rebel? Only a limited group was granted the privilege of beginning a rebellion. Their class background had to be one of the Five Red Categories (People's Liberation Army, Communist Party, workers, rural laborers, or small farmers): "Only the Left will be allowed to rebel; the Right will not be allowed a counterrevolution."[5]

Among the earliest Red Guards in Beijing, the rules were even stricter. The core members of these groups were the children of revolutionary cadres. But Mao himself expanded the movement to a broader slice of the student population by supporting the "rebel" faction of the Red Guards. At a stroke, a mass of ordinary, oppressed people—including some with politically impure family backgrounds—were licensed to rebel. (However, those with impure backgrounds would later face purges.) And who were they rebelling against? The most immediate targets of rebellion were figures of authority in their immediate ambit: teachers, school principals, foremen—anyone who managed and oppressed them. From there, their rebellion boiled over and swept into communities to which they were not personally connected. They rebelled against all old thinking, old culture, old customs, old habits—everything that represented the bad old ways. They wanted to create a break with China's millennia-long history and culture and also with the history of the revolutionary party itself, with everything that happened before the founding of the People's Republic of China, seventeen years earlier. One symbol of this rupture: Tan Houlan led the Beijing Normal University Red Guards to Qufu in Shandong, where they wrecked the temple and tomb of Confucius, who until then had always been a "model for the ages."[6] Another symbol: a poster entitled "The Hundred Uglies," which included cartoons of almost every senior government and party leader, sparing just a select few.

5. The Five Red Categories (红五类) were classes of Chinese citizens based on their political identity during the Cultural Revolution. The Five Red Categories were considered pro-revolutionary forces and included revolutionary military personnel, revolutionary cadres, workers, peasants, and lower- or middle-class farmers. Members of the Five Red Categories and their offspring enjoyed a wide range of political, economic, and social privileges that were denied to members of the anti-revolutionary "Five Black Categories," who were maligned and restricted from participation.

6. Tan Houlan (谭厚兰, 1940-1982), a native of Xiangtan, Hunan Province, was a major leader of the Red Guard Movement during the Cultural Revolution. She was notorious for destroying the Confucian Temple in Qufu, Shandong Province, the hometown of Confucius. She was prosecuted in 1978 and died of cancer at the age of 42.

In a very short time, with the active support of the country's leaders, the existing management of almost every school in the country had been swept aside. The Red Guards started to move out of the schools and into the surrounding communities. They started to move across the country for political rallies and campaigns. For a period of one or two years, the country was in a state of virtual anarchy. This was the height of the Red Guard Movement.

The first time I saw a Red Guard in Nanchang was in August 1966. At first, just a few schoolchildren began wearing red armbands, then some traveled to Beijing to see Mao Zedong's great Red Guard parade and brought back a red flag. We all were waiting at the railway station to greet them. Until that day, Beijing had been a distant legend to us. No one quite believed that it was possible to actually travel there and see Mao Zedong. But suddenly we found that it was.

Suddenly we found that many things were possible. We could travel on buses and trains without paying; our food was free. The young leaders began to feel that anything was possible. Encouraged by the spirit of rebellion, young people were free to doubt everything, to reject everything, to overthrow everything—with the exception of one sacred image, of course. Posters appeared everywhere with Mao's slogan "Bombard the headquarters, burn XXX!" In those posters, XXX could be literally any local leader or local organization. Perhaps young people are naturally inclined to kick off all constraints imposed on them. In 1966, Chinese youth were given a once-in-a-millennium opportunity to rebel.

But right from the start, their rebellion was commanded, or manipulated, by Mao, because the second key characteristic of the Red Guards was their loyalty. They were loyal not to a set of beliefs or to any ideal but to one person—Mao, a living man, though he was seen by many as a god (which explained his mercurial changes and his ineffability). The Red Guards were called "guards" because they swore to protect Chairman Mao; he needed protection because "China's Khrushchev" could be "sleeping in our very beds"—a possibility that showed Mao's fear of conspiracy. "Chairman Mao is our red commander," the Red Guards shouted. "We are Chairman Mao's red soldiers! We will break the head of any dog who opposes Chairman Mao!" Many of China's young people were ready to devote their lives and even to spill their own blood for this cause.

So the rebellion of the Red Guards was not natural. At the very least, its organization and its unfolding were not natural. The course of the rebellion was not directed by the will of the rebels. From the beginning, it was a "commanded rebellion" or a "rebellion to order," and throughout its course it was a manipulated rebellion. When it ended, finally, it was because a stop order was given. This marked a fundamental difference between the Red Guards and the youth rebellions in 1960s France, the United States, and other Western nations. The Red Guards can be seen as the earliest of the 1960s youth movements, but they were also an outlier among those movements. They also were different from participants in the May Fourth Movement or the "right-wing youths" of 1957. The students who were labeled "right wing" in 1957, though still basically aligned with socialism, had wanted to further some of their own ideals of freedom and democracy. But the Red Guard organizations were devoted only to being left wing, red, and loyal to Chairman Mao. They never really had any independent agency, at least none with any stability. All of their actions strictly followed the orders and strategies of Chairman Mao. They carried Chairman Mao's Little Red Book (*Quotations from Chairman Mao*) with them at all times, and they became skilled at debating by lobbing quotations at one another.[7]

They also were ready to accept new "supreme" commands or the "latest orders" at any moment. The reason that they were able to instantly organize and rebel was because they had the support of Mao, the supreme leader, whose power and status at that moment was unprecedented in history. The Red Guards were considered the vanguard of the Cultural Revolution, but perhaps they were in fact its cannon fodder. The driving force behind the Cultural Revolution was not the Chinese Communist Party, but the party's highest leader, who was circumventing his own party. He made use of his own limitless political power and personal charisma to propel the movement. Mao Zedong held eight rallies, in which he stood face to face with 12 million Red Guards, brought in from all over the country. He put on a red arm band himself, telling the assembled crowds, "We must use force!" From that point, the Red Guards carried the fire of revolution out into the streets and even into the smallest and remotest farming villages.

Many of the Red Guards wanted to model themselves after Chairman Mao, particularly the young Mao ("Young we were, schoolmates, At life's full flowering").[8] But the world that they inhabited was very different from the China of the May Fourth Movement. They never realized that the "Chair-

---

7. The Little Red Book (小红书) refers to a red booklet formally known as *Quotations from Chairman Mao*. The booklet is a collection of selected statements from speeches and writings by Mao Zedong. It was widely distributed during the Cultural Revolution, making it one of the most printed books in history.

8. "Changsha," *Selected Works of Mao Tse-tung* (www.marxists.org/reference/archive/mao/selected-works/poems/poems01.htm).

man Mao" that they saw had made it impossible for them to do as young Mao Runzhi—the youth who would become Mao Zedong—did.[9] They believed that they were "criticizing the very rivers and mountains, setting people afire with our words." In fact, it was not they who "ruled over man's destiny" in the "boundless land" of China. It was still Chairman Mao. As has been observed by many before, the spark that started the prairie fire of the Red Guard Movement was a letter of support from Mao Zedong on August 1, 1966, and the movement came to a sudden halt on July 28, 1968, after Mao called a meeting of five Red Guard leaders. This direct link clearly shows how the Red Guards were Mao's creation.

But even if the Red Guards were manipulated, what was their subjective experience? Did they believe that they were free? Even that they were lucky? I believe that they did. As I noted above, for a period at least, they felt that they could do whatever they wanted, even that they were omnipotent. That feeling was related to the third key feature of the Red Guards: the movement was an expression of youthful exuberance and release.

To rebel against authority is perhaps an instinct that every young person possesses. Youth are full of energy and life, and they react against everything around them that represses and restricts, sometimes to the point of violent rejection. Even though in retrospect the Red Guards were clearly engaged in a manipulated rebellion, that was not at all how they felt at the time. And in the process of their rebellion, they displayed all the passion, courage, and intelligence of youth. I remember that all of the "conservative organizations" of Jiangxi Province had the name plaques next to their doors ripped off and smashed, and afterward the Red Guards and various other rebel groups put sarcastic mock plaques in their place. They used whatever materials came to hand, producing reams of fake couplets that hung on either side of the doors, some mocking the institutions, some sarcastically "eulogizing" their demise. These verbal rockets were the first examples I had seen of knowledge of the classics put to modern use on a large scale.

Another night, I accompanied a group to the main square in our provincial capital to take part in a Red Guard rally. Tens of thousands of people were there. Though the atmosphere was a little muted because of factionalism within the movement (the government had not yet come out in support of one faction or another), it was a still a stirring scene, and the celebratory energy was irrepressible. Red Guards around me were dancing and singing:

9. Mao Runzhi (毛润之, 1893–1976) is the courtesy name of Mao Zedong, the founder of the People's Republic of China. The name Runzhi is usually used to refer to Mao during his youth.

"Raise your head and see the pole star, think of Mao Zedong," "Revolution is a great celebration." We felt deeply connected to the people within our own Red Guard group. I was very young, and fell asleep later in the night. When I woke up suddenly in the early dawn, I found that a red flag and someone's coat had been placed over me. Almost everyone else had also fallen asleep, and in the dawn light those boys and girls seemed like the most beautiful people in the world.

But the same boys and girls were swept up in the violence of the movement. Their youthful energy was channeled into violent destruction. And that was the fourth key feature of the Red Guard movement: its propensity for violence. At the beginning of the Cultural Revolution, one of the most common slogans was "Long live the red terror!" Many people were beaten or tortured to death or driven to commit suicide. The violence started with the "criticism and struggle sessions," the extrajudicial interrogations and the beatings. It turned into full-scale pitched battles between factions. On one occasion, I saw with my own eyes a large crowd of Red Guards surrounding the gate of a government office that was rumored to be the hiding place of a conservative faction. Suddenly, a man was pushed out of the gate, and the beating started instantly, before he had a chance to speak. People would squeeze through the crowd, then shout in triumph, "I hit him!" It was some time before the crowd suddenly stepped back, having realized that the man being beaten was "one of us!" By this time the victim was lying half dead on the ground. That was probably the first time I felt fear at the indiscriminate violence.

It seemed that many wanted to use violence to prove their own courage, maturity, and dedication. Ordinarily mild-tempered people became savage. At first they used fists and feet; later they used guns. At first, the dead would be paraded around in their coffins, and the Red Guards would argue over who shot first; later, no one cared who started it. Red Guards loved to stand on the running boards of cars, brandishing handguns. The high school kids, even more than the university students, showed no concern for their own safety or that of anyone else. The Red Guard group that had the reputation of being the best fighters in Nanchang was the No. 5 Middle School "Handful of Die-hards," who were led by a girl known as "Die-hard woman." Violence caused them no hesitation, whether they were victims or perpetrators. On one occasion another Red Guard group had caught someone that they claimed was an "old conservative boss." They shot him in the head in front of a hotel and then went to eat inside, leaving the body in the street. All evening, going in and out of the hotel, they just pretended not to see it.

On July 27, 1968, Mao Zedong sent 30,000 people from his "worker propaganda teams" into the Tsinghua University campus to end the battle between Red Guard factions. One of the factions, led by Kuai Dafu, resisted them because they had not received word directly from Mao.[10] In surprise, Mao asked, "Has the rebel faction really rebelled?" In fact, it was only ignorance: Kuai Dafu did not know that the teams were sent by Mao, and he even sent requests to Mao's office for help in casting off this "black hand." When he saw Mao at a dawn meeting the next day, he cried at his error. When Mao said, "The black hand is me," all resistance immediately collapsed. Thus the Red Guard Movement, which had started at the Tsinghua University Middle School, came to an end at Tsinghua University. Soon afterward, the Beijing Red Guards and their leaders were assigned to positions far outside the capital. The top Red Guards were put under house arrest or thrown in prison by the government and the People's Liberation Army in the 1970s, during the latter part of the Cultural Revolution. The rank-and-file Red Guards were dispersed through a massive program assigning students to jobs in farming communities. By 1980, 17 million people had been sent out of the cities for "reeducation" among poor farmers. Those who did not end up on the farms were assigned to factories or to the army.

A fuller explanation of the concept of "manipulated rebellion" is in order. When I say that the Red Guards acted "under orders" or that they engaged in a "manipulated rebellion," I do not mean to imply that those who gave the orders had complete control over the movement. Nor do I mean that those who gave the orders were able to achieve their goals by using the Red Guards. What I mean is that the Red Guards were able to organize on such a scale because it was so ordered by Chairman Mao, instigator of the Cultural Revolution. The Red Guard Movement was a mini-revolution within the Cultural Revolution. In fact, it was the core of the Cultural Revolution.

The relationship between leaders and ordinary people in the Cultural Revolution is an issue of particular interest. In fact, for the purposes of Cultural Revolution research, they are inseparable. Any history of this period must include both and take careful account of the relationship between them. Within this relationship, we must be clear about which group led and which followed, about whether the leaders or the people played the primary, active

10. Kuai Dafu (蒯大富, 1945–), a native of Binhai, Jiangsu Province, was a major leader of the Red Guard Movement during the Cultural Revolution. He joined the Red Guards when he was a student at Tsinghua University and played an active role in persecuting senior leaders such as Liu Shaoqi, a former president of China. Kuai was prosecuted in 1978 and served a seventeen-year sentence.

role. As I noted above, I believe that the leadership was the agent in this relationship. There are actually two issues here: the first is whether the leaders
played the central role in the movement; the second is whether they achieved
the objectives for which they started the movement or, indeed, whether they
were able to control the movement throughout its duration (to put it another
way, whether they were able to achieve interim objectives).

In *Rationality and Madness: The Masses in the Chinese Cultural Revolution*
(later expanded and retitled *Failure of Charisma*), Wang Shaoguang gives a
detailed analysis and description of the motivations and behavior of the people who joined the rebel factions during the Cultural Revolution in
Wuhan.[11] But he does not give enough attention to the relationship between
the leaders and the masses or to who led within this relationship. He rejects
the idea that the Cultural Revolution centered on its leaders, suggesting that
a Mao-centered reading of the Cultural Revolution requires several assumptions: that its instigators had explicit objectives and a plan to realize them;
that they had transcendental authority to ensure that the plan was executed
as they desired; that most people could understand the leaders' intentions
and plans and whole-heartedly participated in their execution. In short,
Wang believes that if the movement was truly Mao-centric, only top-down,
one-directional communication was permitted.

But those assumptions seem too strong. No individual could possibly fulfill all of Wang's criteria. History, as Engels said, is the composite result of
"intersecting" forces, with no one person able to completely achieve his own
objectives. We can add that if those objectives run contrary to social reality
and human nature, to the point of being completely unrealizable, then it
does not matter how much status or authority a leader might have. Wang
seems to have overlooked the two questions that I posed above. Must a leader
have absolute control over the entire course of a movement and completely
realize all of his objectives in order to count as its "center"? I believe that anyone who plays a "leading role" in a movement (that is, as its primary instigator) can be called its "center" and must bear moral responsibility for its
actions. It is not necessary that the person be its "controller"—that is, to have
achieved his own goals through the movement.

Wang's careful exposition gives reasonable accounts of many of the facts of
the Cultural Revolution. For example, he shows that many members of rebel
organizations were rational and that they had made their own calculations;
rational explanations can be found for why they joined their groups (though

11. Wang Shaoguang, *Failure of Charisma: The Cultural Revolution in Wuhan* (Oxford
University Press, 1999).

for some it was mere chance). However, he underestimates the irrational, or fanatical, aspect of the rebels' behavior, particularly in crowds, when a mob mentality could take hold. The Red Guards were the youngest of the rebel organizations, the shock troops of the Cultural Revolution. Among these young people there was even more irrationality than among other participants, and the high school students were more irrational, more fanatical, than the university students. Some rational calculations were involved when the Red Guards split into two implacably hostile factions and began to battle each other, but there were also many emotional factors: beliefs, passions, and grudges. Neither faction believed that their actions constituted rebellion against Chairman Mao, nor did they believe themselves to be conservative. Each accused the other of those crimes. They were also deeply driven by the theory of struggle. In fact, in this, they were encouraged by their leader: Chairman Mao had become leader through a process of struggle.

The Cultural Revolution involved both class warfare and conflict between different factions within the Chinese Communist Party. The Red Guards believed that they could "turn the world red" through a process of violent insurrection. They must eventually have realized that their "enemy" was very similar to them, that they were all just pawns in a larger game. The problem was that the player who had set out these pawns was never able to move them exactly as he pleased; once the game had started, Mao could not stop the violence without completely ending the movement. But still, the balance of power lay with him, not with the masses. He had the power to sweep the pieces off the board. He could not stop the battles between the Red Guard factions, but he could send both factions out of the cities and to the farms. But we should note that before that happened, the Red Guards did in fact achieve some of the things that Mao had wanted. For example, Kuai Dafu's faction of Tsinghua Red Guards led the movement against Liu Shaoqi.[12] The Nankai University Red Guards formed a group that was dedicated to "rooting out traitors" and defeating the "capitalist class groups" within the party for Mao.

Wang believes that Mao was certainly successful in energizing the masses, probably too successful. But he failed to direct the movement because what the various factions "really cared about" were their own interests. Why did he

12. Liu Shaoqi (刘少奇, 1898–1969), a native of Ningxiang, Hunan Province, was a senior Chinese politician and top Communist Party leader. Liu was the president of the People's Republic of China and Mao's designated successor from 1959 to 1968. He was labeled a "traitor" and "reactionary"during the Cultural Revolution and died after Red Guard persecution.

fail? Why did the Cultural Revolution fail? Were Mao's objectives compatible with the real interests of society and the individuals who made it up? Even if they were theoretically compatible, did ordinary Chinese people—or even human nature in general—support his ideals? Or is there another explanation? Imagine that he had even greater power and status; imagine that he was the leader of a group other than young people or that his strategy had changed somewhat. Could his goals have been achieved then? But how could he have changed his target group? One of his reasons for starting the Cultural Revolution was to harden the next generation of proletarian revolutionaries, to temper them in a storm of violence. He wanted to create a generation of new people. But what was the result of that tempering?

This question demands that we consider fundamental human nature. The future may not bring the same utopia as the past, but it could bring a new kind of utopia, thus the impetus for revolution. The Cultural Revolution failed because no one could resist the "brilliant leader," because no one had the weight to withstand the storm that he unleashed. Liu Shaoqi's organization was not up to it, nor was the old guard of the "February adverse current."[13] The Cultural Revolution ultimately died away because of the indifference of the public. It was defeated by whispers of rumor. The huge response to the Cultural Revolution's call to action gradually died away. Mass political activism reached a peak; then, as after every peak, it declined. It was like the military power of the Qin: as they unified the empire, no other state could resist their power. But by the time of the second Qin emperor, the military giant had become as fragile as glass.

The educated youth who were forced out of the cities into poor, rural areas had been the first Red Guards. In their rural exile, they did suffer a kind of reeducation. In fact, it would not be an exaggeration to call it a second enlightenment. This second enlightenment was more skeptical of the Cultural Revolution than Mao Zedong had ever predicted. The flight and death of Lin Biao—Mao's anointed successor, no less—also shook people's belief in the "brilliance" of their leaders.[14] In April 1976, the first spontaneous mass

13. The February adverse current (二月逆流) refers to an attempt to stop the Cultural Revolution organized by senior leaders at a Politburo meeting in February 1967. It was the first organized, open resistance to the Cultural Revolution.

14. Lin Biao (林彪, 1907–71), a native of Huanggang, Hubei Province, was a famous general in the People's Liberation Army and later a senior politician. Lin became Mao's designated successor during the 9th Party Congress in 1969 after Liu Shaoqi's downfall. He failed in an alleged coup to assassinate Mao in 1971 and died in a plane crash in Mongolia while trying to flee to the Soviet Union.

demonstration in years broke out in Tiananmen Square. Unconnected with any leader or organization, it included many current Red Guards. Though it was quickly suppressed, the downfall of the Gang of Four soon afterward showed how attitudes were changing. In fact, the end of the Gang of Four laid the foundation for social stability at last. Young, educated people had started to look at the world from their position at the bottom. They had suffered and hardened in the farms and the factories. They had learned much about the realities of Chinese society and the realities of the Chinese masses. They also had learned much about themselves. But they had paid an enormous price for this knowledge: they lost their entire youth.

Chinese society today is, of course, very different from what it was forty-four years ago. However, the theme "Brutal China," chosen for the last issue of *Beijing Cultural Review* in 2010, was an insightful one. Many of the essays in that issue showed that even as China becomes wealthy, we can still see authoritarian currents and much violence in Chinese society. We see a failure to value human life both in our social institutions and in many of our citizens. Can this really be unconnected with the savage fanaticism of the Red Guard movement? To open the focus still wider for a moment, is the violence not connected to the Cultural Revolution or to the philosophy of violent struggle that marked the entire mid-twentieth century and reached a climax in the violence of the Cultural Revolution? To avoid future disasters, we must carry out a careful dissection and sterilization of the heritage of the twentieth century, with respect to both its philosophies and its practices.

But I hope that I can also offer an alternative perspective without appearing unduly perverse. We should consider the possibility that in fact the individuals of the Red Guard generation are now the ones who reject the Red Guard philosophy and actions most thoroughly. Today the history of that period may be more attractive to young people than to those who actually lived through it. The Red Guard generation had two distinct experiences in the 1960s and 1970s: urban and rural, triumphant and defeated, destructive and constructive, anti-revisionist and restorative. On an emotional level, one might even call these experiences hope and despair, love and rejection. The personalities of the former Red Guards have been stiffened with a measure of independence. Their past has made them less likely to give quick allegiance to any lofty ideology or "superman" leader. They know the value of the gradual recovery of common sense. They have also learned from the pointless deaths of comrades around them: there can be ugly consequences to exuberant vitality if it is completely unconstrained and particularly if it is allowed to evolve into wanton violence. They are no longer young, these Red Guards;

they may even have become a little conservative. They have now accumulated some things of their own that they believe are worth defending. Of course, they must strive to remain open-minded and to understand the younger generations with whom they share this country.

CHAPTER SEVEN

FROM MOBILIZED MORALITY TO DEMOBILIZED MORALITY

Social and Ethical Changes in Post-Mao China

In the thirty-eight years since Mao Zedong died in 1976, Chinese society has experienced an enormous transformation and our ethical and moral principles have not escaped change. The massive moral shifts are, of course, very much bound up with changes in our economy and particularly our politics. In fact, morality is often dictated by the influence of those two forces. So my account of morality here will inevitably touch on them, particularly our political narrative. I would like to consider the impact of politics on morality and the relationship between the two. I am aware that in an age of enormous change like ours, giving a full description of moral change is no easy thing. I could not hope to do so in a chapter of this length. Instead, I describe one aspect of moral change that I have observed: the shift from "mobilized morality" to "demobilized morality" that I believe characterizes the moral changes over the last three decades. By "mobilized" I mean a morality that emphasizes armed struggle, that is highly politicized and militarized, that is tense, ideological, homogeneous, and lofty in its rhetoric. "Demobilized" morality is more peaceful, popular, and civilian; it is more relaxed, commonsensical, and diverse, and it focuses on moral minimum standards. I then sketch the great distance between the China at the beginning of this transformation process and the China at its end.

The terms I am using are military in origin. According to the *Modern Chinese Dictionary*, the Chinese word for "mobilize" means "to move a country's

This chapter is an edited version of an article first published in *Southern Metropolis Weekly* [Guangzhou], July 21, 2006.

armed forces from peacetime status to a war footing and to orient all of its economic sectors (industry, agriculture, transport, etc.) to supplying the demands of war." Mobilization directly implies war. Everything is oriented toward the war or, rather, toward victory in the war. World War II plunged the world into turbulence precisely because so many European countries mobilized. But after the war, "mobilized" became much more of a political term in China in that its use in the political sphere often overshadowed its military meaning. "Mobilize and struggle to achieve" some goal or another became a very common piece of political rhetoric and political theory.

The dictionary definition of "demobilize" refers to the act whereby "the armed forces and the economic, political, and cultural sectors revert from a war footing to a state of peace" and also to "the release of military personnel from their positions in the armed forces because they reach the end of their service or because a war ends." Of course, mobilized morality has been deeply conditioned by both the military realities of armed conflict and the theory of permanent revolution under the dictatorship of the proletariat. Demobilized morality pertains to a society that is attempting to achieve peace, reconciliation, and harmony—to a shift at the political level from a revolutionary party to a ruling party.

This chapter briefly sketches the course of that shift. It is not an attempt to compare the two types of morality or to work out which is superior. In other words, when I use the word "moral," I do not mean to imply "morally good"; I just mean "morally relevant." Nor do I mean to imply that the end of the 1970s represented the peak of mobilized morality. In fact, it was only the last wave of the tidal wave of mobilization that began earlier in the twentieth century. The age of mobilization reached its peak during the Cultural Revolution, so mobilized morality reached its most extreme and distorted state during that time. It was highly politicized, dominated by the whims of a single leader, and it demanded total, selfless commitment.

These were the most telling of the slogans from the Cultural Revolution:

—Love Chairman Mao without reservation, be loyal to Chairman Mao without reservation, revere Chairman Mao without reservation.

—Always think of Chairman Mao, always obey Chairman Mao, always work for Chairman Mao.

—Think of loyalty, strive for loyalty, bleed for loyalty, give your life for loyalty.

—Beat down every thought of private interests, launch a revolution in the depths of your soul.

Morality had been swallowed up by political ideology. All moral rules had been reduced to a single word: "loyalty." This revolutionary mobilization had permeated morality and many other areas of life. But after 1976, when the Cultural Revolution ended, revolutionary mobilization began to undergo a long decline in importance. Sometimes the outward forms remained while the substantive meaning changed, until finally the forms too faded away.

Meanwhile, demobilized morality is still far from having achieved a mature form. In fact, it is not clear that it has taken a proper form at all—rather, it remains a work in progress. Demobilized morality thus far seems to exist mainly in the negative: the most obvious characteristic of demobilized morality is that it is not mobilized. While it may take on a positive form of its own, it has not yet done so. What this shows is that the last thirty or more years in China have been a time of flux, perhaps even a transition marking the end of China's twentieth century and its entire modern era. These few decades may have been the last gasp of the modern era, and they mean that China is finishing a period of great turbulence and moving toward being a more stable society.

However we characterize this period, its key political events occurred in 1976. That fact was clear at the time and has been confirmed by subsequent history. First, that was the year of the final contest between the political super-giant who was about to pass from the stage (Mao Zedong) and the political giant who was about to take power (Deng Xiaoping). The super-giant naturally once again politically defeated and demeaned his opponent. This time, however, the audience, which had always cheered for the super-giant before, became restive. Nonetheless, a nation with over 1 billion people jittered with every convulsion of the super-giant's dying body, and the people continued to heed his every slurred word.

That marked a moment on a tightrope for the enormous state, because at that point only one person, Zhang Yufeng, Mao's secretary, could even understand what Mao said.[1] It is a matter of great good fortune for China that she harbored no political grudges or ambitions of her own. The political super-giant saw his old rival, Chiang Kai-shek, pass away on the other side of the Taiwan Strait and two of his most qualified and respected comrades in the party, Zhou Enlai and Zhu De, die before him.[2] Finally, serenaded by the terrible roar of the 1976 Tangshan earthquake, he reluctantly left his young

1. Zhang Yufeng (张玉凤, 1944–), a native of Mudanjiang, Heilongjiang Province, was Mao Zedong's confidential secretary during his final years. Besides acting as his secretary, Zhang was also his personal nurse and messenger, passing his orders to the rest of the country.

2. Chiang Kai-shek (蒋介石, 1887–1975), a native of Fenghua, Zhejiang Province, was a military and political leader of the Kuomintang (Nationalist Party) and the Republic of China. Chiang's major accomplishment was his role in China's Anti-Japanese War (1937–

state behind. He had built this new country with his own hands, but it was already in perilous condition. However, the date on which he departed, September 9, seemed to be an omen: in Chinese, 9-9 is *jiujiu*, homonym for "a long, long time," an indication that Mao's legacy would last.

The reason that his death was so important is that without his death, none of what followed could have happened. But this kind of turning point was bound to come eventually. The logic of political power is always to grow and concentrate, but the natural rhythm of life and death cuts across it, and no one can escape that rhythm. In the two years after Mao's death, nothing seemed to change very much. Mao's successor was Hua Guofeng, whom Mao had hastily chosen at the end.[3] There were some ripples. Even Mao's vast personal power and intellectual influence could not protect his widow, Jiang Qing, who was labeled one of the Gang of Four and thrown in jail.[4] But during those two years, it was still Mao's voice that dominated, and his successor

---

45) as China's commander-in-chief and head of state. He was also a well-known and stern anti-communist and a devout Christian. Chiang died in Taiwan in 1975, one year ahead of Mao Zedong. Zhou Enlai (周恩来, 1898–1976), a native of Huaian, Jiangsu Province, was a senior politician and Communist Party leader. After the founding of the People's Republic of China (PRC), Zhou served as the first foreign minister and the first premier of the new government. He had a long and loyal relationship with Mao Zedong, serving as his deputy and right hand. He was highly respected by the Chinese public. Zhu De (朱德, 1886–1976), a native of Yilong, Sichuan Province, was a top general in the People's Liberation Army (PLA) and later a senior politician. After the founding of the PRC, Zhu became the commander-in-chief of the PLA, of which he is regarded as a principal founder.

3. Hua Guofeng (华国锋, 1921–2008), a native of Jiaocheng, Shanxi Province, was Mao's final designated successor as head of state and party leader after the downfall of Liu Shaoqi and of Lin Biao. Despite ending the Cultural Revolution and ousting the Gang of Four, Hua was a loyal follower of Mao's party line. In 1978, Deng Xiaoping sidelined Hua by forcing him into early retirement and then initiated reform policies.

4. Jiang Qing (江青, 1914–1991), a native of Zhucheng, Shandong Province, was the fourth and last wife of Mao Zedong and a leader of the Cultural Revolution as a member of the Gang of Four. A woman with strong political ambition, Jiang married Mao in Yan'an in 1938 and played a leading role in the Cultural Revolution. She was prosecuted in 1981 and sentenced to life imprisonment. The Gang of Four (四人帮) refers to a political coalition of four Communist Party officials during the Cultural Revolution. The group included Mao's wife Jiang Qing and her close associates Zhang Chunqiao, Yao Wenyuan, and Wang Hongwen. The Gang of Four is notorious for having taken advantage of Mao's decision to launch the Cultural Revolution in order to maximize their political power. The members were prosecuted in 1981 for treason and sentenced to death or life imprisonment.

even made that explicit in his "Two Whatevers" policy ("We will resolutely uphold whatever policy decisions Chairman Mao made and unswervingly follow whatever instructions Chairman Mao gave").

The morality of the years 1976–78 was still ideological, still the ideology of revolution. Morality was subordinate to political concerns and overwhelmingly served political ends. And everything—politics, the economy, morality—was ideological, top-down, frenzied. In those two years, there was a mass movement to expose the Gang of Four, an economic drive to "ramp up fast," and a movement for a "new leap forward." The state called for everyone to continue to emulate successful communes—the industrial commune of Daqing and the agricultural commune of Dazhai. The process involved socialist labor contests, with appeals to the revolutionary spirit to drive the population to work harder and produce more. The newspapers deployed stirring rhetoric: "Spirit of revolution and 100 percent effort, strive for speed, make every second count!" "Turn up the horsepower, roll up your sleeves and get to it, get two days' worth out of every day!"

But the great changes started very soon after Mao Zedong died. The first was a series of corrections in the country's politics, which were a massive shock to the Mao era's stark, black-and-white morality of right versus wrong, good guys versus bad guys. They were also to some extent a repudiation of the fanatical, ideological style of politics that had prevailed over the last twenty years or so, not least because those who were rehabilitated had previously been the victims of many purges. A large group of old party members who had been attacked during the Cultural Revolution and earlier were now restored to the party. Some of them had been, in the lingo of the time, "knocked down and kicked so they can't get back up again": Liu Shaoqi, who had been branded "great traitor, great renegade, great scab" and "China's biggest capitalist-roader" at the party's 9th Congress in 1969, was now posthumously rehabilitated. Deng Xiaoping, another of "China's biggest capitalist-roaders," had been repeatedly purged from the party, but after the Tiananmen Incident, he too regained his position.[5] The label "right-winger" was removed from 550,000 people who had been attacked during the 1957 anti-rightist campaign. The party admitted that they had been wrongly labeled, and they were accepted back into the fold. Over 20 million "land-

5. The Tiananmen Incident (天安门事件) refers to the public protest on April 5, 1976, at Tiananmen Square. The incident, which began with crowds assembling to mourn the passing of Premier Zhou Enlai, quickly turned into a public protest expressing anger toward the Gang of Four. The incident was initially defined as an anti-revolutionary movement by the Gang of Four, but that label was removed in 1978.

lords, rich farmers, counterrevolutionaries, and bad elements" also were destigmatized. Their children were no longer listed in separate household registers or discriminated against. The system and the attitudes that had focused on class background and turned those children almost into a separate class of "untouchables" now broke down. Mao's black-and-white morality was moderated, and the "Two Whatevers" policy came in for strong criticism in the debate that sprang up around the essay "Practice Is the Sole Criterion of Truth."[6] In light of the experience of the Cultural Revolution, the party drafted "Guiding Principles for Inner-Party Political Life," an attempt to renormalize the politics of the party, to introduce order and democracy. Before, the country had experienced the extreme politicization of morality, even the swallowing up of morality by politics. Now, politics itself was subject to morality. Political actions had to conform to moral principles and respect the personal virtues.

Up to that time, all changes in China had begun in the political realm. Now there seemed to be a conscious retreat from the politics-first approach. China for the first time tried placing the economy and cultural improvement at the heart of politics. A series of major scientific and education conferences were held, and the college entrance examinations were restarted. In 1978 came the 3rd Plenary Session of the 11th Party Congress, at which the policy reversal was formalized. Class struggle was no longer to be the party's fundamental objective, and the party repeated that "the large-scale and turbulent class struggles of the masses . . . have in the main come to an end." The party's focus shifted to economic reconstruction of the country, and goals were set for a more democratic system and better rule of law. In the Central Work Conference just before the 11th Party Congress, Deng Xiaoping proposed the philosophy of "letting some people get rich first."

Often policy execution and interpersonal relationships were still conducted in the style of an ideological movement, but the sense of struggle diminished. There was a new spirit of "serving the people."[7] Relationships

6. The debate about whether practice is the sole criterion for testing truth (实践是检验真理的唯一标准的大讨论) refers to the national debate on whether to follow unconditionally Mao's instructions before the 3rd Plenum Meeting of the 11th Party Congress. It rejected Hua Guofeng's insistence on Maoist policies and laid the philosophical foundation for the subsequent reform and opening up policy.

7. "Serve the People" ("为人民服务") was a slogan by Mao Zedong defining the goal of Communist Party cadres. It has become the official motto of the Chinese Communist Party and is engraved on the front wall of Zhongnanhai, the Chinese equivalent of the White House.

once marked by wariness bloomed with a new warmth; postures of aggression slowly relaxed. But material wealth and material incentives were not yet a major part of social consciousness, so the primary driver was still affective calls to action. Those calls, combined with the intensity and pressure to conform that remained from the days of ideological movements, were still quite effective motivators. Most people had not yet started to exercise true independence of thought, moral or otherwise. There was still a great deal of hope invested in "the first generation of new, socialist people" and celebration of heroic model laborers. I can give an example from my personal experience. During this period I often took long train journeys, and it was obvious that when the Railway Bureau was engaged in a "movement" to produce "advanced model workers," the quality of service was much higher. Attendants worked themselves into a sweat pouring hot drinks for passengers and tidying the carriages. The steward would organize teams, including passenger representatives, to assess and rate the work of his staff; the bureau would send inspectors, some undercover; and passengers would eagerly join in the process, writing their accolades in the comments books. Train attendants were genuinely happy to receive positive comments, and that served as their motivation to work hard. However, when there was no such "movement," no drive for diligence, the situation was very different. Attendants would appear only at stations, to open the carriage doors, and no one seemed concerned no matter how filthy the passenger compartments became.

The practice of ideological "diligence drives" continued into the 1980s, but the demands that they made became more basic: requirements that anyone could manage and that were more consistent with what people wanted anyway. Eventually it was only the form of these drives that retained the marks of the ideologically pure political movements from which they had evolved. The specific targets were no longer political. In February 1981, the All-China Federation of Trade Unions and other bodies started a drive called the "five conducts and four beauties," aimed at improving public conduct across the country, particularly among young people. The five conducts were good citizenship, courtesy, hygiene, orderliness, and morality; the four beauties were beauty of spirit, of language, of conduct, and of one's surroundings. Soon afterward, three "loves" were added: love of country, love of socialism, love of the party. March of every year was designated "national good citizens' courtesy month," and on almost every day of the month, work units and schools would send hundreds of thousands or even millions of people out onto the streets to do good deeds: sweep the streets, direct traffic, help other citizens, and so on. That kind of moral drive was aimed especially at the education and edification of the young. But unlike during the Cultural Revolution, which had called on the young to be "little generals of the revolution" and the "vanguard of rebellion," the young were now given training in manners and citizenship. They were to be brought up as modern people: rational, moral, enculturated, and disciplined.

In September 1986, the Party Central Committee passed a resolution to develop "socialist spiritual civilization"—jargon for culture and the arts. It said that developing China's culture was as vital a goal as developing the economy. But the moral component of this new culture no longer included the notion of struggle. Instead it was about restraint, grace, maintaining some basic minimum standards of conduct. Professional standards and ethics also were linked in. In February 1986, the Communist Youth League of China (CYLC) Central Committee announced a drive for young people to be more polite in their language, summed up in five words: "hello, please, thank you, sorry, goodbye." They also called on young people not to spit in public. That might seem somewhat trivial to outsiders, but it was a specific response to a real issue.

All of these drives involved the promotion of "model citizens" from whom Chinese people were to take their moral cues. For example, in 1983 the CYLC Central Committee began to publicize Zhang Haidi, a young woman from Shandong who was paralyzed from the waist down but who nonetheless dedicated herself to learning and to helping others.[8] On March 17, China Central Television (CCTV) broadcast a documentary about her, and 200 million people tuned in to watch. It was a genuinely moving story that inspired many viewers to action. The newspapers also reported on events like the "Huashan rescue" and self-sacrificing heroes like Zhang Hua of the Fourth Military Medical University.[9]

8. Zhang Haidi (张海迪, 1955–), a native of Jinan, Shandong Province, is a Chinese writer, translator, and role model. Paralyzed from the waist down at the age of five, Zhang managed to teach herself English, German, and Japanese and received a master's degree in philosophy at Jilin University. She is regarded as China's Helen Keller and advocates for the rights of the disabled.

9. The Huashan Rescue (华山抢险救人的集体) was a volunteer rescue mission by a group of medical school students and workers on May 1, 1983, at Mount Huashan. The mountain trail was overcrowded and a number of tourists fell. The group of medical school students and workers volunteered to rescue the victims and saved many lives. Zhang Hua (张华, 1958–82), a native of Hulin, Heilongjiang Province, was a student at a PLA medical school in Xi'an. In July 1982, Zhang sacrificed his life while trying to rescue an old farmer from a septic tank.

These new heroes were very different from the heroes of a few years before. Many of the heroes of the early years of the People's Republic of China had faded by this time, particularly the heroes of class struggle. But there was one who continued to cast a long shadow: Lei Feng.[10] However, his image shifted as times changed. For example, more weight was placed on his helpfulness and service than his political purity, and as China grew wealthier and attitudes to material goods changed, new details about Lei Feng were revealed: he owned a watch and a leather jacket. Those shifts helped retain his appeal for ordinary citizens.

Another change was increasing concern for the safety of young people. Some of the young heroes of the early Cultural Revolution were martyrs, like Liu Wenxue, who was killed when he intervened to stop a landowner stealing peppers, and the shepherdess sisters Longmei and Yurong, who nearly froze to death because they stayed with their wandering flock.[11] In the late 1980s there was a similar example—a young man named Lai Ning who died while trying to put out a fire—but for the most part government organizations elected not to publicize or promote that sort of thing.[12] There was the realization that young lives were much more important than any material belongings and that they must be protected.

During the 1980s, another subtle change occurred. In 1980, *China Youth* published a letter signed by Pan Xiao that asked, "Why has my life become narrower and narrower?"[13] She described the huge gap that she perceived

10. Lei Feng (雷锋, 1940–62), a native of Wangcheng, Hunan Province, was a PLA soldier. After his death in a car accident, Lei became a national role model in 1963, portrayed as selfless, modest, and devoted to Chairman Mao and the Communist Party. March 5 was later designated as "Lei Feng Memorial Day" in 1963, the date when Chairman Mao wrote the famous article on the front page of *People's Daily*, "To Learn from Comrade Lei Feng."

11. Liu Wenxue (刘文学, 1945–1959), a native of Hezhou, Sichuan Province, was a Communist Young Pioneer who gave his life trying to stop the theft of collective property on his commune. The sisters Longmei and Yurong (龙梅, 1952– , 玉荣, 1955–) were two Mongolian girls who in 1964 at the ages of eleven and nine rescued a flock of sheep owned collectively by their commune during a devastating blizzard in Inner Mongolia. All of the sheep survived, but the two sisters became handicapped due to frostbite.

12. Lai Ning (赖宁, 1973–88), a native of Ya'an, Sichuan Province, was a Communist Young Pioneer member who lost his life trying to put out a local forest fire in 1988. He later became the role model for Young Pioneers.

13. Pan Xiao (潘晓) was the pen name of the writer of an influential article published in the *Chinese Youth* magazine in May 1980. The author claimed to be a twenty-three-year-old woman confused about the current reality and frustrated over her prospects for

between her education and her experience of reality since the end of the Cultural Revolution. *China Youth* then launched a series of essays entitled "What Exactly Is the Meaning of Life?" and within a very short time received over 60,000 letters on the subject. The magazine's circulation that year rose to 3.69 million. Many of the letters revealed rather dismal situations and sentiments, leading the secretary of the Party Central Committee, Hu Qiaomu, to respond: "We have no right to tell them that they have to be singing happy songs all day long."[14] The *People's Daily* also published an editorial saying that the object of the media discussion was to allow

> young people to forget ideology and just tell the truth, to add their own viewpoint and exchange experiences, free from any threat of punishment or moralistic lecturing. . . . For many years, "discussion" has meant nothing but mobbing and shouting down; for many years we have been engaged in "positive education" with little regard for psychological reality. Experience shows that shouting down was a mistake . . . "positive education" has failed.

That was perhaps the first large-scale public debate since the founding of the People's Republic of China that was handled without an explicit plan and without a required political conclusion. It was the first not to be carefully engineered and directed from the top down. It was not a trap to draw out opposing viewpoints, identify opponents, and beat them down. It gave many young people their first opportunity to speak for many years, and the focus was on the process, on communication, not on reaching some political objective. The debate did involve some planning, and it was taken by the Chinese Communist Party to be a part of its propaganda project. In fact, the letter from "Pan Xiao" was not sent by any such person: it was commissioned by the editor from two writers called Pan Wei and Huang Xiaoju. This debate was different from past political drives and very different from purges or violent struggles. Those who expressed nonmainstream opinions or ideas at odds with

---

the future. This article triggered great reaction and sympathy from Chinese society as it touched on society's common fear and frustration after the Cultural Revolution and the advent of the world of economic reform.

14. Hu Qiaomu (胡乔木, 1912–92), a native of Yancheng, Jiangsu Province, was a Communist revolutionary, sociologist, Marxist philosopher, and prominent politician of the PRC. Hu was the first president of the Chinese Academy of Social Sciences, a president of the Xinhua News Agency, and a Politburo member of the Chinese Communist Party. As a resolute follower of Mao, he was well-known for his stern opposition to some of Deng Xiaoping's market reform policies.

the government's official line were for the most part not attacked or affected in any way. For example, one student wrote an essay asserting that "only the self is absolute"—and he is now a philosophy professor. The final conclusion to this public debate, despite efforts to inject more optimistic and noble sentiments, appeared in an essay, "For Those Who Are Thinking about the Meaning of Life," that struck a measured and egalitarian tone. Though their past beliefs were now subject to question, throughout the 1980s young people continued to believe that people should have beliefs, that people should be more concerned with their ideals than with material goods. Young people devoured new ideas from the West like starving people at a banquet as they began to see and to make contact with the world beyond China. Tidal waves of enthusiasm for existentialism and Freud surged through the universities. Two educators who specialized in patriotic rhetoric found themselves subject to considerable pushback from students in the "Shekou debate" in 1988.[15]

By the 1990s, particularly after Deng Xiaoping's speech on his southern tour in 1992, the market economy became an unstoppable force.[16] It was affecting the lives and attitudes of everyone. Since the 1990s, there have been very few movement-style political drives, even on the purely political level. Certainly there have been none that were intended to involve the entire population. The function of politics has been more restricted to the civil service and the body of officials who staff it. As the market economy grew, officials gained control of amounts of financial resources that were simply incomparable to those of past decades. During the transition period, the law had not yet caught up with this new reality, and so corruption became a very serious issue, in the form of rent seeking and influence peddling. The market economy also comes with the requirement for widespread trust and credit, and trust is one resource that seems to be very scarce in China.

15. The Shekou Debate (蛇口风波) was a debate in Shekou, Guangdong Province, in 1988, where three famous scholars, including Li Yanjie and Qu Xiao, debated a group of young students from Shekou, a city at the forefront of China's reform policies. Many controversial issues were raised during the debate, such as whether people should buy imported cars and whether it was right for businesses to pursue material profit. The debate took place against the backdrop of economic reform and triggered a fierce national reaction.

16. Deng Xiaoping's southern tour (邓小平南巡) refers to Deng's tour of the southern part of China in January and February of 1992. The tour was an endeavor to revitalize economic reform after the Tiananmen Square protests in 1989. Deng's resolute pro-reform attitude sent a clear signal to the leadership in Beijing as well as to Chinese citizens and kicked off the next phase of substantial economic reform.

Globalization continued to gather speed in the 1990s, giving everyone the feeling that the entire world was interlinked, all humanity a single family, and that no region or group could hold itself permanently apart. But globalization did not necessarily bring greater agreement or even mutual understanding. In fact, there seemed to be an increase in differences and conflict. The technology of the post-1990s era, particularly information technology (IT) and the Internet, also started to exercise an increasing influence on public morality. China integrated with the world through its computers, and mobile phones spread to every corner of the country. Access to information and opportunities for self-expression exploded. The global village had truly arrived.

There were still a few government drives in the 1990s, calling on people to emulate the warrior for justice Xu Honggang and the dedicated party official Kong Fansen.[17] But for the most part, the government's attempts to improve public morality focused on incremental improvements in everyday conduct. To a certain extent, the government now recognized the independence of morality, its universality, and its relation to history. There was a limited restoration of the reputation of Confucius and his school and traditional social ethics. Ritual Confucianism reappeared, on a small scale. At the same time, there was much greater acceptance of the morality of other countries, including the West. Another important advance was the new recognition of the importance of fairness in our institutions and policies as a major moral issue, perhaps even more important than the moral standards imposed on individuals by those institutions. The voice for "social justice" became louder as people started to realize that before considering the issue of individual morality, we had to think about the morality of our systems. Before making moral demands of individuals, we should make demands of our institutions and the people who play key roles within them.

Another very major change over the last thirty or so years was that people became able to talk relatively freely. That included the freedom to privately criticize the government and even specific leaders, something impossible during the Cultural Revolution, when private speech could easily be a crime,

17. Xu Honggang (徐洪刚, 1971–), a native of Yiliang, Yunan Province, is a PLA soldier who risked his life to save a woman from a robbery in 1993. Though severely wounded, Xu did not give up pursuit of the robber. After his recovery, he received honors from top leaders in Beijing and was made a national role model. Kong Fansen (孔繁森, 1944–94), a native of Liaocheng, Shandong Province, was a local Communist Party cadre in Tibet. He was highly respected in his locality for his hard work and integrity. He was killed in a traffic accident in 1994 and was portrayed as the role model for all Communist Party cadres.

sometimes even a capital crime. A line popular during the 1980s said, "You pick up your chopsticks and eat the pork, lay down your chopsticks and abuse the cook." It captures two of the great changes: a radical improvement in material wealth for everyone and a huge expansion in freedom of speech. People became keener to tell the truth and to create and maintain a social environment in which one could tell the truth. Ba Jin was someone who argued publicly for this, and his ideas were widely welcomed.[18]

People also began to find heroes and models who were not individuals groomed and presented to the public in government propaganda drives but private citizens who emerged spontaneously. In fact, the new type of hero may even have had to fight the government at some point. For example, Gao Yaojie, a retired doctor from Henan, has become known for her work on HIV/AIDS prevention.[19] She exposed the serious epidemic in Henan caused by "blood merchants" and spent many years visiting rural villages to educate residents on HIV prevention and to deliver donations and medication to HIV sufferers. When she raised the alarm about the epidemic and was searching for its cause, at first the authorities silenced her. It was only later that her work was promoted and her findings confirmed. Eventually CCTV named her one of its 2003 "persons of the year." Gao drew her inspiration from a rather unique source: her maternal grandfather had been a member of the Qing Dynasty Hanlin Academy. She had received a classical education from the age of three years, and she was able to recite long sections of the classics from memory. Some of the concepts that she found in the classics were burned into her mind. "I am a disciple of Confucius," she said. "All living things have their duties, and mine is to be a good doctor." There are many similar examples of heroes and ordinary good people who drew their inspiration from sources other than official rhetoric: Buddhists, Christians, and Muslims made great contributions in their jobs and as volunteers.

Another feature of the heroic figures celebrated by the government in this period was that their achievements were no longer casually exaggerated. Now

18. Ba Jin (巴金, 1904–2005) was the pen name of one of the most prominent literary figures in China of the twentieth century. Ba, who addressed many social issues of the times, was persecuted during the Cultural Revolution.

19. Gao Yaojie (高耀洁, 1927–) is a Chinese gynecologist, academic, and AIDS activist from Zhengzhou, Henan Province. Gao, who spent time under house arrest in China, has been honored for her work in public health by the United Nations and many Western organizations. Her dispute with the Chinese authorities on the transmission and the seriousness of the AIDS epidemic in China hindered her further activities and resulted in her departing for the United States in 2009.

the publicity focused on their real achievements, often connected with their position or their professional ethics. Their status as a good citizen, good member of society, or good person also was recognized. For example, Zhong Nanshan came to public attention as a doctor fighting SARS in 2003.[20] He and his colleagues in Guangzhou were never held up as lofty heroes; instead, they were praised as conscientious doctors, committed to their work. Zhong Nanshan said, "In our job, the greatest political ideal is to do what we can to prevent and treat disease." The selection of role models began to take on more bottom-up features as well. Since 2002, CCTV has selected a "person of the year" through public vote. Over 1 million people are said to cast votes, and the program attracts an audience of tens of millions. Though the selection still incorporates political considerations, it has produced a much broader range of heroes. In 2003 one of the persons of the year was a Japanese lawyer, Oyama Hiroshi, who for over forty years has represented Chinese victims of war crimes in Japanese courts, never accepting any payment and indeed paying court fees himself.[21] In 2004 Tian Shiguo earned the title by proving his devotion to his mother by donating a kidney to her.[22]

Politics exhibits inertia, and so does morality. Many people still retain the old sensitivity to stirring political drives, and they can produce striking short-term results. But in the long term, moral growth cannot be nurtured with idealistic campaigns. Moral maturity has its own rhythm and order, and the best that we can do is to prepare the way for its coming. There is nothing that we can do to artificially speed up the process. Mass mobilization has become very difficult in a country where people no longer depend entirely on their "work unit" but are financially independent and have income from a range of sources.[23] Any ordinary person can tell you that the response to

20. Zhong Nanshan (钟南山, 1936–), a native of Nanjing, Jiangsu Province, is the Chinese pulmonologist who discovered the SARS virus in 2003. He is most well known for managing the SARS outbreak in Guangdong Province. He was voted one of China's top-ten scientists in 2010.

21. Oyama Hiroshi (Wei Shanhong, 尾山宏, 1930–) is a Japanese lawyer who voluntarily helped Chinese World War II victims sue the Japanese government for compensation. He was awarded the "Touching China" honor in 2003.

22. Tian Shiguo (田世国, 1965–), a native of Zaozhuang, Shandong Province, is a Chinese lawyer who donated a kidney to save his mother. Tian received the "Touching China" award in 2004.

23. Work unit (单位) refers to a place of employment in the PRC. In the pre-reform era, work units were state-owned social institutions comprising schools, factories, and hospitals that provided employment as well as social services and housing for urban residents

political calls to action now is far from what it used to be. Everyone knows tacitly that Cultural Revolution–style political movements are a thing of the past, but we allow them to persist in an attenuated form. Part of this new accommodation is a new attitude toward government: "Policies come from above, policy neutralization comes from below."

There were also some less obvious changes in the rhythm of ordinary life that were to become the "new normal" in subsequent years. The power of ideology to mobilize masses of people was now waning, so beginning in the 1990s bureaucratic institutions arose that relied on the self-interest of citizens. Even when local drives and campaigns were used, they now often appealed to and manipulated the public's financial interests.

Over the last thirty years or so, we may have experienced the biggest and most comprehensive changes in China's history, in everything from material standards of living, cultural life, the economy, politics, technology, art, and the environment to public attitudes. From the most intrinsic to the most extrinsic, from the Chinese people's traditional rootedness in the soil of one place to today's flowing tides of humanity, everywhere we see unimaginable change. If you had visited Beijing in 1976, you would have seen a city of bicycles. Everyone would have been wearing the same blue and grey clothes. People lined up outside stores to buy goods, and there was much counting of cloth coupons, rice coupons, and other paperwork. Huge banners printed with slogans were hung on every wall, and the city was full of assemblies and marches. Beijing's good restaurants could be counted on your fingers, and after nightfall the lights in the hutongs were little brighter than fireflies. But if you had visited in 2005, you would have found a city of cars—though slow-moving cars at many intersections. Clothing now comes in a kaleidoscopic variety of styles and colors; supermarkets are everywhere, with produce stacked on shelves for anyone to buy. Skyscrapers race for the sky, and at night the neon is almost blinding. There are still queues: low-paid workers wait through the night to be assigned low-cost housing; people from other parts of the country put up makeshift tents outside hospitals to stay close to sick friends and relatives. But overall there has been a massive increase in material standards of living, and the greater options and possibilities enjoyed by everyone are an obvious fact of twenty-first-century life.

---

in a planned economy. In the post-reform era, due to the proliferation of private enterprises, the phrase "work unit" refers either to state-owned enterprises or simply one's place of employment.

More fundamental changes have occurred in thinking and attitudes. There has been a sea change in our level of tolerance for different ideas and lifestyles. In 1983, a woman named Wang was executed for the crime of "hooliganism" because she was found to have had sexual relations with over ten men. She said: "Free sexuality is a lifestyle that I have chosen. My conduct may be too radical today, but in twenty years people will not see it that way." Twenty years later, the profligate "Muzi Mei," a blogger who wrote about her sex life, was not accused of any crime and in fact became an online celebrity.[24] Then there was "Sister Lotus," another online celebrity who specialized in boasting about her appearance, and *Supergirls*, a song-and-dance show that became a national sensation.[25] It is not sufficient to say that such behavior could never have happened thirty years ago—it was in fact unimaginable thirty years ago. Any slight hint of similar tendencies would have been subject to strident attacks for being "vulgar" or representing the "bourgeois lifestyle." Today these fads, spread by our new technologies, reflect the huge changes in our values.

There are even some popular rhymes that describe the changes and express worries over our moral trajectory:

—*In the 50s we gave our sincere hearts; in the 60s we gave our red hearts; in the 70s we gave our loyal hearts; in the 80s we gave our good hearts; in the 90s we gave our charitable hearts. We gave them; now they are gone.*

—*In the 50s people helped people; in the 60s people beat people; in the 70s people yelled at people; in the 80s people ignored people; in the 90s people cheat people.*

—*First-class citizens are "civil servants"; their sons and grandsons are blessed. Tenth-class citizens are "masters"; they make revolution like Lei Feng.*

And there are many more besides those given above.

Box 7-1 lists headlines that appeared on November 29, 2005, under the rubric "Social News" on the Sina website. Of course, headlines are designed to be eye-catching (that being another characteristic of our time), and negative news tends to dominate, but I think they still offer us a window into our

24. Muzi Mei (木子美), real name Li Li, is a freelance writer who in 2003 revealed her sex diary online. She quickly became famous but has also attracted a huge amount of controversy.

25. Sister Lotus (芙蓉姐姐), real name Shi Hengxia, is a self-proclaimed dancer and beauty. She published a number of her dance photos online, attracting a huge amount of attention as well as controversy. *Supergirls* (超级女声) is a talent show for Chinese female singers. The show is broadcast on Hunan TV, and the competition is determined by viewer voting. It is considered a Chinese version of "American Idol."

Box 7-1. *Headlines from "Social News," November 29, 2005*

Corrupt police boss shot; 10,000 sign petition against shooter's execution

Ningxia police catch armed robber wanted for murder using bone dating techniques

Heilongjiang drug mules dealing on train; over 10,000 amphetamine pills found taped to legs

Teacher smacked by high school students repeatedly; principal can only give students extra lessons

Chengdu resident criticized for registering "love flu" trademark (sounds same as "bird flu")

Yangzhou domestic worker firm offers wet nurse service; fees as high as RMB3,000 per month

Diary of a car thief: must steal every day or can't forgive self

Unemployed Beijinger, 26, rapes and kills 84-year-old to relieve boredom

Beijing police shut down over 500 phones across the country implicated in prostitution

Policeman sprints 100 meters to catch thief after being stabbed in chest

Millionaire proposes in BMW; female students look for money when choosing husband

Father puts "spare the rod" philosophy into practice: 400 clips round the ear to make a great pianist

Man drugs construction worker with sleeping pills in his meal, steals digger

Advertisement in Zhuhai features image of RMB notes, hangs for a full week

University student mistakes hemlock for honeysuckle in herbal tea; one dead, eight hospitalized

Farmer in Zhenan, Shaanxi, buys bride but can't buy love; woman kept under watch to prevent escape

Apartment complex manager beaten by 20-30 residents for interfering with their building in shared spaces

Middle School attached to China Conservatory allows students to pay to audit classes; rakes in over 10 million in five years.

times. If an adult who died in 1976 was brought back to life today, would that person be able to understand those headlines? If the person was given the full context, wouldn't he or she be stunned into silence? Massive change does not necessarily require centuries. In just thirty years, we have witnessed a sea change. Today it would be rare to see millions of people gathered for a parade. We do not see a million workers throwing down their tools to greet visitors from overseas. No one sees huge masses of workers on construction sites with the red flag flying high above them. Now those sites are buried under highway overpasses and strings of skyscraper hotels. Everything has started to boom, to normalize, but it is perhaps just a little bland. There are at least a few people—a minority, certainly, but a real minority—who are not so concerned with these benefits and who miss the passion that has been lost. They may even wish to dedicate themselves once more to something higher, to throw themselves into a great cause with the spirit and fire that used to be mandatory.

The shift from mobilized morality to nonmobilized morality also meant a shift from the morality of an atypical era to that of a normal era; from a morality of high goals to a morality of minimum standards; from a morality of uniform values and models to a morality of diverse values and models. In terms of time, it was a shift from the twentieth to the twenty-first century. Eric Hobsbawm calls the period from 1914 to 1991 the "short century" and the "age of extremes." For China, our short century runs from 1919 to 1989, from the May Fourth Movement to June 4, 1989, at Tiananmen Square. It was, of course, an age of extremes, but it was different from traditional society and different from other ages of extremes, so I will give it another name: "age of mobilization." It is the age of mobilization because of the constant efforts to arouse the people, to mobilize the masses, to make "the people" the lead actor on the stage of history—to make the people, for the first time, agents of history. It was characterized by a series of political movements: from movements of intellectuals, student movements, and worker movements down to peasant movements. It saw a shift from peaceful movements to armed movements. During this period, movement often followed movement with no break in between, and the techniques of political mobilization became increasingly frenzied. It started with enlightenment; it turned to armed liberation. There was always a top-down driver of mobilization, always a distinction between the mobilizers and the mobilized. A set of inspiring goals was used to motivate and rally an often lethargic populace, and over time a set of highly refined techniques was developed to stimulate mass engagement. Now it looks as though these must all be put aside for the time being, though their aftereffects still persist within our culture.

One aftereffect is uncertainty about the present. Though mobilized morality is now in the past and can be fairly precisely defined, demobilized morality is still ongoing, and its principles are not fully clear. As yet it is defined mainly in negatives, and it is uncertain whether it will develop into a stable moral format for a stable society—that is, whether it falls within the scope of a morality to which human will and behavior can successfully adapt. The most that we can say now is that it feels like demobilization—reversion to a relatively normal, nonheightened state, to a tradition. It is also a form of diversification: though people need a convergence in their fundamental values, there is some inevitable spread in values and lifestyles. Of course, it is always possible that a new mobilized era will return. Given the long-term trends, "remobilization" seems highly unlikely, but history is full of reversals.

The most serious problem and potential danger in our current moral regime still lies in the rural parts of China. The state destroyed the social order and natural power relationships that existed in rural villages and took full control, down to the level of the individual. But with the introduction of the household responsibility system, it just as quickly retreated again, leaving China's small farmers in a completely uncoordinated state. Later the government rebuilt the rural institutions, added many more officials, and costs rose dramatically, increasing the burden on rural residents. The media and many well-meaning people have wrung their hands over the plight of farmers, but the important question is this: What can farmers do for themselves? Farmers still do not have institutions and stable representatives who truly work for their interests. They do not yet receive equal treatment as citizens of this country. That is especially clear with respect to the millions who have traveled to the cities to find work: the value of their labor has not kept pace with the growing economy. They have lost virtually all ability to negotiate their own wages and job security. And when minimum material standards are threatened, it is very difficult to maintain minimum moral standards.

Fundamental moral beliefs surely exist in the minds of most people at any time. They are not completely shaped by the tides of politics or the booming economy. We can still hope for a healthier moral environment, and our hopes rest on the shoulders of the most ordinary of people. The moral environment depends on the inherent moral strength of the general public. Politics can play an important role, of course, and it should do what it can to support and protect the natural positive moral force of the public. But moral strength cannot be forced, and attempts to artificially induce moral sentiment are likely to fail.

Public opinion and policy in today's China have both reached a turning point. The focus is moving from "letting some people get rich first" toward making everyone rich—or at least toward giving everyone a reasonably equal standard of living. It is moving from "efficiency first, fairness second" to social justice as a primary consideration. As we go through this transition, the important questions are these: How can we avoid losing the progress that we have already made? How can we avoid using extremist techniques? How can we avoid threats to social stability from unexpected events?

PART IV

CHINA'S ONGOING MORAL DECAY?

CHAPTER EIGHT

MORAL CRISIS IN CHINESE SOCIETY

China's tragic collision with the West began in the nineteenth century, when we were swiftly plunged into a state of constant struggle for our very survival. China experienced wave after wave of "enlightenment and revolution," steadily increasing in intensity. The self-strengthening movement was interrupted by the first Sino-Japanese war; as a result of the war, China had the Hundred Days' Reform, which came to an unfortunate early end because it was led by writers, not politicians. The Xinhai Revolution was, as revolutions go, relatively bloodless. However, once the Manchu Qing ruler had abdicated, no one was willing to take the time necessary to cultivate a democratic republic. Rather, people desperately cast around for a shortcut, copying from other countries whatever seemed to be the fastest and most successful solutions to the problems of the state. That left them wide open to the influence of dishonest ideologies and militarized violence. By the start of the New Culture Movement, people believed that the only way to create a new, rich, strong China was to reject everything and remake the country. To be sure, some enlightenment was necessary, but now all of China's historical and cultural traditions were subject to virulent attack. And the first target was the "three guidelines and five constants": the foundation of traditional social morality. The three guidelines and five constants do indeed need periodic updating, but in the early twentieth century people seemed to want to completely abandon traditional morality in its entirety, in the belief that the old

This chapter is an edited version of a chapter first published in *New Principles* (Sichuan People's Publishing House, 2013), pp. 35–40.

had to be destroyed to make way for the new. Moreover, there were now fashionable imported theories and ideologies behind which we could rally.

This abandonment of traditional morality and the repeated attacks against it can be seen as reaching a climax in the Cultural Revolution. At the beginning of the Cultural Revolution, the campaign to "smash the four olds" (破四旧) swept up the entire population. Tradition, which was clinging only by a thread, was once again given a battering, in all its manifestations: old thought, old culture, old customs, and old habits. That battering included destruction of many ancient and historical books, artifacts, and sites. The tombs of some honored historical figures were wrecked, and sometimes even their remains were dug up. Millions of families had their homes searched; children were ordered to report on their own parents and sometimes even to take part in beating members of their own families; husbands and wives were encouraged to report on and attack each other. Politics completely supplanted morality. The only criterion for moral right and wrong was loyalty to a political leader, Mao Zedong. In the latter part of the Cultural Revolution, the whole nation was drawn into mass criticism of Confucius and Lin Biao.[1] Confucius's desire to restore the old rites was linked to Lin Biao's alleged desire to restore the old capitalist order. In the history promoted at that time, the conflict between Confucians and Legalists was played up, with the Legalists being the heroes and Confucians the villains. In this version of history, even the first Emperor of Qin was a hero.

The campaign against Confucius and Lin Biao was not violent, but it was an attempt to dig out the "deep roots," or the spirit, of traditional culture. The goal was a complete break, not just with traditional systems of ownership but with traditional concepts. At the same time, however, it also attempted to link with another Chinese historical tradition: there was massive promotion of the tradition of legalism and autocracy. Intellectuals, including many writers who had previously been committed Confucians, opted into the anti-Confucian squad.[2] Among ordinary people, Confucius,

1. "The Criticize Lin Biao and Criticize Confucius Campaign" (批林批孔运动) was a political propaganda campaign started by Mao Zedong and his wife, Jiang Qing, the leader of the Gang of Four. It lasted from 1973 until the end of the Cultural Revolution in 1976. The campaign, which produced detailed Maoist interpretations of Chinese history, was used as a tool by the Gang of Four to attack their enemies, including Premier Zhou Enlai.

2. For example, Feng Youlan was a philosopher who before the revolution had been engaged in revitalizing neo-Confucianism. After the revolution, he repudiated his former views and declared many times that Confucius represented only the interests of the exploitative landowning class. During the anti-Confucius/anti–Lin Biao movement, he was forced to declare that Confucius was an apologist for the philosophy of the slave-owning class.

the Confucian school, Confucian rites, and Confucian moral principles became dirty words. The effects of that demonization can still be felt today, and the harm that it has done to public morality cannot be overstated.

Traditional culture and the traditional morality underpinning it were attacked repeatedly by liberal writers during the period from 1919 to 1989. In the twenty-five years since 1989, they have been seriously eroded by the onslaught of the market economy. After a century of repeated criticism and attacks, traditional morality is now extremely weak. There has been a small resurgence of our historical and cultural traditions, led by Confucianism, thanks to the painstaking efforts of a few contemporary believers. But they are still only on the margins of mainstream society.

Observe the society of modern China: what we see is a diseased society. In the recent anti-Japanese demonstrations (this time regarding the territorial dispute over a group of uninhabited islands known in Japan as the Senkaku Islands and in China as the Diaoyu Islands), which had been tacitly or explicitly approved by certain authorities, violence and rioting started at the slightest encouragement or the slightest relaxation of controls. We see the weak taking knives to those even weaker than them, with some unhappy souls even killing children.

There are two especially worrying aspects of our moral miasma. First is its level of severity. Official corruption is not limited to the highest levels. Even lowly civil servants—village heads, town mayors, local bank managers—are able to accumulate tens or even hundreds of millions of yuan in bribes. A district bureau chief may own dozens of houses. Violence is similarly unrestrained: there are people who kill their own spouses, parents, siblings, and even children. Second is the scale of the moral disruption. This is not just a problem of government corruption; it is a "failure of society," as one sociologist has put it.[3] Wherever the smallest bit of authority is granted or the smallest loophole exists in the rules, there is an immediate, unseemly scramble to abuse it to gain some nominal advantage. So any authority leads automatically to corruption, and now that urge infects even areas where there is no authority: people try to manufacture authority to generate corruption.

There is also widespread indifference to others, a lack of concern for human life, for public decorum, and for the law. People who see a child or an elderly person fall in the street will no longer go to help, sometimes with piti-

3. Sun Liping, "Tsinghua Professor Sun Liping: Society Is Quickly Heading toward Collapse!" *Renmin*, February 17, 2011 (http://wenku.baidu.com/link?url=e2wcSYkN-QiBzFdWAKKmKD9AqbM2ud9acqBrs2Fo9tdcWH8W4y5JrJF605W-VFR6cUmy1ID TCtonPh-cco3sLh6CEKjX_gQu6qEyuIXtRbA7).

ful consequences. There have been repeated accidents involving kindergarten buses; when trucks crash, passersby do not save the victims but steal the freight instead; popular holiday beaches end up covered with litter. Some of these, such as littered beaches, may be only minor moral failings. But when they are pervasive, they are still a worrying phenomenon.

Fundamental trust and fundamental kindness are being lost in our society, sometimes at a shocking pace. There is a serious crisis in the government's public credibility, to the extent that now many people seem to instinctively disbelieve any message that comes from official sources. Private acts of kindness or charity are also met with immediate suspicion of improper or ulterior motives. At best, charity is seen as an attempt to bamboozle or to buy celebrity. We are losing the most basic social propriety and the most fundamental moral principles.

Take, for example, teaching and medicine, the two professions that traditionally have imposed the strictest moral requirements on their practitioners and have commanded the highest esteem. These professions have suffered from the same destructive forces, and we now see major problems with the reputations of teachers and doctors and serious disruptions in the teacher-student and doctor-patient relationships. The most important question concerns government officials, who occupy the most vital and influential positions in our society. Are they acting as government officials should?

One key indicator of confidence in our society and willingness to do our duty is whether people—particularly our social elite—are trying to jump ship. And we do indeed see signs that many are trying to leave this country and this society. Meanwhile China's thinkers—and society at large—are deeply divided over how to resolve these problems. The debate is muddied by extremism and emotional responses. One economist has written that "the contradictions in China's economy and society are approaching a critical point. If we cannot resolve the underlying causes of these contradictions through a process of controlled reform, then support will increase for extremist solutions."[4] Clashes of extremist views could easily spark widespread violence. There is even the danger that China could be pitched back into sustained violent turmoil.

What is the reason for all these shocking lapses, for this moral failure? Where does it come from? Our many problems and scandals are something that we, as a society, should be ashamed of. They are a source of sorrow for

4. Wu Jinglian, "China's Economic and Social Contradictions Are Approaching a Critical Point," *Caijing*, November 15, 2012 (http://magazine.caijing.com.cn/).

China. But I do not think that our current problems mean that Chinese people are especially bad or that our national character is bad. Human nature does not vary much in this world. There are civic problems in China, but they are caused by our history, our culture, and our political system. The longevity of our ancient civilization shows that traditional Chinese moral habits bear creditable comparison with those of any culture in the world. But we must admit the severe damage caused by the destruction of our moral principles over the last century. Moreover, we are now in a state of transition: the old has been destroyed, but the new is not yet established. In the midst of these wrenching changes, a litany of severe moral problems has emerged. But a society's moral habits can be changed, and so can a nation's moral character. To realize these changes, we need good systems. Skillful use of the lever of politics is vital.

CHAPTER NINE

CHINESE PEOPLE:
WHY ARE YOU SO ANGRY?

Twenty years ago, Lung Ying-tai wrote an essay entitled "Chinese People, Why Aren't You Angry?"[1] She called on people to feel anger at the damage being done to the public interest and to the environment. She urged us no longer to be silent, no longer to dumbly accept, but to take action: to express our anger loud and clear to those doing the damage, to the public, and to the state's legal apparatus.

I support this kind of anger. It is a necessary step on the path to creation of a citizen society. In fact, it is one of the factors that keeps a society healthy. This kind of anger, wielded rationally, is beneficial to our society, and it is an expression of the dignity and responsibility of individuals. But what I want to talk about today is another side of our behavior, another side of our very real propensity to anger and rage. We could call it our "savage" side. This kind of savage anger benefits no one at all.

This chapter is an edited version of an article first published in the *Beijing News*, December 11, 2005.

1. Lung Ying-tai (龙应台, 1952–) is a Taiwanese essayist and culture critic. As a mainland immigrant to Taiwan after the Civil War, she writes extensively on cultural and emotional ties between mainland China and Taiwan. Her books have attracted a huge number of readers in China. In 2012, she was appointed minister of culture of the Republic of China in Taiwan.

We see savagery often on our streets. It starts with a verbal conflict, escalates to involve fists and feet, and seems to be satisfied with nothing but blood—sometimes with nothing but death. Very often it is triggered by some very minor issue. On November 8, 2005, a student at Lingkun Middle School in Wenzhou was taken to the principal for a scolding because he had been messing around in the classroom. The principal apparently gave the boy a clip around the ear (though accounts vary), and the child's parents later demanded that the principal accompany the child to the hospital, where the doctors found that he was perfectly healthy. On November 11, the principal visited the student's home to discuss the incident. While he was there, even as the student himself tried to restrain his father, the father attacked and killed the principal. It is reported that the father's wife had left him a few days previously.

Not long before that, a young man in Fujian with chronic prostatitis became enraged because his condition was not improving and transferred his anger to the traditional Chinese medicine doctor treating him. He stormed into the doctor's clinic and attacked him with a knife, pursued him as he tried to flee in a taxi, and finally killed him.

Earlier in 2005, a Beijing policeman visiting Taiyuan got involved in an argument with a local policeman at a traffic light. The Taiyuan policeman apparently was unable to calm down after that encounter, so he gathered a group of people, and they beat the Beijing policeman to death. A few years ago, a Beijing taxi driver had a 30 yuan bonus deducted from her pay. She protested the deduction without success, then, unable to control her anger, took one of the company's vehicles to Tiananmen Square and drove it into a crowd of pedestrians, killing and injuring several. After the crash, the driver was overcome with remorse. She requested the death penalty and asked that her organs be donated after her death. But not long ago a similar tragedy played out again in Huairou. A farmer taking his daughter out on his bicycle got into a dispute with a truck driver. While they were at the police station sorting it out, the farmer saw the driver making a phone call and suspected that the driver was trying to call in favors to resolve the issue in his favor. Enraged, the farmer got his car and used it to ram other cars and pedestrians.

Again in Beijing in 2005, there was a shocking and harrowing incident on a bus: a bus conductor got into an argument with a passenger over the stop at which she had boarded the bus. The passenger, a thirteen-year-old girl, claimed to have gotten on one stop later than the conductor thought, making her fare 1 yuan less. The argument escalated into a physical fight, and the conductor grabbed the girl by the neck and choked her. The girl was taken to a hospital, but the doctors were unable to save her.

A young girl just entering adulthood, she was the pride of two aging parents. Before her were university, a job, relationships. When she grew up, she would marry and have children of her own, who would go on to have her grandchildren. But that chain of life was broken in that instant on the bus. Did the person who killed her bear some terrible grudge against her? Was there some dispute that made it impossible for him to accept her existence? There was none.

So why this savage anger? What problem was there that could not be worked out with words? To push the question to its absolute limit: If a girl does insult you, you can always insult her back. If she hits you to the point that you are driven to respond, then you might give her a smack in return. But why respond with violence that ends her life?

Looking at these acts of violence, we see that some of them seem to start with unmotivated suspicion, some with normal disputes, and some with genuinely unfair treatment—though not treatment that justifies self-protection through violence. Some of the victims were party to a dispute, but others were blameless victims of random rage. Who the victim is does not affect the outcome: injury and death. What we feel most of all when we look at these events is the yawning disparity between the causes of an incident and its consequences. That gap between cause and consequence is generated by savagery.

We can feel the overlay of savagery in our ordinary lives. It is not the unique preserve of any particular region or any particular group of people. Savagery exists in every area, in every profession, in our remotest hamlets and our most prosperous metropolises. It exists between strangers, between doctors and patients, between teachers and students, even among those whose job it is to uphold the law. Has this savagery started to infiltrate our very bloodstream? At the very least, we can be sure that it pervades our everyday lives and cannot easily be eliminated. And a large part of it is displaced, vented on bystanders. We are all victims of this poisonous atmosphere, but we may also become desensitized to it or even contribute to it.

The savage have one feature in common: they attempt to relieve their anger through violence. They try to use violence to solve their problems. This habit of using violence to solve problems is an attitude of the weak. It is a habit of a person used to acting as part of a collective, not as an independent, responsible citizen. To put it plainly, it is an artifact of a personality that oscillates between being a subject and a member of a mob. A citizen of a modern, rule-of-law society should react to disputes calmly, through rational argumentation. In the face of inequity, she may show proper, rightful anger and may work hard at fighting inequity, within the framework of the law and through rational devices. When the legal system is flawed, that may be very difficult, but we can still commit ourselves to pursuing that course of action. If many people commit themselves to this approach, then it may gradually become easier.

But if we choose another course, the course of merely acting out our rage, then the routes to legal resolution become narrower and narrower. We should all prepare ourselves to fight our battles within the parameters of the law, though it demands of us more courage, more strength, more passion, and more endurance and patience. If one moment of release is likely to cause endless suffering, and if the situation is not that serious in the first place—not a matter of fundamental principle—then we might as well try applying the wisdom of the ancient Chinese thinkers, the wisdom of conciliation and tolerance: "On reuniting, with one smile, we'll wash away the hate."[2]

Of course, we are all emotional beings; at times we cannot avoid feeling anger. Realistic social systems should take that fact into consideration. Wherever they constrain or repress any group, they should offer mechanisms for mitigation and outlets for frustration. But on the personal level, we should also consider what types of anger are healthy, and when our anger is healthy and appropriate, we should consider what kind of outlet is most suitable for expressing it.

Many factors have contributed to our atmosphere of savagery. Human nature, history, and our current era have all played a part. The Austrian ethologist Konrad Lorenz believed that aggression was a fundamental part of human nature. And there have been eras of widespread savagery in China before, mainly during times of change. In the twentieth century, China, along with the rest of the world, experienced great violence and bloodshed. Our cultural tradition of peace and compromise was abandoned, and entire generations of Chinese people were raised in a culture that revered violence; we often say that they were "raised on wolf's milk." Instinctively, we often are not inclined to try to resolve disputes through the law, but that is because the law often did not give us that option. But in today's world, if we wish to protect our safety and our dignity, rule of law is the only option. No matter how difficult, we must try to understand and control the urge to savagery. Doing so will allow us to build the rule of law and thereby promote lasting social stability, and it will help us to properly value our own and others' lives. But just as important, it will help us to retain our fundamental dignity and standards as citizens and as human beings.

2. See *Selected Classical Poems by Lu Xun* (www.coldbacon.com/writing/luxun-scp.html).

CHAPTER TEN

"Absurd Bans" and the Need for Minimum Moral Standards

An online poll recently claimed to identify China's "ten most absurd bans." They included the following:

—Officials are strictly forbidden from using public funds when playing mahjong for money.

—Customs officials may not cover up smuggling.

—Teachers in middle and elementary schools are strictly forbidden from indecent contact with female students.

—Drivers may not drive motor vehicles while under the influence of alcohol.

Some of them had been announced with great pomp and inserted into formal professional guidelines, standards for government authorities, or handbooks for educational institutions.

Tsinghua University sociology professor Sun Liping commented that though these bans may look absurd, they are not so crazy when we look at the facts. Violations of even these basic standards are commonplace. What that shows is that Chinese society repeatedly and continually fails to observe minimum moral standards. That failure threatens the very foundations of our society. When minimum standards are habitually disregarded, we cannot simply blame the forces of change during a period of social transition. Moral failure also speaks of our stability as a people. It is undeniable that opportunism, fueled by the fluid state of our developing legal system, has swept away whatever restraining power minimum social standards used to have.

This chapter is an edited version of an article first published in the *Beijing News*, February 12, 2006.

The opportunism that we see is marked by a willingness on the part of opportunists to use any method to achieve their ends. Opportunism admits no sacred or inviolable principles; the sole criterion is whether an action results in some gain for the actor. But ultimately there will be a reckoning for such wanton disregard for basic minimum standards of conduct.

I very much agree with Professor Sun's analysis, that these absurd bans actually have a rationale. In a sense, we can see them as alarm bells. In some areas of life, habitual dismissal of minimum moral standards already constitutes a serious threat to our society. This failure of moral standards is related to the historical break in the transmission of Chinese culture. Specifically, it is widespread moral relativism or nihilism, which leads to the sense that the ends can justify any and all means. That is why what we now face the urgent need to establish universal minimum moral standards.

But we can take Professor Sun's analysis a little further. Why exactly do so many people see these bans as absurd? I think the reason is that the bans touch not just on behavior that is immoral in the context of a specific industry or profession but on behavior that should be beyond the pale for every citizen, for every member of society, under any circumstances. Such behavior transgresses the minimum standards for a person *as a person*. These minimum standards are not just moral rules; they are fundamentals of law. Indecent contact with minor girls, driving under the influence of alcohol—these are not rules for certain professions. They should go without saying for every person and every citizen. Anyone who disregards these rules should suffer criminal prosecution and penalties.

Ethical codes for specific professions should take these universal strictures for granted. They should build on universals in the context of their particular industry and develop standards that are more specific, more dynamic—in fact, stricter. For example, it is not enough that civil servants do not use public funds for improper purposes. They should discharge their professional responsibilities, be effective administrators, and improve life for the citizens in their care. It is not enough that teachers do not indecently assault their students. They must educate them and transmit knowledge and understanding sufficient to meet the required standards. That is why "Indecent contact with female students is strictly forbidden" is an insult to the vast majority of teachers—even though we know that some teachers fail to observe that rule. What this situation tells us is that we urgently need to clarify our moral minimum standards. We need a developed theory of minimal ethics that we can deploy as a shield to protect the normal workings of society.

Of course, every individual has his or her own minimum standard of conduct, some higher, some lower. But there is still an objective set of minimum standards applicable across the community. A person who drops below this social minimum may still have his or her own minimum standards, but we would no longer call them *moral* standards, because morality demands its own set of objective minimums.

We can divide objective moral minimum standards into three levels. The first level includes the basic natural and social responsibilities that every person must meet: do not harm or threaten the life of others, do not cheat others, and so forth. These are the fundamentals, what we normally mean when we talk about moral minimums. The second level includes standards associated with the law and our social institutions, with the responsibilities of citizens: obey the law, support the rule of law, oppose infringement of civil rights, exercise one's own civil rights, and so forth. The third level includes professional ethics and the morality of specific areas of activity: ethics of government officials, teachers' ethics, Internet ethics, and so on.

Of the three levels, the first is the most fundamental. The third level is usually an extension of the first two. To some extent, the third level is an instantiation of the first two levels in a specific area, but professional or specific ethics often also include additional rules relevant only to their field. For that reason, ethics at the third level usually seem stricter than those at the first level. For example, government officials must take on responsibilities commensurate with their authority; those responsibilities are in addition to their natural and social duties and their duties as citizens. An official's professional responsibilities will become heavier as the level of power with which he is entrusted grows. An official with great authority can be a major influence on other people and on society at large, so his responsibilities will be more stringent.

In my 1994 book *A Theory of Conscience*, I examined from a first-person perspective the fundamental responsibilities that every person must undertake as a person and as a fitting member of society. These responsibilities correspond to the moral minimums. In that book I try to construct a modern duty ethic that is egalitarian, universal, objective, and reasonable. In 1998 I published another book, *Minimalist Ethics*, a collection of essays that I had written exploring moral minimum standards on two levels: those of individual responsibility and social justice. The terms "minimum standards," "moral minimum," and "moral minimum ethics" have now started to become much more widely used and understood, both among writers and among the public. The new popularity of these terms reflects increasing worry and interest in reconstructing our social morality and the need for an ethics of minimum standards.

It is a simple enough subject; it requires no higher-order logic or abstruse argument. Minimum standards stand in contrast with higher ideals or values. The idea is that people may pursue any of a number of lifestyles or values but that minimum standards apply equally to everyone. They refer to lines that may not be crossed: you cannot compel other people by force, you cannot kill, you cannot rob, you cannot swindle, and so forth. You must see people as people and "do not do to others what you would not have done to you." As one common saying puts it: "Everyone loves riches, but riches must be obtained in the right way."

The logic of minimum moral standards is straightforward, but the task of arguing and proving these basic rules is a difficult one. The ethics that preceded them—the morality of classical China and the morality of the twentieth-century transition—were both aspirational ethics: they called on everyone to be saints or to be ideal modern citizens. Parallel to these aspirational ethics ran a countercurrent of moral relativism and nihilism, and it is that countercurrent that has become popular once again in the post-aspirational era. Aspirational ethics, of course, have great value. They inspired a small number of great individuals to marvelous moral achievements. Still today they have the power to attract people and to motivate them to make great moral efforts. However, lofty aspirational ethics are simply not the right kind of system to promulgate equally to the body of citizens of a modern society. They cannot serve as a dominant social ethics based on universal moral constraints.

A universalist ethics of minimum moral standards may conflict with aspirational ethics, and moral universals also stand completely opposed to moral nihilism. For that reason, a universalist minimum-standard ethics often is attacked from both sides. But no matter how hard it is to stick to and support this middle path, it is vital for our social morality that we do so. Any individual who chooses to pursue higher moral goals must start out from this same baseline; at the least, their pursuit must not lead them to violate moral minimum standards.

China has been through a wrenching break with tradition followed by an era of turmoil. Now it is in a period of fast transition to a market economy, and the pace of economic and technical advancement is blinding. But our morality has not just failed to keep up, it may even be regressing. The process has been described as a "moral slide," a "moral cliff," and even a "moral collapse." Whatever the truth, it is now seriously damaging the foundations of our society. For example, the ethics of the "gardeners" of our society (teachers) and our "white-coated angels" (doctors) often are seen as an important ethical bellwether, and the professional minimum standards in these two professions have been severely eroded and damaged. A basic moral order is the foundation for our lives as individuals and as a society. Every society and every person must be rooted in a functioning moral order. Damage that foundation, and everything that is built upon it, however bright and splendid, will ultimately be lost.

PART V

ETHICAL DISCOURSE IN REFORM ERA CHINA

CHAPTER ELEVEN

WHY SHOULD WE REPEATEDLY
STRESS THE PRINCIPLE OF LIFE?

In 2011 I published a volume of essays called *The Great Virtue of Life Giving*. The book starts with the questions of war and the death penalty and goes on to reaffirm a moral principle that I have written much about: the preservation of life. In the first essay, "A Public Call to 'Kill,'" I write about a survey that I had seen eight years earlier, in August 2004. Conducted by the website Sina, it asked respondents about their attitudes toward war. Many people expressed extreme opinions, along the lines of "killing anyone who is not of my race," and even extended their lack of mercy to women, children, and prisoners of war. At the time, I wondered whether it was not just an example of "verbal violence": merely people expressing fantasies that would not reflect their real behavior. But a few recent events have led me to question that view. For example, in September 2012, there were demonstrations following an incident at the Diaoyu Islands, the rights to which China and Japan both claim. I saw then that in our society, verbal violence and physical violence are very closely linked. The febrile atmosphere created by violent statements can very easily tip over into violent action. The slightest provocation—or sometimes just a slight relaxation of vigilance—can send violence spreading like wildfire. The violence is not always directed at outsiders. Often the victims are compatriots, and it is Chinese property that is smashed and looted. That surely gives us cause for worry. We must think very carefully about whether China can survive another century of fruitless bloodshed. If another period

The chapter is an edited version of an article first published in *Caijing*, October 2012.

of turbulence were to engulf this country, we would lose all the economic progress that we have made and endanger the life of every living person.

Am I being unnecessarily gloomy? I hope so. Some violent behavior certainly seems to pass quickly; today the world is peaceful once again. But we need to look not just at the present but also at our history. Often our history still exists within us, in the legacy of our language. We still need to make preventing the worst outcomes our first priority. In the "thousand-year tradition" of our long history, population pressure, economic failure, and political corruption have sometimes made human life rather cheap. The "hundred-year tradition" of modernity was a tradition of even more violent tendencies and violent action. Violence colonized our language, clothing itself in the rhetoric of "glory."

I remember reading an essay by Shen Congwen in which he recounts watching the army march out of his town in western Hunan to find and arrest local bandit gangs.[1] They would come back with a crowd of prisoners: bandits but also camp followers, farmers who had been mixed up with the bandits, and sometimes even farmers who were just in the wrong place at the wrong time. With no easy way to identify who was who but determined that someone should die, they lined the prisoners up and gave each a number, "one, two, one, two." Thus divided into two lines, half of the prisoners would be summarily shot. No trial, nothing but this random "selection." What was most shocking was not that the executioners seemed to think that this slaughter was perfectly justified but that the victims themselves barely protested. What lay behind such cruelty, lack of respect for life, and apparent indifference to one's fate? People at the time lacked a belief in the sacredness of life (they did not have a religion to teach that life is sacred), but there is also the objective question of living standards. If people cannot live well, if they are unable even to feed and clothe themselves, then that may well be a reason for not treasuring their own lives. Throughout Chinese history, particularly near the end of a dynasty, we can see the pressure that the human population put on its living environment. Those were times when life became cheap indeed.

In the twentieth century, there emerged a "new language" in which widespread death and bloodshed was of no importance compared with political ideals and victories. The new language lent mass violence a legitimacy that such violence had never enjoyed before and provided an ideological flag to

1. Shen Congwen (沈从文, 1902–1988), a native of Fenghuang, Hunan Province, was one of the great modern Chinese writers. He was known for combining modern and classical Chinese in his writings. It was believed that Shen was to be awarded the Nobel Prize in Literature in 1988, but he passed away earlier that year.

protect it. In the modern period of nation building, racism and nationalism also were common.

We can examine the case of twenty-one-year-old Cai Yang, who smashed up cars and assaulted people in Xian, in the light of those historical influences. Reports suggest that people from Cai's village knew him to be a violent person. He often would attack his father: "He knocked his father down with a single blow." He presented a split personality to outsiders: sometimes he would politely greet guests to the house, sometimes he would suddenly hit and start shoving them. But when he came to the city, his behavior was relatively calm. Perhaps the imposing city suppressed his violent urges for a while. His uncle said that he was stupid and never could learn any skills, but he still managed to make 200 yuan a day. But he was not successful with women, and he was desperate for a relationship. He liked to watch TV shows about the war against Japan and to play war-themed computer games. On September 15, the day of the anti-Japan demonstrations in Xian, he was caught up in it quite by chance, but once he was involved, he became wildly overexcited. In the surveillance footage, we see him nimbly dodging and darting, flailing a bicycle U lock at the skulls of victims all around him. He seems unaware that they are real, innocent, fragile people. When he is told that he has badly injured many people, he still keeps on insisting, "I'm a patriot, down with Japanese products!" "I'm a patriot, I despise you." You might say that this is just another young person, much like millions of others. But that is precisely where the danger lies. If we do not work out the reasons for their thoughtlessness and learn how to prevent it, then this kind of incident will happen again and again.

When we look at incidents like the anti-Japanese violence that broke out in so many cities in the middle of September, a few points can be made. First, there has to be a legitimate "reason"—or a rallying cry—if many similar incidents are to break out in many different places. Sometimes this reason leads the police to fail in their duty to keep order. Second, there must be a crowd. A crowd gives individuals within it the boldness that they need to act, and they begin to compete, becoming ever more extreme. Of course, these two factors are linked: it is the cause or slogan that brings people out to the streets in the first place, and crowds—or those who wish to form crowds—often seek some flag or cause to rally behind. Third, the incident has to begin in a relatively safe environment. If the venue is not initially safe, then individuals will feel threatened and avoid it. If the demonstration were on a real battlefield, then there would be far fewer participants—certainly far fewer people would spontaneously join the action. Fourth, random violence is very difficult for individual victims to predict and avoid. But it is relatively easily controlled. It erupts suddenly, but it also quickly dies. Organized violence has a much clearer target and tends to last longer.

But no matter how organized the violence, it is a danger to those around it. The topic of physical safety has long been a concern of mine. It appeared in my doctoral thesis *Contract Theories and Social Justice* (written in the 1980s and published in 1993) and in my book *A Theory of Conscience* (published in 1994). I will not go over old arguments here. When I was trying to write a follow-up to *A Theory of Conscience*, to offer a reinterpretation of social justice in traditional China, the very first essay that I wrote was about the relationship between peace and the political order. I wanted to use the resources of traditional philosophy to explain and prove that an orderly polity is vital because it plays such a large role in ensuring our physical safety. The principle that a state first and foremost must have the capacity to be a state—that it must have a certain level of state power in order to maintain order in the state—has a somewhat conservative flavor. But we should realize that when outstanding thinkers and politicians are apparently conservative, the underlying reason lies in the principle of protecting life. What they conserve is not just the political status quo, it is society. They do not conserve just narrow interests; they conserve and preserve life. In the future I hope to write something explaining that when the Confucians fought to maintain social order, they did so not because they wanted to protect their own privileges and interests or because they had some natural weakness. It was because they saw the moral principle of protecting life as paramount. Of course, those who defend the principle of life must also be open to defending the principle of political freedom, perhaps even of economic equality—all the more so in modern society. But no matter the era or society, protection of life must be the most important principle. When we pursue freedom or equality, we must not do so if it means sacrificing life. And of course that goes double for the pursuit of false ideologies, which actively seek to harm people's safety.

I also wrote a little book for children and parents called *Treasure Life*, in which I discuss the ethics of conduct during war and how the right to existence works in international politics. I cast doubt on whether a state has the right to take life through the death penalty, even when there are no other forms of punishment available. As I see it, it is such a miracle that among the stars of this great universe, we have rational human life on this little planet that we must treasure this remarkable gift. Every second of every hour, inexhaustible nature is telling us: The great morality of the universe is Life. Humanity has survived thus far, but now it is time for us to respond to nature. We must do it for ourselves and for all of life, for all living things, because humankind has grown to the point where our actions do not affect us alone. They have a massive impact on the Earth and on other lives. In some ways humankind is now the master of the Earth, so we must properly protect and nurture the life in our world.

And I am not yet talking about environmental ethics. All of this pertains just to the question of protecting human life. Protecting human life involves two conditions. First, people need to be protected from direct attack—deliberate injury or killing. They need to be safe, not subject to attack by others or to arrest or harm by the authorities. Second, they must not be cut off from the basic necessities that they need to maintain themselves physically. The basic goods and environment needed for maintaining physical life must be provided. The government has primary responsibility for ensuring that these conditions are met.

The first condition means that those with power must avoid war, maintain a stable society, and not allow any person or authority to kill or physically harm other people. The second condition means that those with power must provide for the basic requirements of life: they must protect us from natural disaster and famine. If a failure of governance or of policy leads to the deaths of tens of millions of people from hunger, causing desperation and even cannibalism, then that is a crime that cannot be forgiven. That is something that no civilization in the world has had to experience.

But here I want to consider first of all the question of preventing direct physical attacks on people. I want to consider the causes of the anti-Japanese violence that we saw in September. The Cai Yangs of this world do not create the theories or "reasons" that motivate them to do what they do. They may spout slogans, but those slogans were given to them by other people. In fact, it often seems that those who provide the "reasons" and those who act are two completely separate groups. Often the people who invent the reasons do not commit violence themselves—leaders do not get their hands dirty. If the reasons or theories that they produce become part of our social consciousness, a part of the dominant patterns of social thought, then many people will naturally act on them.

But in the September demonstrations, there was in fact one professor, Han Deqiang, who took violent action himself: he struck someone and gave his own "reasons" for doing so.[2] We can examine some of the points that he made:

2. Han Deqiang (韩德强, 1967–), a native of Shaoxing, Zhejiang Province, is a leftist and Maoist professor at Beijing University of Aeronautics and Astronautics. He became

—*I didn't hit a person, I hit a race traitor. . . . I wanted to hit this traitor.*
This illustrates the primary strategy of those who attack and kill: first they
slander the target of their attack. They label the target "bandit," "traitor,"
"counterrevolutionary," "anticommunist," "worthless dog," and so forth.
Then they can self-righteously call for violence against the target. Some of
these categories of dehumanization are highly specific products of political
theories. How many people were killed during the Cultural Revolution for
harboring "counterrevolutionary" thoughts? Some were even tried in real
courts and executed for allegedly doing so. But today we would think it
criminal even to call such a thing a crime. Some insults, such as "traitor,"
require careful discussion and perhaps even a judicial process to determine
their applicability. People have no right to apply these labels just because
they think that the labels are correct, even less to take punitive action
themselves.

—*When an elephant is on the road, you can't spend your time worrying about
ants and grasshoppers. . . . An ordinary citizen is an ant or a grasshopper. They
may be stepped on by the political movement. There is no way to avoid it.* It
seems that Han is inclined to value the state and its leaders above everything
else. A political state will inevitably allow for differences in political power
and differences in role. But the right of existence surely applies equally to
everyone. Everyone has a right to live. The most important message of the
principle of life is that life itself is precious. It is not precious as a method or
as a tool but as an end in itself. If we follow this line of argument, we can see
that all human life is equally precious. All humans are worthy of respect, and
all have the same right to continue their existence. Han's theory allows for the
sacrificing of individuals in order to achieve some greater goal or to realize
some ideal. Given this goal, the ends justify the means and human life can be
used as the means. But that is wrong. Even if a goal is great and can be
achieved, it would still not be acceptable to harm the innocent. In fact, any
goal that would require harming innocents is dubious at best.

The principle of life is a universal principle. It applies in all cases to all
people. It is not dependent on the validity of any goals or objectives or any
other factors. So the same principle also applies to another case, which hap-

---

famous when he beat an old man who criticized Chairman Mao on the street during an
anti-Japanese demonstration in 2012. He labeled the old man a "traitor" and claimed that
all traitors deserve to be beaten. Han's action and words triggered a tremendous angry
backlash from Chinese citizens for his ignorance of the law and lack of respect for freedom
of speech.

pened in July 2012: the beating of Wu Fatian.[3] Violence is never an acceptable way of resolving differences of opinion. Certainly spectators should never violently involve themselves in a dispute. The journalist who started it, a woman, had arranged the meeting with Wu in advance. And she was actually legally sanctioned as a result: she was detained for a several days by the police. Professor Han struck an elderly Chinese man out of rage and kept calling him a "race traitor." Clearly, Han failed to see the humanity of his target and certainly did not see him as worthy of respect because of his age. In this incident we can also see the issue of privilege at work. If one is a member of the majority, striking a member of an ethnic minority or a foreign visitor is virtually danger free. Actually going to another country and protesting—for example, protesting at the Yasukuni Shrine in Japan—would be quite another type of action.[4] It would take courage to go into the midst of the "enemy" and protest. It would show strength. Within our own society, the equivalent question is whether we can allow those with whom we disagree to come and raise their protest in our city squares and leave unmolested. Or do we beat them to a pulp? If we beat them, is that a great victory for us?

In the two examples above, the violence was not as serious as that of Cai Yang, but the arguments of the perpetrators were even more worrying. If we attempt to resolve differences in viewpoints or beliefs and conflicts of interest using our fists and feet, then we will certainly move on to resolving them with guns and cannons. We will end up using all the force at our disposal, including nuclear weapons. A physical blow will evolve into mass bloodshed, even to mutual destruction. One of the painful lessons of the twentieth century is this: the biggest killer of all is institutionalized violence under the banner of righteousness and justice. I do not wish to see another hole torn in the fabric of the world in the name of some "good reason." We can try very hard to understand and respect the beliefs and positions of another person, but we cannot decide to use violence against other people because they hold a belief

3. Wu Fatian (real name, Wu Danhong), an associate professor at China University of Political Science and Law and well-known Internet personality, had apparently challenged a female reporter from Sichuan who was constantly arguing against his views on the Weibo social media platform to meet and continue the dispute in person. At the appointed time, supporters of the reporter arrived and assaulted him. This incident led to much debate over which party was at fault, what actually transpired, and how an online dispute could turn into a call for actual violence.

4. Yasukuni Shrine (靖国神社) is a Japanese shrine where many World War II war criminals are buried. Official visits to the shrine by Japanese politicians constantly trigger fierce diplomatic and nationalistic reactions from South Korea and China.

or a position different from our own. And we certainly should not be hitting the elderly for such a reason.

There is no such thing as a perfect system, and there is no such thing as a perfect person. But we can distinguish between better and worse, between right and wrong. And when we are considering standards of behavior, distinguishing between right and wrong is vital. We must be very cautious when judging people. Every individual is a complex, multifaceted being. But when judging behavior, we can be more absolute. Killing is killing; violence is violence. Killing another person, unless it is done only for the purpose of self-defense, is a crime. Beating and injuring others should be condemned and punished. This is the principle of protecting life and the principle of complying with the law. More vital still is that we must be extremely cautious and reflective about any proposed "theory" or "reasons" for violence. A Cai Yang, not driven by any particular theory, may harm a few individuals. But an ideology that legitimizes violence has the potential to harm thousands, even millions of people. It can infect and create many young "Cai Yangs," who become the tools of that ideology.

In conclusion, why do we repeatedly stress the principle of life? In simple terms, it is because serious threats to life repeatedly arise. They never fully disappear. The twentieth century wrote these lessons in blood, and they are there for us to read, but we still easily forget them. Moreover, ideology has its own internal momentum, which means that it often obscures the lessons of the past. New "reasons" for violence are constantly invented. We are still weighted down by a political legacy that leans strongly toward violence. This legacy will continue to encourage violence, adoration of power, and the use of any means to achieve its stated ends. All of these factors have conspired to prevent our society from developing an unconditional, instinctive rejection of violence. It is not yet "just basic common sense" to oppose all violence against innocents.

People hold many and various high values. We variously pursue the good life. But we need a commitment on the political, legal, and economic levels to protect all human life. This is a precondition for people to be able to realize their own values and their own good life. It is a precondition for human life. So it is of the principle of life that we say: This is the greatest principle of them all. Life above all else. Preserving life should be given priority over all other principles, because it is the most fundamental. Only this principle demands that we reaffirm it every year, every month, and every day. It must be repeated until it is beaten into our very conception of society. It must become the most fundamental criterion defining the conduct of every single person.

CHAPTER TWELVE

On Possible Ways to Contain the Corruption of Power

The abuse of power to obtain money and personal advantage has long infuriated people in China, where there has always been talk of punishing the corrupt. In 2005, a court in Yangquan, Shanxi, stunned the whole country with a sentence of fifteen years for Wu Baoan, a Communist Party secretary who gave out official positions in return for bribes. In late July, a court in Beijing gave a suspended death sentence to Ma De, a former party secretary in Suihua, Heilongjiang, for accepting bribes and confiscated his entire fortune. But the problem remains a severe one. Many anticorruption strategies have been proposed, but a full solution will certainly require a set of broad-ranging, systemwide changes. Here I summarize my take on corruption in six main guidelines:

—*First: Make it harder.* We should make it difficult for those in power to act in corrupt ways. Doing so requires a clear, comprehensive, detailed system of laws and regulations, from strict modern accounting practices to a constitutional system of checks and balances. Such a system would force those in power to use their authority in the public interest and leave them unable to pursue their private interests. It would ensure that no significant amount of funds or resources (including institutional resources like official positions) can be diverted on the command of one person; such decisions should not rest in one set of hands. If such a system could be established, how many abuses of power would it stop? Strict rules may seem to officials like chains and petty restrictions, but it is precisely those restrictions that prevent

This chapter is an edited version of an article first published in the *Beijing News*, December 3, 2005.

officials from ending up in jail or worse. Some corruption happens simply because an opportunity is too easy to pass up. Many officials say, "Even if you don't want it, it's hard to avoid." And once the rot sets in, it spreads fast.

—*Second: Make it riskier.* The first condition is prevention, but this condition is about applying real penalties so that officials dare not abuse their position. Officials who try to extract bribes should not only find it impossible, they should also be named, shamed, and punished. In this way, they would serve as an example for any others who might be tempted. In terms of warning off potential criminals, certainty of prosecution is much more effective than harsh sentences. As Chen Yi wrote in his poem: "Do not lay your hands on what is not yours, for you will surely be caught."[1]

—*Third: Make it unnecessary.* This principle is expressed by some as "high salaries make for clean governance." But exactly how much compensation a "high salary" should offer is a question that needs careful consideration. The wealth of the country and the state of our society are all factors. Official pay must be linked in some way to the prosperity of the community, so that we do not end up with absurdly rich leaders of impoverished villages. Of course, it would be unrealistic, even dangerous, to attempt to force officials to live impoverished lifestyles. They should have a standard of living that corresponds to their position and is generally higher than average for their community. That would boost officials' sense of self-worth and might even contribute to the proper use of their authority. We should just be careful that the gap between the lifestyles of officials and of everyone else does not become too big.

—*Fourth: Make it contemptible.* This condition is not often mentioned, but it is very important. It speaks to the question of values, of what sort of people we want to be and what sort of lives we want to lead. The main issue is how to improve and maintain the character and esthetics of our corps of officials. How can we ensure that they are not fixated on the material, concerned only with money? In traditional China, there certainly was corruption, but all officials had been selected through the imperial examinations. They had a high level of education, and their tastes were cultured. Their pursuit of wealth was not quite so single-minded: they had other interests, such as music, games, calligraphy, and painting. They would invest time and

---

1. Chen Yi (陈毅, 1901–72), a native of Lezhi, Sichuan Province, was a senior People's Liberation Army (PLA) commander and later a politician of the People's Republic of China (PRC). In 1955, he was named one of the Ten Marshals of the PLA, along with Zhu De. Chen also served as the mayor of Shanghai and as the second Chinese foreign minister after Zhou Enlai.

energy in these higher pursuits and not solely in the accumulation of material wealth. But can you imagine that today? When someone spends millions to obtain an official post that pays little but offers him the opportunity to become rich through corruption, what are his objectives? Can they be anything but to wring every last drop of material gain out of that post? If the buying and selling of official posts becomes business as usual, then what will that do to the morals of officialdom as a whole?

—*Fifth: Make it shameful.* We need to cultivate a sense of social empathy, particularly empathy for the poorest and least advantaged of us. The money that corrupt officials siphon off does not fall from the sky. It is taken directly out of the pockets of ordinary people. Wu Baoan was the party secretary of just one county, but within eight months of taking his position he had accumulated over 5 million yuan. Suihua is one of the poorest parts of Heilongjiang, but Ma De was able to embezzle over 6 million yuan there. How could they forgive themselves for such theft? There have been cases of taking money directly out of social security funds, retirement funds, and life insurance funds. This money was earned by the sweat of ordinary workers' brows; it was their lifeline in case of emergency. How could the embezzlers forgive themselves? Wu Baoan and Ma De both came from very ordinary families. They were perfectly able to see that many people were still living in great poverty. If they had had the smallest bit of empathy in their hearts, they could not have taken those huge sums.

—*Sixth: Limit material desires.* There have always been conflicts between human desires and human rationality, between greed and morality. A general ban on self-interest is unworkable, but regulating material desires through moral rationality is both possible and morally right. What is required is a sense of duty associated with citizenship and a sense of respect for the demands of one's position. This ethic of obligation will then serve as a regulator of self-interest, preventing officials from using inappropriate means to satisfy their desires. The perfect resolution would, of course, be the condition that Confucius described: "I could do what I wanted without ever being improper." But very few ever make it to that level of balance, so in the meantime we have to work on self-control. Those who want to be officials will at least have to be able to refuse to do what is improper even when it might benefit them. The most elementary moral demand that we can make of our civil servants is that they do not use their official powers for personal gain.

Of the six conditions listed here, the first two rely primarily on *rules*. The first condition, "Make it harder," uses positive rules about duties and limitations; the second, "Make it riskier," uses negative, punitive rules. The next two conditions work on *motivation*. "Make it unnecessary" is an adjustment of external incentives; "Make it contemptible" is an adjustment of internal motivation. External motivations always lose their traction at some point, so internal motivation is needed to ensure willing and unconflicted compliance. The fifth and sixth conditions are concerned with *morality*. "Make it shameful" is an appeal to empathy, which is an individual virtue possessed by every person but too easily forgotten. "Limit material desires" implies long-term training in moral reasoning, which can inhibit improper desires.

We can also categorize the first three as the application of external normative rules concerned with the building of institutions and the other three as the development of internal normative tendencies, producing internal regulation through the development of character. The latter three conditions are more fundamental, because ultimately it takes good people to engage in good conduct: a properly oriented heart produces proper behavior. However, the first three are the first areas to work on—particularly when corruption is severe. These institutional levers are direct, sure, and fast. They will be effective for the vast majority of people.

External and internal motivation are naturally mutually reinforcing. Consistent external regulation is conducive to self-regulation, as it helps individuals to develop the habits of self-regulation. Systems that rely entirely on the character and determination of individuals are unlikely to be effective for the majority of people. But external motivation must be matched by the development of corresponding internal tendencies, otherwise institutions fail. Rules constrain only those who are willing to be ruled; threats deter only those who are willing to be deterred; incentives work only on those who want to be motivated.

Rooting out corruption requires multiple, integrated policies. I am certainly not claiming that my six conditions represent an exhaustive list or a complete solution to the problem of corruption. On the contrary, even if all six were successfully imposed, I am not sure that they would eradicate all official corruption, because there remains the problem of power itself. One of the many causes of corruption is the very nature of power. That is to say, one of the effects of power may be to encourage transgression and corruption. However, the alternative to power is anarchy, and that would leave us only one step away from the "law of the jungle." We must give some people powers that exceed those of ordinary people so that they can govern; without power they cannot govern. And those who are given power will always be people, not saints, so the chances are that they will abuse that power unless they are constrained by proper checks and balances. So humanity needs political order and political power, and it also needs to discipline and constrain the use of political power. These are responsibilities of which humanity will never be free.

So a basic philosophy of government would probably have to include a constitutional set of checks and balances. Some of those checks and balances would be external to government: monitoring by the public, the media, nongovernmental organizations, and citizen groups. Some would be internal to government, coming from structural features of the institutions themselves. In this chapter I have looked only at the problem of the abuse of power in the pursuit of private interests. I have not considered the pursuit of extreme power simply out of ambition or the desire to realize some political ideal. Those urges must be controlled through institutional constraints on power.

CHAPTER THIRTEEN

CHALLENGING THE DEATH PENALTY

The papers had reported that the Supreme People's Court retracted permission for any court other than itself to approve executions. That got me thinking about the death penalty once again. What is the death penalty? What does the death penalty mean? What objectives does capital punishment seek to achieve? Can it achieve those objectives? What emotional needs does capital punishment meet, and what reactions or consequences is it likely to cause? Is it a reasonable criminal penalty? Is the death penalty in harmony with the "harmonious society"? Can it be reconciled with efforts to "keep up with the times"?[1] I think that we need to reflect deeply on these questions and approach them in the light of real experience.

What Does the Death Penalty Mean?

At one time, not that long ago, executions were carried out in public, not just in China but in Europe as well. In fact, the public was encouraged to watch. At the start of his essay "Reflections on the Guillotine," Albert Camus recalls a murder: in 1914, shortly before the start of World War I, a laborer in a frenzy had killed a farmer and his entire family, including the children, and had

---

This chapter is an edited version of an article first published in the *Beijing News*, November 13, 20, and 27, 2005.

1. "Keep up with the times" (与时俱进) was a political slogan articulated by Jiang Zemin at the 16th Party Congress to encourage party members to abandon old dogmas and adapt to the new reality of Chinese society.

stolen all of their money and valuables. The crime sparked outrage, and Camus's father was especially enraged by the killing of the children. So he decided to go to watch the execution of this criminal himself. That day he got up before dawn and went to the other side of Algiers to see the execution. However, on his return he did not speak. In a state of great agitation, he lay down on his bed, but he soon started vomiting. After witnessing the execution of the man, he found himself thinking not of the murdered children, but only of the trembling person whom he had seen thrown on the block to have his head chopped off. His attention had been redirected. That is the story of Camus's father at an execution. Camus tells many similar stories, both in that essay and in his other works: *The Stranger, The Plague, The First Man.*

There are many similar accounts. In his autobiography, *The Story of My Life*, the renowned American lawyer Clarence Darrow writes that his understanding of and attitude toward the death penalty also came largely from his father. When he was seven or eight years old, a murder was committed in the next town. In those days the murderer was hanged outdoors in broad daylight, and his father had pushed right through to the front of the crowd to watch the moment of death. But when he saw the rope adjusted around the man's neck and the black cap pulled over his head, he turned his face away. Darrow's father felt ashamed for the rest of his life to think human beings could be so cruel as to punish criminal behavior by killing another person.

These fathers did not say anything or write anything. They experienced their pain, revulsion, and shame in silence. But their reactions to capital punishment left a deep impression on their children. And after their children grew to adulthood, the children said the words that needed saying. The children wrote the lines that their fathers should have written. So the question that we need to ask here is what was it in the spectacle of the executions that produced the changes in the minds of these fathers? Why were these fathers so full of enthusiasm on the way to the killing grounds, worried only about getting a good view, and then so deflated and affected after the event? What did they see? Why did it shock them so? Why did it cause this extraordinary reversal in their attitudes? Why did curiosity and righteous indignation turn to revulsion, shame, and hatred? It must have touched a nerve deep in their souls, one that is usually never exposed.

The first shocking thing may be the speed with which life is turned into death. In the blink of an eye, a living person becomes a corpse. In life, people can speak and move. Even if they are silent, with only their eyes blinking and a stray hair moving as they breathe, they are still living. But in an instant, a person dies. That person will never move again, never speak again. That person can never return. We suddenly become aware of the absolute division between the living and the dead, of the impenetrable border that separates us.

The next shock may be the realization that all of this has been done by a human hand—which is to say that we could have chosen to do otherwise. The one who is killed is a person; the ones who kill him are people. The one who is to die has killed another or has done some other unacceptable act. As a result, a mechanism has sprung into action, condemning that person to death and bringing the person to a guillotine or a scaffold, where he or she is turned into a dead body. The person becomes a piece of meat, soon to rot, no longer a person at all. In fact, before this moment, the person has been treated as "dead meat." And this may be the most shocking thing of all: this has happened as a result of a calm, technical, rational process, a rational process that perhaps has involved repeated back and forth communication before coming to an end. It is defended by massive, powerful institutions and carried out in the name of the state or the people. It is "lawful killing," in the strictest meaning of the term.

Capital punishment shows us with great vividness and clarity how unique and fragile the life of a human animal is. It shows us just how badly the human body can be abused. And we see that in an execution, the end of life is totally artificial and yet absolute. No matter how advanced our execution procedures may become, they will never alter this fact: capital punishment is the instantaneous, permanent ending of a person's life by a powerful state apparatus that has other punitive options.

I will not say that all witnesses to an execution have the same strong reaction as the two fathers talked about above. Every person and every reaction is different. But I do believe that all spectators, no matter how excited they might be to watch or discuss the events of a killing, will still feel a trace of unease when they later calm down and think back on what they have seen. And I think that we should be more sensitive to this unease. I believe that we should talk about it and reflect on it deeply.

The year 2005 was the centenary of many major events, but something happened 100 years earlier that I think many people have forgotten. In 1905, the Qing court approved a proposal made by Wu Tingfang and Shen Jiaben to end permanently the use of three especially cruel forms of capital punishment: execution by slow slicing, beheading and displaying of the head, and mutilation of the corpse. Later, extracting confessions by torture and unnecessarily cruel corporal punishments also were forbidden, and investigators and jailers were instructed to carry out their duties humanely.[2] After a century of progress, have we managed to improve on this state of affairs? Today, abolition of the death penalty has become the standard, particularly over the last few years. As of 2013, 98 countries had abolished capital punishment for all criminal offenses and 7 had abolished it for ordinary criminal offenses; a further 35 had abolished the death penalty in practice—that is, there had been no executions for at least 10 years. That is a total of 140 countries.[3] Most of the countries in the world have now ended the use of capital punishment. Of the countries that still have capital punishment, most use it very rarely.

The second five-year reform program published by the Supreme People's Court on October 26, 2005, officially gave the authority to approve the death penalty to the Supreme People's Court alone. It also updated procedures for trying capital punishment cases and for the approval process. It instituted procedures for capital punishment appeals and for the presentation of evidence and witnesses in court and required improvements in the handling of witnesses in all capital punishment trials. It required courts to ensure that confessions have not been forced and that evidence has not been gathered illegally. Appeals procedures have been tightened by requiring key witnesses to appear in court. For the most part, this is simply a procedural recapitulation of laws that already exist, but it is still a development to be celebrated. We can safely predict that the number of executions will drop sharply and in particular that controversial cases (including miscarriages of justice) will be sharply reduced. In fact, I believe that this may be the intention of the program. But some of its other objectives could be made more explicit. China today is said to account for 70 percent of the world's executions. As one judge asked, can we not at least reduce that figure to something like 20 percent, a figure more comparable with the proportion of the world's population that lives in China? To go further, because of the specific issues with the death penalty discussed above, I believe that we should at least consider making the abolition of capital punishment one of our goals.

2. Wu Tingfang (伍廷芳, 1842–1922), a native of Xinhui, Guangdong Province, was a Chinese diplomat and politician of the Republic of China. Wu served as foreign minister and later as acting premier during the early years of the Republic of China. Shen Jiaben (沈家本, 1840–1913), a native of Wuxing, Zhejiang Province, was a politician and judicial scholar during the late Qing Dynasty. Shen was in charge of the 1905 revision of the Qing Code, which abolished several inhumane and cruel punishments.

3. Amnesty International, "Abolitionist and Retentionist Countries" (www.amnesty. org/en/death-penalty/abolitionist-and-retentionist-countries).

Can the Death Penalty Serve the Purposes That We Give It?

The debate over capital punishment centers on two main issues. The first is the question of its teleology: can capital punishment serve its purpose—does it produce the effect that we want? The second is the question of deontology: is execution a reasonable type of action to take in the name of justice? Here I consider the first question.

First, I want to exclude from consideration the abuse of the death penalty. I do not consider here the use of capital punishment for political or private ends—for example, to expand one's power or to purge one's enemies. That is not to say that all of its abuses can be easily prevented, but I would like to think about the death penalty in the best possible light. The positive objective of the death penalty is to reduce crime. First, it prevents crime by the criminal himself, because he will not be able to commit further crimes. It is also said to have a deterrent effect on potential criminals, which could prevent hundreds of other crimes.

In order for the death penalty to have a deterrent effect, it must inspire fear. Now, there are a very small number of fanatics who do not fear death; there are also some who will take extreme risks in response to some insult or some opportunity for gain. As Laozi asked, with these people, "what point is there in threatening them with death?" There also are many criminals who simply do not think through the consequences of their crime; they commit what can be called crimes of passion, or nonrational crimes. At the time of the crime, they do not think about anything at all. They may fear the consequences afterward, but by then it is too late. Human beings are not always rational actors. But it is nonetheless true that many people do fear death and are rational under normal circumstances. In this case, the death penalty could have a certain deterrent effect. But is this effect large enough to make up for the fact that the death penalty itself is an evil that ends human life? Is it large enough that no other criminal punishment could have the same deterrent effect?

The question of deterrent effect seems to be one that we could address empirically. However, the fear that the death penalty produces is a psychological feeling. How are we to know how many people did not commit crimes because of their fear of execution—or how many people committed crimes because they knew that they could not be executed? Because of this problem, the argument usually takes the form of indirect, observational data on whether crime rates rise or fall following the introduction or abolition of the death penalty. This kind of methodology is open to serious question, and it remains controversial. Some surveys in other countries seem to show that the death penalty reduces the rate of violent crime, and some research seems to reach the opposite conclusion. The most striking piece of evidence is that in many countries where the death penalty has been abolished, rates of violent crime have fallen rather than risen.[4]

So the idea that the death penalty is an effective deterrent seems to be little more than a myth. The evidence for deterrence is lacking and possibly does not exist at all. And the experience of China over the last twenty to thirty years also fails to support the deterrent effect. Over this period, the death penalty has been imposed for more crimes and death sentences have been imposed by judges with increasing frequency, but have the number of major crime cases increased or decreased? We can ask ourselves this question: has the expansion of capital punishment brought sufficient improvements in safety (to say nothing of psychological health) to justify its use?

Given the cruel nature of capital punishment, the burden of proof should lie with its supporters. Execution is a form of absolute violence. If this state violence does not achieve the goal of reducing total violence, then we must say that in terms of its utility, there is no reason for it to exist. And it remains controversial whether quick execution is indeed more of a reliable deterrent than imprisonment for life.

Another issue is that it is human nature to become gradually inured to even the powerful psychological lever of execution. Sometimes a less dramatic penalty can have the same deterrent effect. The precise details of what level of threat is necessary will of course vary from country to country and from era to era. There is a saying, "When the world is in turmoil, law must have a heavy hand." There is a certain rationality to that, but we should not take it too uncritically; we may end up locked in a vicious cycle of turmoil and increasingly severe punishments, because severity in the law can sometimes have the opposite of its intended effect. On average, the psychology and behavior of ordinary people is to a large degree a function of the social, political, and legal environment in which they find themselves. Cruelty in the law often creates cruelty among the people. The eighteenth-century Italian legal philosopher Cesare Beccaria wrote,

> The countries and times most notorious for severity of punishments were always those in which the most bloody and inhuman actions and the most atrocious crimes were committed; for the hand of the legisla-

4. Liu Renwen, "The Temperature of the Death Penalty," *Beijing News*, July 20, 2013 [http://star.news.sohu.com/20130720/n382154353.html].

tor and the assassin were directed by the same spirit of ferocity . . . the severity of punishments ought to be in proportion to the state of the nation. Among a people hardly yet emerged from barbarity, they should be most severe, as strong impressions are required; but, in proportion as the minds of men become softened by their intercourse in society, the severity of punishments should be diminished, if it be intended that the necessary relation between the object and the sensation should be maintained.[5]

Many well-intentioned people worry that abolishing the death penalty will mean that crime will become rife because there is insufficient deterrent. But as Beccaria says, "Crimes are more effectually prevented by the certainty than the severity of punishment." Montesquieu made much the same point:

> If we inquire into the cause of all human corruptions, we shall find that they proceed from the impunity of criminals, and not from the moderation of punishments. . . . There are two sorts of corruptions—one when the people do not observe the laws; the other when they are corrupted by the laws: an incurable evil, because it is in the very remedy itself.[6]

In the end, applying consistent and appropriate punishments swiftly and unerringly is much more effective a deterrent than simply increasing the savagery of the punishment. In fact, inappropriate forms of "justice" may even have the unwanted effect of corrupting those who enforce them. I am not saying that the death penalty has no deterrent effect whatsoever, but the size of this effect is extremely hard to demonstrate. The death penalty brings an irrevocable end to a human life, and I have very little faith that its deterrent effect is large enough to provide us with good reason to support it.

Even more worrying to me is another type of impact that it could have on the human spirit and human conduct: it could make us less concerned with the value of human life and even encourage violence and cruelty. It could strengthen the impulse to resolve problems by physically destroying people, thereby driving violent behavior. We cannot deny that the death penalty, the most extreme violence that can be imposed on a person, has a certain symbolic meaning. Marx tells us that "there is history—there is such a thing as

5. Cesare Bonesana, Marchese Beccaria, *Of Crimes and Punishments* (www.constitution.org/cb/crim_pun.txt).

6. Charles de Secondat, Baron de Montesquieu, *The Spirit of Laws,* translated by Thomas Nugent, 1752 (www.constitution.org/cm/sol.txt).

statistics—which proves with the most complete evidence . . . murders of the most atrocious kind, following closely upon the execution of criminals." If capital punishment in fact increases the amount of savagery in society, then it may have the paradoxical effect of making us less safe. And if a society is violent, then it may be necessary to use the lever of the law to gradually soften it.

So the argument for deterrence is highly dubious. We cannot be sure how large the deterrent effect is or whether it can do enough good to outweigh any potential negative effects on people or its own inherent cruelty. There may be an element in human nature that leads to violence. Violence has been a major part of our history, and in the twentieth century's wars and revolutions it flourished. That means that respecting and protecting life must be a more fundamental goal today, although it is a difficult one to realize. How do we promote being sensitive to and cherishing all human life, including our own? How do we soften the callousness and cruelty that we see around us and form a more peaceful and conciliatory society? It seems to me that if we show extreme caution when dealing with the life of any person, even a convicted criminal, then we give less reason for even the criminally inclined to resort to violence.

In What Sense Is Capital Punishment Just?

So deterrence does not seem to be a convincing argument in favor of capital punishment and in fact seems at odds with the notions of civilization and progress. But there is another substantive argument in favor of capital punishment, which is that death can be a rightful response to and retribution for crime. No matter what its social impact, the execution of a criminal can be a form of closure for the friends and relatives of a victim and can bring a proper resolution to public outrage. That is, there is an argument for capital punishment that stems from a sense of justice: the execution itself is just. Its social impact is irrelevant; execution itself is a proper correction and must be supported.

There are two different aspects of justice: distributive justice and corrective justice. Distributive justice concerns the distribution of benefits, which are those things that everyone wants. Corrective justice can also be said to be a kind of "distribution," but what is distributed is criminal punishment, which is something that everyone wants to avoid. The demand of all forms of justice is that we treat all people equally and fairly insofar as that is possible: benefits in return for contributions, punishment in return for crime.

For thousands of years, the idea that a murderer should die, that those who take life should forfeit their own, has been regarded as part of the natural order. Before that, in a more primitive time, the retributive theory of "an eye for an eye, a tooth for a tooth" was put into literal practice: anyone who wrongly harmed the body of another person would suffer exactly the same injury in punishment. But as civilizations developed and particularly in modern times, most forms of corporal punishment have been replaced by imprisonment for varying lengths of time. The enforcement of the law should not and need not bring enforcers down to the same level as the criminals. Enforcers, having powers at their disposal that far exceed those of the criminal, have no need to apply the same physical tortures that the criminal applied. They can use other methods of punishment. Ironically, while most forms of corporal punishment have been abolished, many countries have retained the most serious, the most cruel, the ultimate corporal punishment: the death penalty.

If the principle of matching the punishment with the crime were to be properly applied, then nonviolent crimes such as corruption or burglary would be most properly dealt with by imprisonment of the criminal and recovery of the property that the criminal stole. That would be a better fit than destruction of the person. But just as distributive justice must acknowledge that, in reality, absolute equality is impossible, corrective justice is subject to certain constraints. It can use only a finite system of defined crimes and defined punishments of limited levels of severity to respond to the infinite variety of possible criminal behavior. For example, a murderer may murder many people or may kill in an especially horrific way, but the maximum possible response of the law is to kill one person: the criminal. And it may not use inhumane execution procedures. That is because the justice system and the criminal exist in an imbalanced relationship: one represents right, the other evil; one has much more power than the other. The justice system seeks justice for the victim, but it may not use the methods of a criminal to achieve it. When determining guilt, justice must adhere strictly to a set of procedures that ensure openness and fairness. During the administration of justice, the enforcers must never bring themselves down to the criminal's level. And that remains true even during the punishment phase, after the judgment of guilt has been made.

From another perspective, committing a crime—for example, killing another person—is the equivalent of leaving and rejecting society. Even if the criminal is not caught, he is still on the run. He may be in a state of fear and despair that cannot be revealed even to his closest family members. And if the crime is one that is likely to attract the death penalty, then he lives with the constant fear of death. In some ways, that state of waiting for death is worse than death itself. So the mantra "a death for a death" does not express real equivalence between crime and punishment. A criminal on the run who is captured immediately becomes no bigger than an insect. The machinery of the state can crush him like a bug at any time during the process of arrest, detention, and judgment. The very power of the state and its attempt to serve justice raise an obvious question: Does justice really require that this person be squashed like a bug?

The most persuasive argument for executing a murderer is the principle of taking a life for a life. But how exactly is killing the murderer supposed to make up for or cancel out the life that he took? The victim is dead, and we grieve the death of that person. If killing a criminal could recall a victim to life and that were the only way to do it, then I suspect that everyone would approve of the death penalty. Killing the criminal so that the victim might live would truly be "a life for a life," rather than just a death for a death. But that is not possible. Life and death cannot be exchanged. So must we institute "a death for a death"? Can "a death for a death" give true closure to the friends and family of a victim? Culture and personal factors play a large role in determining exactly what kind of punishment will give some kind of satisfaction to the family of a murder victim. There has been more than one case in which Chinese authorities have executed the murderer of a foreign national, only to find that the family of the victim did not approve of the execution at all.

There is also the issue of public acceptance to consider. Public reaction includes a proper moral anger, but there are other complicating factors. Some of those who have researched the death penalty, including Karl Bruno Leder, believe that many of the people who advocate strongly for the death penalty do so for reasons that have nothing to do with justice. Their motivation is deeply rooted in the nonrational, in a deep psychological need to vent their repressed urges. Historically, the precursors of the death penalty were blood feuds and human sacrifice. Neither of these phenomena is rooted in justice. Blood feuds are a way of expiating one's own feelings of guilt; sacrifices are a release mechanism for individual and social fears. Every potential execution attracts a group of highly stimulated people, and their moral anger is always mixed with other emotions: a lust for extremes and simple bloodlust. But in our age, we have the option of not satisfying or releasing these desires through executions.

Human justice can never be perfect. That is why Buddhists talk of karma and Christians repeat the words "Vengeance is mine; I will repay." Laozi wrote: "When we try to chop wood in place of the master carpenter, there are few of us who escape hurting our own hands instead." He perhaps believed that there was still a kind of natural justice in the darkness, so there was no need for people to use extreme sanctions in pursuit of perfect human justice. And strictly speaking, all human beings are connected to one another in some way. We all bear a kind of joint responsibility and shared pain for the death of every person. In some sense, the blade really does fall on all of our necks, and the bell tolls for every one of us.

Mercy and love are higher principles than justice. We have an obligation to separate crimes from criminals. We can give a full and unequivocal condemnation of crimes, but our attitude to criminals should be as Confucius said: "When you have found out the truth of any accusation, be grieved for and pity them, and do not feel joy at your own ability."[7] We also need to consider the people who are most often executed. When we examine their backgrounds, we find that the majority are those from the margins: the poor, the isolated. Even if we ignore the distorting effects of money and power on the justice system, among those cases where the death penalty is one of the legal sentencing options, it is used far more on the disadvantaged than on anyone else. Capital punishment makes the strong stronger and the weak weaker; in fact, it is barely a factor for the advantaged in society. And is that not precisely one of the reasons why those who have power and a voice are not especially concerned about the death penalty?

Capital punishment is a method of justice that has been used throughout history. But as our culture has developed, we have reached the point that it is impossible to see the death penalty as just in any sense. Perhaps now it is just only in a symbolic way, as it represents the ultimate penalty: an expedient that can be used in the most extreme cases. For example, if because of a real and pressing danger, failing to execute a prisoner would constitute a risk of violence against the public, then the death penalty could be considered. But it is not a tool to be used frequently in the long term in a normal society, in a society that is committed to making itself more civilized.

---

7. *The Analects*, attributed to Confucius [Kongfuzi], 551-479 BCE, by Lao-Tse [Lao Zi], translated by James Legge (1815–1897) (http://china.usc.edu/ShowArticle.aspx?articleID=373).

CHAPTER FOURTEEN

THE MORAL, LEGAL, AND RELIGIOUS ISSUES OF CIVIL DISOBEDIENCE

In the Western tradition, the practice of civil disobedience has historically involved legal, moral, and religious (or spiritual) elements. That is true in particular in cases of successful movements that used civil disobedience as a tactic. In this chapter, I consider the practice from those three angles, from the most apparent to the least obvious.

First of all, civil disobedience is a form of illegal behavior. That is its most obvious characteristic. Civil disobedience is protest in the form of open, non-violent violation of some law: disruption of traffic, occupation of an office building or commercial area, or similar actions. It interrupts the normal working of society as maintained by the law, so it attracts a lot of attention and may cause serious unrest. The illegal behavior is sometimes a violation of the very law being protested. For example, refusing to pay a tax that the protestor believes is unfair, ignoring specific government prohibitions, or refusing to serve in the military to protest a war. Sometimes the illegality is not directly connected to the cause. Disruption of traffic is generally not an attempt to protest the transportation system; it is just a way of attracting public and government attention. Often unrelated disobedience occurs when the target of the protest is not a specific law but a more general injustice or when the consequences of breaking the protested law directly would be too serious and the losses caused too great.

But the lawbreaking involved in acts of civil disobedience remains true to the spirit of the law. By that I mean that though laws are broken, the law-

This chapter is an edited version of an article first published in *Orient*, no. 2 (2002).

breakers do not take the breaking of the law too far. They remain close to the boundary between legality and illegality, usually breaking only non-vital laws. They do not advocate violence, so they avoid the kind of behavior that criminal law treats as the most serious. They break laws only because of their concern about an issue that cannot be resolved under the existing legal system or when resolution is too slow, and they remain willing to resume law-abiding behavior at any time. An important feature of civil disobedience is that the lawbreaking involved is never done for its own sake. Though sometimes the law broken is the very one being protested, the objective is to change the law or repeal it through the proper constitutional process. Usually, civil disobedience honors the constitution. Often the argument made is that the specific law being targeted for protest is unconstitutional and that the protestors are breaking the law only for the purpose of upholding the constitution. The leaders and protestors who take part in civil disobedience campaigns are willing to accept the legal consequences of their actions by submitting to the lawful punishments given to them for their illegal behavior. Their lawbreaking is done openly. There is no attempt to evade the law or run from the law.

The second important aspect of civil disobedience is its moral dimension. Civil disobedience is the pursuit of some moral goal connected with public (civil) morality. Thus it is a behavior of engaged citizens, not simply a protest by disaffected or violent elements and definitely not the slavish obedience of "subjects." The disobedience is motivated by the morality and duties of a citizen; it is an act of responsibility, involving full consideration of the consequences of one's actions. Civil disobedience is an act of conscience, and it encourages the rest of society to act on the dictates of conscience as well. Protestors make judgments based on their own conscience that they or some class of people in society are the victims of unfair treatment. Generally, civil disobedience is not used in disputes over money but in issues of more fundamental rights or citizenship.

The protestors' belief that they must protest comes from a strong sense of injustice. They protest on behalf of themselves but not just themselves, so their objective is often not to defeat their opponents, still less to eradicate their opponents. They want to eradicate the offending behavior, not the offenders. Their protests are an appeal to the consciences of their opponents and of observers, in the hope that they will feel the same sense of injustice. The protestors appeal to a universal moral sensibility, so they are willing to make sacrifices themselves first, willing to use their own moral conduct as a tool to elicit moral action from others. Of course, the protestors believe that they stand on the side of justice, but they do not claim that they are morally superior. They are just trying to do good. This moral orientation naturally demands that they eschew violent tactics or plots. Moreover, as Gandhi observed, this form of clean protest, involving moral consideration of both its ends and its means, is unlikely to do much damage. Even if the judgment of the protestors is wrong and the goal is mistaken, it is the protestors themselves who suffer most during the protest. Even if their protest fails, they are not morally degraded by it. And certainly they will not suffer the fate of some movements that succeed in their objective but find that it brings moral and spiritual degradation.

Finally, looking at the practice of civil disobedience in the twentieth century, we see that religion and spiritual belief are a major supporting feature. The most representative examples—for instance, the Indian struggle for independence from British colonial rulers, led by Gandhi, and the U.S. civil rights movement, led by Martin Luther King Jr.—had a strong religious basis and support, and religion also played a role in regulating the movements. Civil disobedience can occur only given a certain convergence of external environment, social systems, and personalities. High levels of moral quality and moral strength are required for civil disobedience. That means that the barriers to entry for civil disobedience are high. A group that has been oppressed or abused must still retain the spirit of love; a group that has been treated unfairly must still want to uphold the principle of fairness. While a group must have the strength to protest, it also must be scrupulous about remaining within the limits of moral permissibility. That requires deep reserves of spiritual strength. But such groups have absorbed a concept that in terms of human history is very new: the resolution of disputes without resorting to violence or force—indeed, a determination to decide issues without making them a question of personal victory or defeat. We cannot use violent methods to end violence; we cannot end evil with more evil. Protestors who use civil disobedience have a transcendent element in their psychology, leading them to believe that there is an eternal justice that will defeat all opposition. Therefore they have a powerful motive for supporting and promoting justice and enduring temporary setbacks or even failure in the temporal world. So while it is possible to discuss civil disobedience purely in theoretical terms, when we look at the practice—particularly the successful practice—of civil disobedience, we are immediately confronted with spiritual beliefs. They are an element that must not be overlooked.

But, civil disobedience is fundamentally a legal concept—or, to be more precise, it is a concept based on the rule of law in a constitutional system. The supporters of the U.S. civil rights movements were able to organize, develop, and strengthen because of the rule of law. Genuinely competent leaders were able to emerge, participants were able to develop a mature consensus, and the wider public was able to understand the protest through fair and unbiased reporting. All of these processes were dependent on a strong, stable, rule-based society. And the ultimate success of the movement also was possible only because of the rule of law. The direct objective of the U.S. civil rights movement—its definition of success—was to pass a civil rights bill. Once that bill passed, civil rights were genuinely enforced. In any society that respects the rule of law, there are bound to be examples of this kind of legislation, born out of painful struggle. Of course, genuine friendship between races and national solidarity did not instantly spring into being because a law was passed, but at the very least the most obvious humiliations were largely ended. The original intentions of civil disobedience also were faithful to the constitution or faithful to some natural law that forms the moral underpinnings and spirit of the law. Natural law can also motivate efforts to change specific existing laws based on the demands of justice and moral conscience.

It is interesting that a number of Chinese legal theorists have thought about the Western concept of civil disobedience in the light of the Chinese situation and have all reached the same conclusion: that China needs more constitutional law and better rule-of-law institutions. They say that China needs that spirit of faithfulness to the constitution and more abidance of the law, not more law breaking. Of course, this is not just about individuals: the government's willingness to follow the constitution is an important part of any discussion of constitutionalism and rule of law. For nearly 100 years, we have missed opportunities to build stronger rule-of-law institutions in China. I recall Liang Shuming (see chapter 3, note 20) and his unusual commentary on the May Fourth Movement. When there were arrests after students burned down the Zhao residence and beat people, Liang expressed anger at the authorities and praised the students' patriotism.[1] But he also objected to the "completely uncritical forgiveness" of the students that was expressed throughout Chinese society. He said that he hoped that the students who rioted would be properly tried in court—that the prosecutors would prosecute, the court adjudicate, and the students pay the requisite legal penalties:

---

1. The burning of Zhaojialou (火烧赵家楼) refers to the razing of the residence of Cao Rulin, the transportation minister of the Republic of China during the May Fourth Movement in 1919. Cao was believed to be a traitor who made concessions to Japan at the Paris Peace Conference regarding China's sovereignty in Shandong Province. The student protestors failed to capture Cao but burned down his residence to vent their anger.

If the prosecutors were truly unable to determine what had happened, then we should where possible turn ourselves into the police and confess. We should make this sacrifice, because if we do not, then we will lose even more. By any logic, beating people and burning houses is crime. That much is undeniable. Cao and Zhang may be guilty of terrible crimes. But until those crimes are proved [until they are prosecuted and convicted], they will have their freedom. We may be acting out of patriotism and concern for our state, but that does not mean we are free to do as we please. We cannot say that what we have done is right, or that criminal behavior is now allowed.

Liang Shuming thought that the situation had been caused by failing to consider others and thinking only of one's own interests. He saw that as a bad habit formed during thousands of years of autocratic rule: vacillation between heedless rampage and mindless obedience. He thought that the Chinese people did not know how to balance their own ideas against other people's on an ongoing, case-by-case basis. If that character flaw could not be fixed, then the current political system would be unworkable, let alone any more evolved system that might emerge in future. He said that his first idea was to have the students go through a proper trial, then have the minister of justice request a special pardon from the president, a process that would ensure both that the law was followed and that the students did not suffer any more than they should. But on reflection, he realized that serving their sentences would be better: heroes who accepted the law could be celebrated for all eternity. However, at the time, Liang's viewpoint was seen as eccentric and left him rather isolated. Nearly a century later, we still face a long struggle to develop our legal institutions and to foster attitudes of citizenship among Chinese people.

One final point worth noting is that we must look at the weakness of the individual against the institution and the weakness of the minority against the majority. Often those who launch and participate in civil disobedience are members of minorities or underprivileged groups. It is often desperation that makes them willing to break the law in order to attract attention to their cause. They feel that the normal functioning of the legal system cannot help them, so they have to try something else. Because members of the majority or of privileged groups usually find it difficult to empathize with the desperation or anger that the protestors feel, the disobedient actions of the minority mean that in the short term at least, they will have to pay an even greater price. Without strong moral sentiments and spiritual guidance to constrain them, desperation and anger are likely to be expressed in other, more explosive ways. Such anger is like a fire that can consume the self and others. Terrorism, both international and domestic, is of this type. It is often driven by a desperation that believes that normal, peaceful channels of conflict resolution do not work. Of course such action is morally culpable, but it is also deserving of sympathy. It is important that we think hard about what is implied by the word "desperation." In dynastic China, there was no rule of law, and perhaps for precisely that reason the state took a particular interest in helping the voiceless poor and those with no means of support. We should learn from that system: even as we work to build institutions of law that properly realize civil rights, we should remember that both we as individuals and the government ought to show concern for the weakest groups. We should give them practical help and hope in order to relieve their desperation and help them build basic confidence. Of course, that does not alter our main task: building rule-of-law institutions, fostering moral feeling among citizens, and raising levels of cultural and spiritual awareness.

CHAPTER FIFTEEN

ECOLOGICAL ETHICS

Spiritual Resources and Philosophical Foundations

The people living on this planet today live in societies that are modern or are just becoming modern and in which economic growth is the overriding value. Hundreds of years of growth in the West and decades of growth in China have brought massive gains in material prosperity, and living standards are gradually rising throughout the world today. However, economic growth has also caused severe degradation of the natural environment, which represents a threat of unknown proportions to future generations, to the living things around us, and to the whole Earth.

For anyone who understands it, this situation is extremely worrying. It prompts much searching for philosophical and political resources that can be developed into effective responses and solutions—resources that might be found in ancient teachings on sustainable practices and in popular religion, primitive beliefs, theological details, and even the philosophies and ideologies of other countries.

This search for cultural resources is what this book [*Environmental Ethics*] is devoted to. The goal and the thread connecting the essays in this volume is the search for philosophical and spiritual resources to support environmental ethics, be they Chinese or foreign, modern or historical. The essays present belief systems, religions, aesthetics, and values that can support environmental ethics and describe the various forms that environmental philosophy takes in the modern world. These essays support the project of building an envi-

This chapter is an edited version of a chapter first published in He Huaihong, ed., *Environmental Ethics* (Hebei University Press, 2002), pp. 1–23.

ronmental ethic that meets the needs of modern China; an ethic that fuses the wisdom of our historical tradition and the urgency of our current realities; an ethic that also takes a global perspective. This volume is our contribution to environmental protection and green lifestyles in China.

Distinguishing Behavioral Norms, Spiritual Beliefs, and Philosophical Theories

This volume has two sections: "Spiritual Resources" and "Philosophical Foundations." Spiritual resources are traditional, cultural beliefs that have a positive environmental value. They may in theory include any belief or concept that is relatively mature and stable in any culture, but because our own time and scope are limited, we restrict our consideration to resources in the major world traditions represented in China. Philosophical foundations are modern ethical theories and systems developed over the last few decades, mainly in the West, concerning the ethics of the environment and the natural world.

The division between the two parts is not absolute. The two areas are deeply interconnected. Nevertheless, spiritual resources and philosophical foundations are still recognizably different, and in this volume we have particular motives for separating the two that should be explained here in this introduction. In the Spiritual Resources section, we focus on ideas and resources that are widely accepted, even pervasive, and deeply rooted in strong traditions of belief. These ideas have become integral to the lives of peoples, cultures, or specific individuals or groups, embedded more or less deeply, more or less powerfully in their beliefs. Some of these ideas affect not just educated elites but entire societies. They are expressed not just as rational claims but also as a mix of emotions, will, instinct, and rationality. They combine with other concepts in a range of structures to produce stable beliefs, which have their own history, closely allied to individual and cultural lifestyles.

Philosophical theory, on the other hand, is the product of rational, systematic, scientific argument on the rational or academic level. Its fierce debates and careful proofs are circulated among researchers themselves and educated readers. Formal environmental ethics are a product of only the most recent few decades. In simple terms, the difference between spiritual resources and philosophical foundations is that spiritual resources are generally more deeply rooted, more widely accepted, and have had a greater and more lasting impact on society. But spiritual resources also lack the clarity and purity of environmental philosophy.

Environmental ethics and its key tenets are strongly oriented toward the practical. Of course, ethics is always concerned with influencing people's behavior and lifestyles, but environmental ethics is even more so. Its most obvious feature is that it is always a strong call to action. It does not exist merely to satisfy the interest or curiosity of scholars, so it is difficult to imagine a detached, indifferent environmental ethic. It is always calling for something. It always demands spiritual, emotional, and intentional investment from its followers. Above the doorway to environmental ethics we could inscribe, "Enter not, indifferent ones." Environmentalism is a science that requires not just knowledge, but action. As such, it is not merely a system of knowledge; it can also become a belief: a lifelong, complete belief, an ultimate concern akin to religious faith. It is precisely because environmentalism is like a faith that we need to identify and separate out the spiritual resources from the other elements of the theory. And though we do not in this volume directly discuss environmental action, it is our objective to furnish for this kind of action as broad as possible a range of spiritual resources and philosophical theory options.

To summarize, environmental ethics is unlike other systems of knowledge in two striking ways: environmental ethics is practical, and it is a belief. Environmental ethics is not an indifferent, detached system of knowledge, rooted in pure love of knowledge. It is a theory that was forced into existence by a crisis and severe problems requiring practical action. As such, it may in turn force you to do something: perhaps to change your personal lifestyle or to engage in collective green action. In this sense, environmentalism can truly be said to be an "urgent" science. For those who are fully engaged in environmentalism, it brings not just the pleasures of knowledge but also worry about the current situation and the powerful urge to do something—no matter what that something is. It may also demand support from corresponding beliefs and changes in lifestyle. Environmentalism, therefore, is an undertaking: first a commitment to beliefs and then a commitment to act.

Environmental ethics is therefore ultimately organized around action and practice. The goal is not to interpret the world but to change the world. However, the kind of change that it aims for is not to defeat the world. It is not an attempt to make the natural world adapt to humanity. Rather, it is an attempt to change the motivations of humans, along with their actions and lifestyles—to make people adapt to the natural world, to live in harmony with it. Timely and forceful direct action is an extremely important form of environmental protection. But locating and developing spiritual resources and philosophical beliefs that can support green action also is vital. After all, the only guarantees that action will be timely and forceful lie in the actors' attitudes: in their understanding, viewpoints, commitments, and beliefs. To improve the state of environmental protection in China will require behavioral norms, spiritual beliefs, and philosophical theories that relate to the environment. These three necessary elements make up the scope of this book. Below, we look in more detail at each of these three elements.

"Behavioral norms" refers simply to what people can do and cannot do to nonhuman living things and to the natural world. They are the moral constraints and restrictions on our conduct toward nonhuman life and nonhuman objects. There are two types of behavioral norms. The first is binding on groups—companies, ethnic groups, nations—and includes both soft restrictions, such as declarations, petitions, and statements, and harder green regulations, such as treaties, conventions, and laws. The second type of norm is binding on individuals, and some are already part of criminal law—for example, the hunting of certain kinds of wild animal—but the main norm of this type is simply the promotion of a green lifestyle. These norms, along with the theories and spiritual beliefs that underpin them, form the substance of an environmental ethics.

"Spiritual beliefs" refers to the most fundamental and deepest layer of beliefs and attitudes that make people obey restrictions and constraints, whether it includes just one spiritual belief or a complex set of beliefs. These beliefs form a person's underlying internal motivation for action. Any environmental ethics that lacks supporting beliefs is incomplete. At the same time, these beliefs probably do not only motivate attitudes and actions toward the natural world; they probably also support attitudes and actions toward other people and toward society. They may in fact be a comprehensive ethic, personal philosophy, or set of religious beliefs. They are the beliefs that underpin a person's sense of life's fundamental meaning.

"Philosophical theories" in this volume refers mainly to contemporary Western theories of environmental ethics. These theories developed directly from the study of ethics, but they have greatly deepened and broadened the scope of the traditional field of ethics. Some emerged from the fields of ecology and environmental science but bring a philosophical approach to these fields.

If we approach environmental ethics historically, we can also develop a slightly different analysis, including "behavioral norms," "spiritual beliefs," and "related thought." Here, "related thought" replaces "philosophical theories" in a sense, because dynastic China had no systematic philosophy of the environment. Unlike "spiritual resources," which refers to beliefs, "related thought" means rational ethical theory in pre-modern civilizations that does not deal directly with environmental matters but is very relevant to it. Related systems of ethics can also help people to abide by some norms of environmental ethics, and they can integrate with environmental rules to enrich and on some level ground those rules even though their original scope was not the environment. In dynastic times, there was not yet an articulated system of environmental ethics. Traditional thought on the environment is scattered throughout other writings, not centralized in one place. It was never systematized into a coherent philosophy. But traditional theories and values did include environmental concepts on a deep level, and they are quite compatible with an environmental ethics.

In this volume, our prime objective is neither the "related thought" of traditional China or explicit behavioral norms. We include only one example: in the section on Confucian environmental thought, there is a brief exploration of some behavioral norms and some related areas of thought. This is not to say that those aspects are unimportant. The importance of behavioral norms hardly requires explanation, and the importance of related Confucian thought can be seen in the fact that economic growth was not a primary value for the Confucians, so the Confucian value of moderation was able to serve as an important protection for the environment in traditional China. The spiritual resources for environmentalism in Confucianism may not have been quite as rich and ambitious as those of Daoism—never mind a systematic modern theory—but because the Confucians controlled the levers of the political system and the governing social philosophy, they were probably able to achieve more with Confucian environmental ethics than the Daoists ever did.

We can distinguish more carefully among the various types of spiritual resources and philosophical theories that this volume discusses. For example, spiritual resources can be divided into religious or nonreligious resources. Religious resources can be divided again into monotheistic or polytheistic beliefs, or into major religious traditions or primitive beliefs. Nonreligious resources include the Chinese traditions of Confucianism and Daoism and aesthetic traditions in the arts such as naturalism and romanticism. Philosophical theories can be sorted into anthropocentric or non-anthropocentric varieties. Anthropocentric theories can be further divided into classical or modern theories or into strong or weak anthropocentrism. Non-anthropocentric theories include animal liberation, animal rights, biocentrism, and ecocentrism.

Spiritual Beliefs and Philosophical Theories

As noted above, we distinguish three aspects of environmental ethics: spiritual beliefs, philosophical theories, and behavioral norms. This volume includes essays on two of those aspects. That is not because we ignore the will to act and consensus behavior but because of this consideration: we wish to find as much spiritual motivation and philosophical theory as possible to provide deep support for environmental protection and green action.

We can consider the relationship between the three aspects of environmental ethics. Spiritual beliefs are fundamental values. They are the deepest, most basic part. Fundamental change in human conduct or lifestyles is ultimately a question of a "change of heart": it requires the insight to develop a correct view of the relationship between humanity and nature. That insight gives us the powerful motivation and determination that we need to act on environmental issues. Philosophical theory also requires motivation at the spiritual level, particularly on the part of the initial developers of a theory. But as presented to readers, theory appeals primarily to our rationality. Theory can be used to make policy arguments; it helps us build broad-based environmental awareness and consensus through a process of public debate. In this sense, theory can be seen as an intermediate stage between spiritual motivation and behavioral norms. Finally, behavioral norms are the necessary result. Behavioral norms emerge naturally from motivation and theory. Action also is necessary: without norms of action, ethical theory and spiritual motivation lose the practical quality that properly characterizes environmental ethics and both beliefs and theory lose their meaning.

The importance of spiritual resources in the development of philosophical theories can be seen in the work of many of the originators of early environmental theories: Henry David Thoreau, Albert Schweitzer, and so forth. Here we focus the discussion on the direct connection between spiritual resources and environmental practice for ordinary people and members of aboriginal communities. The following is extracted from an essay entitled "In Environmental Action, Brainwashing Is the Most Important Thing"[1]—

---

1. I read the essay online; I do not know where it was first published. The word used in the essay's title, "brainwashing," is not quite right. But the author was expressing the realization that the most important part of protecting the environment was changing people's attitudes. Returning to an older sense of humility and respect for nature and its flora and fauna would be one possible program among others. This also means respecting the beliefs of local people and using local, traditional resources. The essay also touches on another very important issue: environmental campaigners must take into account the eco-

Between 1995 and 1998, I went several times to Dêqên in Yunnan to stop the felling of primary forest. In November 1999 my wife and I came again to where Xi Zhinong and a few other environmentalists from Yunnan had set up home, near the Mainri Snow Mountains (Meili Xue Shan, 梅里雪山).[2] We found that attitudes among the local residents toward nature had changed greatly from what they used to be. Xi said to us, sadly, "The most important thing is helping ordinary people to recover a state of mind that they used to have. They have to start getting used to the idea of protecting nature in their culture, in their religion, and in their way of life. Otherwise the forests here are soon going to be destroyed, and the black snub-nosed monkey and other species will be driven to extinction."

In 1996, Xi Zhinong and a group of university students involved in Green Camp[3] came to the area around the Mainri Snow Mountains, where an elderly local Tibetan told them, "Fifty years ago, the Tibetans in this area did not hunt. You would often see herds of 20–30 red or dwarf deer trampling through the farmers' fields, but they were protected by Tibetan custom. Their religious strictures did not allow them to hunt: killing a single deer was believed to bring disaster to a family. The entire community protected the wildlife and lived at peace with it. There was also very little chopping down of trees at that time. Tibetan Buddhism taught that if too many trees were cut down, the rains would fail and the springs would dry up. The spirits of people who cut down trees without good cause would not go to heaven, and bad luck would dog their families for generations."

Xi Zhinong and his group of green campaigners started trying to use the traditional beliefs and religious culture of the Tibetans to find common cause on the protection of the environment. They started local, aiming to protect the area around the Mainri Snow Mountains. [One of the peaks] is the most sacred of the eight divine mountains in Tibetan Buddhism. The American explorer Dr. Joseph Rock, who had

---

nomic needs of local residents. That is why environmental projects often are coupled with targeted anti-poverty measures, to the point that today, green campaigners often double as poverty campaigners; often they are poverty workers first, green campaigners second.

2. Xi Zhinong (奚志农, 1964–), a native of Dali, Yunnan Province, is a Chinese wildlife photographer and environmentalist. He is highly respected among environmentalists and has received a number of environmental protection awards.

3. Green Camp (绿色营) is a nongovernmental environmental protection agency dedicated to the protection of wild monkeys in Yunnan Province.

seen many of the Earth's magnificent sights, declared [this peak] the "most beautiful mountain in the world." Over the last century, a dozen or more teams have made attempts on the summit, but they have all mysteriously failed. In 1991, a joint Chinese-Japanese team's vehicle rolled, and 17 lives were lost to the mountain. The Japanese team was particularly frustrated by that failure. They signed agreements with the local authorities giving them priority in future attempts at the summit. They sent daring expeditions in 1996 and 1999, but both ended in failure. In early 2000, they got ready once again. . . .

The local Tibetan residents were strongly opposed to all attempts to climb the mountain. Every time a new expedition crunched off over the snow toward the summit, a crowd of Tibetans would throw themselves on the ground at the base, praying to the god of the mountain not to be offended by the intrusion. Another group would gather at the offices of the county government, demanding that the county authorities sack officials who were supporting the Japanese attempts to climb the mountain. Xi Zhinong and his colleagues petitioned and worked every committee and system they could: the State Ethnic Affairs Commission, the Yunnan Provincial Government, the Tibetan Autonomous Region Government, the county authorities, as well as all the major media. But they were never able to stop the ascents. Instead, it seemed to be the mountain that heard their petitions each time and stopped the climbers in their tracks.

On the afternoon of the very last working day of 1999, the Beijing authorities finally ordered a stop to any further expeditions on Mount Meri. The state had intervened at last. The Tibetans around Mount Meri were very grateful to Xi Zhinong, and Xi experienced for the first time how powerful a tool religious taboos could be in the fight to protect the environment.

Of course, mountaineering has value. As the great British explorer George Mallory replied to the question of why he wanted to climb Mount Everest: "Because it's there." But there is another truth that must be recognized and that was affirmed by Aldo Leopold: So long as there is wilderness out there, even if you never visit it once in your life, just knowing that it exists brings psychological comfort. Wilderness has its own value. Environmentalists are not always against mountaineering, but as Shen Xiaohui, a veteran forestry commissioner, once said:

Why can't we keep just a few virgin summits, untainted by human footprints or human trash? Why not keep the dignity, privacy, and mystery of a few mountains? And leave a patch of sacred land for our religions and for our descendants? We have to realize that giving in to our desire to conquer everything, to prove our own omnipotence is not the right choice. It is better to control our desire and to prove that there are things one cannot do. That is how we rectify the relationship between humanity and nature. We have to keep ourselves in check, otherwise it all ends in tears.[4]

Shen also writes:

The contribution of religion to environmental protection over history cannot be overestimated. Mount Tianhu in eastern China and Dinghu Mountain National Nature Reserve in the south are both sacred Buddhist mountains. In the northwest, the Xinglong Mountain Nature Reserve is a Daoist center. Without religion, the forest ecosystems of these national parks would never have been preserved as well as they are. Even today, Tibetan Buddhism is still a major force in the protection of the Tibetan environment. One researcher who has spent many years in Tibet says the most striking lesson he learned there is that wherever the religious tradition is strongest, the environment is well-protected. That is something that should give us pause for thought.[5]

Shen might support a mission statement like this: in order to protect ecological diversity, we need to protect the diversity of traditional cultures. Uniformity is weakness; diversity is stability. That is a basic principle of ecology.

This kind of local spiritual belief has deep roots, and it can be a powerful force when coupled with the lifestyles that have been practiced by local people for generations. Even when it has suffered years of constant interference and suppression, it can still be quickly revived and deployed. And given the level of degradation that our natural environment has suffered, we are now willing to use any resource and method to protect it, no matter what its origin.

Now, nearly a century after we abandoned primitive beliefs, it is time to think about the consequences of that abandonment. Beliefs like pantheism and worship of plants and animals offer a spiritual viewpoint that modern people often forget. For a large fraction of the population, they may also be

4. Shen Xiaohui, *Seeking Dreams on Snowy Peaks* (Shenyang Publishing House, 1998), p. 154.

5. Ibid., p. 120.

the only thing that is not about self-interest, the only thing that has spiritual force. Dismissing them as "superstitions" and rejecting them can place us in a state in which we are controlled only by our material desires, without any spiritual reverence. This kind of psychological state is fatal for the environment.

So even in this "post-religious" age, we do not necessarily have to go and preach in some artificial way. We just need to protect the existing "ecosystem" of old beliefs that still persist in people's hearts and minds. We should value the spiritual undergrowth like we value physical vegetation, rather than attempting to weed it with no heed for the consequences. If the spiritual beliefs within people are strangled and there are no new shoots of spirituality, then their hearts will become bald, barren places. They will end up entirely given over to material desires, and that would be a catastrophe for the natural world. It would ultimately make our forests equally bald and equally barren. It is also important to note that for many people, the prod of the spiritual element is sufficient to move them to take action to protect the environment, without the mediation of any articulated philosophical theory. They just do what they should do and don't do what they shouldn't. And the motivation offered by these spiritual resources is strong and sustained.

The role of philosophy and theory is nonetheless still important. Good theories can also be internalized, slowly fermenting to become a fixed part of an individual's attitudes and even a spiritual belief. Philosophical theories appeal primarily to people's rationality. They offer rational reasons and arguments, and they can play a major role in influencing public debate and government policy.

Ecological or environmental ethics has been one of the fastest-growing areas of study in the last few decades in the West. The earliest inspirations for environmentalism in the nineteenth century, such as Thoreau and John Muir, were oddities. Even in the first half of the twentieth century, the founders of the discipline, such as Schweitzer and Leopold, had few peers. Today, environmental ethics is a subject that attracts input from masses of researchers and huge public interest as well as green activism. Environmentalism may have started late, but it has grown fast, and the field now has its own dedicated research organizations, influential theories, and celebrated thinkers. Environmental ethics is a new, interdisciplinary field of study in which theory and practice are very closely linked. It therefore faces many practical challenges, and it often draws its material and its nourishment from real cases. At the same time, the broadening of theoretical study can help in the resolution of real problems and benefit the further development of environmental ethics itself. It can also inform the wider study of general ethics.

Green ethics has been deeply influenced on the level of theory by philosophy and general ethics; it also raises its own challenges to those fields of study.

Environmental ethics is unique among the various fields of applied ethics. Political ethics, economic ethics, legal ethics, educational ethics, media ethics, international ethics, and life sciences and medical ethics all deal with relationships between people. Only environmental ethics faces a different question: the relationship between humans and the natural environment. As a result, it has produced a rich and distinctive literature. Most of the other fields of applied ethics represent extensions or applications of general theories of ethics. Environmental ethics has its own, unique, philosophical theories: from modern weak anthropocentrism to theories centered on animals, life, or even ecosystems. Within the field, there is vigorous debate over these different viewpoints.

And it is perhaps only in environmental ethics that we find a division between two different approaches to theory: one is a generalist approach, the other is environmental exceptionalism. The formative influence of general ethical theories and general philosophical theories on environmental ethics is plain to see. For example, in the area of animal ethics the two main theories are extensions of general philosophical positions. Animal liberation is a teleological ethics, applying utilitarianism to animals and stressing that we must respect animal sensations, happiness, and comfort as much as we do those of humans. Animal rights is a deontological theory extending the theory of human rights to animals and stressing that we must respect the rights of animals just as we do those of humans. This reflects the fundamental divide in modern normative ethics between deontology, or duty ethics (particularly the theory of rights), and teleological, or consequentialist ethics (particularly utilitarianism). Another example comes from the three main ecocentric approaches. Leopold's land ethic can be seen as a duty ethic: it develops the duties of humanity toward nature from the conception of equal membership of a community. Holmes Rolston's environmental ethics is a form of value ethics and duty ethics: it proposes deducing humanity's duties toward nature from the intrinsic value of nature itself. Arne Næss's deep ecology is a classic teleological ethic, though it is not the utilitarianism that has occupied a central place in modern consequentialist ethics. Rather, it is an ethic of self-actualization (or perfectionism or potentialism), which is a very ancient idea that can be traced in a relatively systematic form right back to Aristotle. In deep ecology, the scope of the theory is broadened from people to all living things. It is a thus a form of virtue ethics, or good-life ethics.

The division in philosophy between theories focusing on the individual and theories based on whole systems also finds its echo in the microcosm of environmental ethics, offering us another way to categorize environmental ethical theories, for example, into theories that give centrality to animals or individual living things or theories that give primacy to the ecosystem as a whole. Some writers on environmental ethics have also applied moral philosophy directly to environmental issues. An example would be applying John Rawls's theory of justice to the question of international and intergenerational environmental justice.

But environmental ethics has also developed its own distinctive theories, which in some cases present serious challenges to traditional general ethics. In part, that is because of the object and scope of the theory. General ethics is concerned with and seeks to regulate relations between persons; environmental ethics shifts that concern to relations between humans and nature, including plants and animals. The internal divisions within environmental ethics seem to be more naturally delineated with reference to this expanded scope: anthropocentric, zoocentric (centered on animals), biocentric, and ecocentric.

The expansion of the ethical scope may look like just a quantitative change, but in fact it qualitatively alters our view of ethics. In fact, it forces a change in the traditional definition of ethics—or develops a whole new ethics. History has seen many expansions of the scope of moral theory from one specific group to another (from a race to a citizenry, from slave owners to slaves, from men to women, and so forth). But if an ethics that was not centered on humans—ecocentric ethics, for example—were to be fully realized and widely accepted and acted on, it would be a bigger change than any previously seen. All people, including infants, those with developmental issues, and those with mental health issues, can be moral subjects just by virtue of their being human beings. But plants, animals, and other components of the natural world do not have that capacity. In order to deal with their almost total lack of moral agency, new concepts must be developed: "moral patients," "moral agents," "moral status," and so on. But why should humanity, made up of moral agents, give moral concern to animals, which lack rationality; to plants, which lack perception; and even to mountains, rivers, ice, and stones, which lack life itself? What is the source of this moral attitude and moral duty? We would need a major reinterpretation of ethics to accommodate this change. We would have to explain the subjects and objects of morality, moral duty and its sources, values, rights, perfection, self-actualization, and many other important concepts in ethics. Animal-centered ethical theories ask us to put ourselves in the position of an animal, to experience its pleasures and pains. Biocentric theories hope that we can appreciate the rhythms of plant life. Ecocentric ethics asks us to "think like a mountain," to abandon the self and to look at all of nature.

All of these types of ethics hope that we will step out of our habitual logic of human self-interest. Just as we rid ourselves of racism, we should rid ourselves of speciesism and sentience bigotry. These are completely new ideas, unlike any from past human history. They call for the shattering of ideas ingrained over thousands of generations and demand that we look at ourselves and the world from a new perspective. The revolutionary implications are obvious. If humanity can sort out its own issues—if we can properly regulate all of our internal relations—so that we can then shift the focus of ethics to the human-nature relationship, then that would be a great day for humankind! But perhaps this narrative is still excessively anthropocentric? At the very least, we can say that at this stage in human history, even if we are still engaged in regulating human relations, we cannot completely ignore the relationship between humanity and nature. Proper settlement of human issues must include proper settlement of human-nature relations. A full conciliation with nature, a "unity between heaven and man," is a dream that we will never abandon. It is a goal toward which we must fight.

Clearly there are beneficial exchanges to be had between spirit and action; theory and practice; spirit and theory; religious and secular spiritual beliefs; general ethics and specific ethics. In the West, we have seen scholars who sought the spiritual roots of ecological crises level severe criticisms against Christianity, and those attacks sparked a green revolution within Christianity. When environmentalists tried to extend universal human rights into environmental ethics, they encountered great difficulty trying to apply rights theory to beings with no consciousness. But new arguments were developed: instead of starting from the rights of these nonhuman entities, we can derive human obligations toward them from their own intrinsic value. In turn, some of the approaches used actually informed broader human rights theory. Anthropocentrism, meanwhile, calls for the application of a two-group system, like the division between the aristocracy and the peasantry: first the conduct of the aristocrats must be noble; second, one must not do to others what one would not have done to oneself. This model can be used to define the human–nature relationship, and it is worth considering.

The invention and development of environmental ethics is a modern, even contemporary development. Two factors reveal the mark of modern society. First, it was the modern, anthropocentric ethic of economics and the satisfaction of material desires that first caused the tension between man and

nature—the ecological crises that forced the environment into our consciousness. Second, the dominant ethics of environmentalism has been based on
equality, which is one of the major features of modern thinking; for example,
the pursuit of equality has become vastly more important than the pursuit of
excellence. The ethics of our times is one that seeks equality and is deeply
concerned with the underprivileged. In today's world, evidently humanity is
the privileged group. Humans can use their rationality, wisdom, and tools to
achieve total dominance over every other living thing. In traditional society,
people pursued spiritual or cultural achievements, which are distinctively
human forms of excellence. There was little concern with the relationship
between humans and other things. In modern society, people primarily pursue excellence defined by things. They are little concerned with spiritual or
cultural matters. But modern society also provides us with another spiritual
and philosophical resource: the urge for equality. This fundamental ethical
urge can be applied in zoocentric, biocentric or ecocentric ethics, all of which
posit some form of equality between humans and nonhumans. Each of these
different ethics expands the scope of equality: to animals, plants, or the
whole of nature. Even weak anthropocentrism is concerned with equality on
some level.

The origins of the urge to equality can be traced back to the shift from
polytheism to monotheism: Arnold Toynbee and many other historians have
discussed how polytheism and the designation of nature and certain natural
objects as sacred have been very important in the preservation of the environment. In the eyes of early cultures, nature was a world of spirits, a world in
which everything had a soul. Their reverence for and awe of nature meant
that they did not act on it however they wished. But monotheism ended the
sacredness of nature. Humans may have become closer to god, but they drew
further away from nature. But a mature monotheism did bring the concept
of universal love or equality among all humans and a compassion for all living things. At first, this concept was purely spiritual, but it developed into a
temporal as well as spiritual notion and entered into our social and political
vocabulary. In modern times, equality has been realized to some extent in our
institutions. Polytheism and pantheism are nearer to nature, but they have
inherent within them an ordering of different levels; monotheism is distant
from nature, but it has within it the concept of equality. So the interactions
between spiritual and philosophical beliefs and their relationship to environmental practice are rather complex. This is something that we must recognize: if we are to understand those interactions, careful analysis is needed.
Simplistic judgments will not suffice.

For billions of years, the Earth's ecosystems have been unconsciously, naturally "seeking" ever greater fitness, and through countless experiments and improvements the Earth finally produced humans, its most brilliant creation, with our consciousness and our intelligence. In that sense, humans are indeed the "paragon of animals." But as Rolston writes, that is also reason for us to be grateful to the natural ecosystem that produced us, just as a flower might be grateful to the tree and to the land. We may be the paragon of animals, but we are not the master of animals. Today we are using our intelligence to sort out our position in the natural world, to properly adjust our relationship with nature, to be kind to nature and all nonhuman entities. This is how we earn our title of "paragon." And there are rich resources in our past and present that can help us to better understand and adapt to our relationship with nature. They just await discovery and proper use.

Building Consensus for Green Action

We have noted that spiritual resources that can support environmental action come from a wide range of sources. Many and various too are the environmental philosophies that explain the relationship between man and nature and our obligations toward nature. So is there not a need to build consensus? Is it even possible? If the answers are positive, then on what level do we build consensus?

Over the past twenty or more years of fast economic growth in China, many environmental problems have emerged. We can even be said to be facing an environmental crisis. This dangerous situation has forced environmental philosophers to explore all kinds of ideas, spiritual resources, and solutions, both ancient and modern, to help us resolve our environmental problems. There is much to be learned from the problems, solutions, and spiritual and philosophical resources used in other countries. However, China's problems are both similar to and different from those of other countries. Our solutions must be coordinated with those of other nations and must tackle global issues; at the same time, they must be crafted in the context of our own cultural traditions, social institutions, and specific environmental problems. We have to mobilize all of the spiritual resources that we can and present theories of environmental ethics that are compatible with the realities of today's China if we are to promote a wider awareness of environmental issues among Chinese people.

Contemporary environmental philosophy overseas has arisen from the issues in other countries. It is adapted to the social institutions of other countries and founded on the historical and cultural bedrock of those countries. There are bound to be differences between them and China in terms of the priority of issues, the seriousness of problems, and the supporting argumentation. But of course, we all live on the same planet. We face global problems as well as local problems, so the task of forging common goals while respecting local differences is always going to be a major concern. Moreover, China is a multi-ethnic state that encompasses many different histories and belief systems. Broad-based cooperation is needed to solve our increasingly grave environmental problems, but respecting reasonable beliefs and ways of life is a precondition for activating various philosophies and spiritual resources and bringing them into our consensus. This will remain a major area for research and discussion in the long term. Environmental work requires participation from every member of society, and the consequences will have a huge impact on all of us, on our children, and on our mother Earth. Building consensus for green action is vital, because action can be properly motivated and coordinated only through consensus. But surveys show that Chinese people are still rather lacking in environmental awareness, or rather, that disparity in awareness among people is very great. The importance of creating a shared understanding is thus very clear.

The kind of consensus that we build depends very much on the level on which we want to build it. In this age, can we achieve consensus on the level of spiritual beliefs? I don't believe that it's possible. Can we identify the spiritual beliefs that will be most conducive to environmental protection, then require every person to have faith in them? Can we turn everyone into a Christian, a Buddhist, a Muslim, an animist, or an atheist? Without even going into the constitutional issue of freedom of belief, religious diversity is a widely accepted principle in a modern society. It is already—or is fast becoming—a simple fact of life. It is likely to be seen as the ongoing "normal." All people have the right to retain their own fundamental beliefs and their own fundamental understanding of the meaning of life and their ultimate goals, so long as they do not interfere with the equal right of others to do the same. By the same token, they may also act on their beliefs. This concept is already one of the shared fundamentals of our society. Spiritual beliefs are those beliefs that are totalizing, that pervade every aspect of our lives and represent our ultimate life goals. And they exist on their own plane. They cannot—and should not—be forced, and modern society increasingly accepts that fact.

So perhaps we could look to build consensus on the level of theory. But we must ask ourselves once again exactly what kind of consensus it is that we are looking for. Is it just consensus among academics? Clearly not. We want a far-reaching agreement to which the whole of society will assent. And we want a consensus that is oriented toward action. There is no need for a theory that is precise, consistent, lofty, and all-encompassing or even one that contains some "ultimate truth." At this point, we perhaps encounter a difficulty. It is possible that we might be especially drawn to one particular theory, by its truth or because of our own spiritual beliefs. But we may find that when we attempt to promote this theory to others, they do not find it persuasive. We want to coordinate action and bring others around to our way of thinking, but our preferred theory is not reaching the greatest number of people. We may have to step down in theoretical terms, to use a "lower" theory in order to generate broader agreement. We may keep our highest spiritual understanding and hope that it will influence others in quieter and more subtle ways. But in our rational arguments, we must consider their effectiveness in persuading others, at least at first.

Many great environmental advocates have run into this problem. John Muir, one of the forces behind the establishment of U.S. national parks and a passionate protector of wilderness, wrote many essays about the rights of orchids, rattlesnakes, alligators, and other creatures before he came to California. His views at that time were biocentric—rooted in the importance of life itself. But when he was faced with the task of persuading the U.S. government and people that they should save the forests and wilderness, he made his arguments primarily in terms of their value to humanity. He said that they were valuable for restoring the human spirit, showing us beauty, and protecting our watersheds and catchment areas. His arguments were in fact anthropocentric. He moderated his views—we could say that he "climbed down" from his original position. Leopold and many others are said to have used the same strategy when trying to coordinate environmental action.

Is this dishonesty? I think not. This strategy was to some extent forced on Muir, but there was also a good reason for it. Muir was a pioneer, but his beliefs and the beliefs current among the American public at the time were still compatible in many areas. At the very least, there were elements that could be exploited to build consensus. And in order to achieve success in his plan for environmental action, he had to start with the basic understanding of environmental issues shared by realistic people. In other words, when we attempt to build broad social consensus, we may have to start with finding the lowest common denominator. We may have to start by asking the public to understand the problems and crises in the environment today. This understanding may at first be people-oriented; indeed, it may be stated in terms of the interests of the people involved. It is just that they had not previously considered their real interests in the broad and long-term way in which those interests are now presented.

We want to create a level of alarm among the public, to make them feel that they ought to do something—or more precisely, that first of all they ought *not* to do something: they ought not to cut down forests and pollute rivers. People should make an effort to stop doing the things that cause such harm to the natural environment. It is particularly urgent in China. We cannot allow any more pollution of our lakes, rivers, and oceans. We don't have any unpolluted rivers left. People must stop hunting endangered species like the Tibetan antelope and snub-nosed monkeys and stop destroying their habitats. The populations of these animals have plummeted over the last decade or more, and they are now on the brink of extinction. We must stop destroying grasslands if we are to reduce sandstorms, and on and on. The first thing that we need to do is to generate a consensus to put an end to our most damaging behaviors and build the will to act on that consensus.

This process will inevitably be one of finding common ground, but the shared ground will be small. One may think that such a small patch of common ground will not be large enough, but it is wrong not to look for it. In terms of theory, the best option for building a broad consensus seems to be a form of weak or enlightened anthropocentrism. There exists a striking contrast: within the world of environmental ethics studies, it seems that non-anthropocentric theories dominate, at least in China. Most people engaged in environmental ethics reject human-based ethics in favor of some other form. But in the real world, the opposite view prevails. When asked, most people espouse an anthropocentric view. Even enlightened anthropocentrism is rare. Many people are completely devoid of environmental awareness. So in realistic terms, to advance our environmental work, we must first build a powerful anthropocentric ethic that includes environmental consciousness. Injecting holistic, long-term thinking into anthropocentrism is a necessary step along the way. Of course, we may be able to build many different levels of consensus. The broadest level could extend to the whole community, but there could also be greater consensus among more restricted groups, perhaps on higher issues. That way we could have concentric circles of agreement and political action, all with the environment at their heart.

If we take a broader perspective, we see that environmentalism is not just an issue of the human–nature relationship. It also touches on relations between people and between people and systems and on the relations of a person with him- or herself. It touches on human values and goals, on what we ultimately want and pursue. If material desires and economic well-being really are the foundations of society, then exactly how much material stuff should we have? How much is enough? Does the human–nature relationship and real harmony depend on changing our modern lifestyles and values? What sort of institutional guarantees or changes are necessary? Which should come first, changes in attitude or institutional changes? Thus we see that environmental ethics must engage with politics, economics, sociology, psychology, the law, and all of the humanities.

Wang Lixiong has written an article titled "Leaving the Green Ivory Tower," commenting on current environmental problems and future possible solutions.[6] Wang discusses the Xilin Gol grasslands, where the local herders remember that when they were young their biggest problem was the sheep and cows disappearing into the tall grass. Now the grass is gone because of lack of water due to environmental degradation, and they can see rabbits running a mile away across the scrub. On the way to Baiyangdian Lake, Wang needed water for his radiator. He had to let out a lot of rope before he reached the water at the bottom of the well. A local saw him and his colleagues and told them that you used to be able to lie at the edge of the well and drink directly from the water.

If we just look at the environment around us, the degradation of nature and the depletion of natural resources are very apparent, and they affect everyone. The question Wang raises is this: If humanity genuinely tries to protect the environment, can we solve our environmental problems? He believes that we cannot and that the reason relates to what is referred to in environmental circles as the distinction between "light green" and "deep green." "Light green" involves environmental protection but nothing more. "Deep green" is a view that the real route out of our environmental crisis lies in fundamentally changing human lifestyles. Industrialized civilization is founded on several ideas. One is materialism, in which social progress is measured in terms of material wealth, the pursuit of which has given rise to the contradiction of trying to extract limitless growth from limited resources. Another is consumerism, in which sensory enjoyment becomes the meaning

---

6. The essay appears in Wang Lixiong, *The Spiritual Journey of a Free Soul* (China Film Press). Wang Lixiong (王力雄, 1953–), a native of Changchun, Jilin Province, is a Chinese writer, scholar, and advocate for environmental protection. He was one of the founders of the Friends of Nature (自然之友), the first nongovernmental organization to focus on environmental protection. He is best known for his political prophecy novel, *Yellow Peril*, and for his writings on religion and ethnicity in Tibet. More recently, Wang also offered a provocative analysis of ethnic tensions in Xinjiang.

of human existence. Deep green thinkers believe that our environmental problems are to some extent problems of human attitudes. So long as humanity's dominant philosophy and lifestyle remain unchanged, mere environmental protection cannot save us. So the deep green objective is for people to reject the excesses of consumerism and return to lives of restraint, simplicity, and spirituality. But is this really possible? Wang is not optimistic about the prospects. He believes that it will require changes in our social systems if the deep green philosophy is to advance out of the ivory tower and be applied in modifying lifestyles. If our systems do not change, then environmental protection will remain at the light green level. Deep green will remain a dream, and we will be unable to attain our objective of saving the Earth— or more precisely, of saving ourselves.

Wang's essay raises important questions that are worthy of serious thought, but it presents a rather pessimistic view. Of course, even if it is correct, so long as these problems are properly handled, they need not stop the development of the will and commitment to act. As Liang Congjie, director of Friends of Nature, said, every person can do his or her part—all people can do "whatever is in their power to do." Dealing with our severe environmental pressures may indeed require a two-pronged solution, with changes in both our systems and our attitudes. Attitudes can be addressed by having ecologists and others correct public misunderstandings about the environment and encourage people to take up environmental protection for themselves and make it part of their own lifestyle. Changing social systems demands institutional innovation and adaptations to which many fields must contribute.

Even if institutional changes are the primary mechanism, such changes still depend on people, though they may compose only a small minority at first. So it seems that the first priority must still be conveying to people an awareness and a sense of crisis. In the United States in the 1940s and 1950s, Aldo Leopold's books received only a very muted response. Sometimes it was hard for him to find a publisher. Then in the 1960s, Rachel Carson's *Silent Spring* sounded a sudden wake-up call, showing that the ecological damage to which people had become inured now represented a major threat to all life. As a result, the field of environmental ethics grew explosively in the 1970s. In China, we worked for many years under the assumption that we were fighting nature, that we had to overcome it, that we must "make the mountains bow their heads and make the rivers stand aside." One lovely and popular song, *The Little Swallow*, speaks of building a factory in the countryside because "the spring here is so beautiful" and expresses the hope that the listener will come next year because then "the spring here will be more beautiful"—because there will be more smoking chimneys and roaring machines. Even in the 1980s, there was very little environmental awareness. But by the 1990s nature was beginning to take its revenge, punishing us for the damage that we had done. Also, following work by individuals, green organizations, and government agencies, there was significantly more and deeper popular understanding of environmental ideas.

To return to the themes of this volume, our exploration centers on people's attitudes and philosophy. This volume does not address social institutions or specific ethical rules. It attempts to distinguish two levels of environmental thought—spiritual resources and philosophical theory—and on that basis to help people with different cultural backgrounds and beliefs find common ground. At the very least, it tries to supply a list of philosophical options as candidates for forming that common ground. My further hope is that readers can find in this book support for their own ideas and theories and that they will be inspired to seek in their own particular lifestyle and cultural background the spiritual resources and positive reinforcement that they need to support their own environmentalism. They can then develop more consistent environmental rules in coordination with others across society, while also being open to other spiritual beliefs.

Today, China is still a long way from developing a fully worked out environmental philosophy or environmental ethics of its own. As in the economic sphere, we are still a developing nation. Today's world is globalized in terms of both our economies and our environmental problems. We have no option but to take a global perspective. We cannot but borrow from the experience and the intellectual insights of the first industrialized nations, which encountered their own environmental problems long before we did. This is the only way in which we can start to piece together an ecology and an environmentalism for China—the only way in which we can reach deep and lasting agreement on the question of action, so that we can avoid the pitfalls that other countries have hit before us. Ultimately, we need to work on every level of our consciousness: beliefs, emotions, rationality, experience, intuition. We must not reject any idea on any level that could help us in our fight to improve the environment. And we must hope that no matter how minimal it may be, we can find some broad-based consensus and broad-based will to act.

PART VI

CHINESE ETHICAL DIALOGUE WITH THE WEST AND THE WORLD

CHAPTER SIXTEEN

The Possibilities and Limits of Moral Philosophy

What can moral philosophy do? What expectations can we have of moral philosophy? We can list three things that people often hope moral philosophy will do: clarify moral concepts; provide arguments or foundations for moral rules; and reflect on human life and give some explanation of it or reveal its meaning. Most people have little doubt that moral philosophy can successfully accomplish the first task. Even those who are very skeptical of the utility of moral philosophy believe that it can achieve something in the line of clarification. And it seems that we can provide some weak defense of its ability to achieve the third goal as well. Reflection generally does offer some form of meaning, even if that meaning is not final or absolute. The greatest controversy and doubt seem to hang over its ability to formulate arguments for moral rules—which, because moral rules involve other people and the community, is its most important job. Often arguments for moral rules are presented in a part–whole structure: an argument for a part is taken to be an argument for the whole, and vice versa.

This chapter addresses mainly the second objective. First it surveys the approach of Bernard Williams, then uses a case study to discuss the limitations and possibilities of moral philosophy. But the aim of the chapter is not to derive some conclusion through meticulous argument—it is to bring to light a problem and present it as clearly and incisively as possible.

This chapter is an edited version of an article first published in *Fudan Journal*, no. 4 (2006).

Bernard Williams and the Meaning of "Moral Philosophy"

Bernard Williams is skeptical of and presents a powerful late-modern challenge to normative theory. He defines "moral philosophy" as the attempt to provide grounds or arguments for moral rules. In *Ethics and the Limits of Philosophy*, he writes that morality should be understood as a particular development of ethics. It is a set of views about obligations derived in a particular way, based on particular assumptions. Therefore, he says, under most circumstances he uses the term "ethics" to mean the scope of this area of study and the term "moral philosophy" to denote the narrower system.[1] He believes that there are two basic types of moral philosophy. The first is the relatively formal and abstract Kantian philosophy; the second is the richer, more concrete Aristotelian philosophy. Both search for an Archimedean "place to stand," a place on which to ground morality.

In *Ethics and the Limits of Philosophy*, Williams explores one of the limits of philosophical research. He claims that the character of philosophy is reflective and summative; it makes arguments that are rationally persuasive. But we must not forget that our age is very different from that of Socrates: modern life is so reflexive and self-conscious that philosophy can no longer be distinguished from other kinds of activity such as law, medicine, and literature. Williams goes so far as to say that philosophy tends to destroy moral knowledge inherited from traditional culture, so that ethics can be objective only so long as it is ignorant of philosophy. But he says that he wants to focus his attention on the most important or most interesting developments in moral philosophy, though he says he is very suspicious of the use of moral philosophy. Or more broadly, he is very doubtful that philosophical grounds exist for moral rules and concepts. He doubts the intelligibility of moral values and the concepts that they invoke. He also doubts the possibility of philosophical arguments for ethical rules. In particular, he does not believe that philosophy can "ground" or "prove" morality to an amoralist or a skeptic. That does not mean that Williams himself was either an immoralist or an amoralist. He does not reject the kinds of behavior that morality generally prescribes, and he often supports the institutions praised by moral common sense, such as liberal democracy. What he rejects is this idea: that philosophy can provide evidence for morality through exegesis of moral concepts.[2]

1. Bernard Williams, *Ethics and the Limits of Philosophy* (Harvard University Press, 1985), p. 6.

2. See Denise Peterfreund, *Great Traditions in Ethics* (Peking University Press, 2002). Peterfreund explicitly lists Williams as an "ethics skeptic." The following description is

Williams believes that the motivation to adhere to moral standards arises from a person's character. Most people want to adhere to moral standards; if people did not have this desire or need, there is no way that philosophical argument could implant that desire in them or demonstrate that they must hold these ideas. Williams gives the example of Callicles, who is not persuaded by the eloquence of Socrates in the *Gorgias*. He suggests that philosophy can at most give those who already have that desire within them an explanation of the meaning of their motivation. Williams not only believes that philosophy is powerless to persuade the amoralist, he also thinks that this project is unnecessary: that there is no need to persuade such a person. We could use other, non-philosophical arguments to shape people's actions into something that the majority of us can accept. Or we have only to rely on this fact: most people can follow moral rules without any need for arguments at all.

Williams believes that skepticism about a certain kind of knowledge could cause everyone to reject that knowledge. But ethical skepticism does not cause entire societies to reject ethics, though it might make one person reject one kind of ethical life. Ethical skeptics are different from skeptics of scientific knowledge. Ethical skeptics can admit the existence of a kind of ethical knowledge; they just deny that it has any force to decide a person's action. Skepticism of ethics is skepticism of the force of ethics. Unlike ordinary skeptics, ethical skeptics may simply wish to leave behind all discussion of morality but still go on living their life. There is no reason to think that people who do not want an explanation of ethical life necessarily want to live unethical or immoral lives. But Williams wishes to leave open the possibility of all kinds of life, even unethical lives. So the problem is not in what we should say to the skeptic. Better to say that we may want to explain ethics to those who are already living an ethical life. And we can offer them political institutions to support this kind of life. To be sure, Williams's skepticism is not a general or extreme skepticism but a rather mild skepticism. He writes, "A skeptic, after all, is merely skeptical. As far as possible, he neither asserts nor denies."[3]

Williams asks: Is there an Archimedean point for philosophy? And is there a solid foundation that allows philosophy to argue for morality using a method that all people will accept, with the force to make all people adopt ethical standards? Kant believed that the Archimedean point was the concept

---

taken from this volume. *The Oxford Dictionary of Philosophy* says that Williams takes a relativist position on ethics. He rejects Aristotle's and Kant's belief that virtue develops by training the rationality of the heart.

3. Williams, *Ethics and the Limits of Philosophy*, p. 27.

of "rational" behavior. Aristotle believed it was "living a specifically human life." Williams is especially skeptical of Kantian ethics. He doubts that all those who reject morality are really irrational or unreasonable. Though he seems to agree that a society without morality would be unsustainable, that does not mean that people who reject moral language and practices are irrational. For example, a person may study mathematics and use logic to reflect on other areas of his life. He may rationally plan his future. This kind of person can understand moral language but thinks that moral language has no influence on his decisions about how to act. Williams also criticizes utilitarianism, but his primary position is to reject all moral theories that use philosophical argument. His meaning is perhaps that philosophy must halt before ethical rules begin. Williams did not support either egoism or egocentrism, nor did he think that rejecting moral theory meant embracing egoism. Rather he thought that personal plans were more important than some ethical objectives. After arguing that there is no Archimedean point, Williams expresses the hope that there is a way of thinking that can encourage people to adopt humane rules. He suggests that this way of thinking is truth, honesty, and the meaning of the individual life.

However, what we are concerned with here is one aspect of Williams's suspicion of moral philosophy, one of the most powerful and challenging aspects of his views. So the question we posed at the beginning of this chapter can be rewritten in a more focused way: Does moral philosophy offer supporting arguments and grounding for rules of conduct? Williams thinks that it is impossible—and unnecessary—for it to do so. The arguments of moral philosophy cannot persuade the skeptic, but even if they do, it does not matter, because even skeptics generally live orderly lives. Skeptics already are obeying moral rules; they just maintain an ongoing interest in asking questions and exploring the truth. Moral philosophers not only lack the ability to convince them, they ought not to try—at least, they have no need to do so. There is no need to pester skeptics with arguments; just let them be. They do not pose any serious threat to society. (There is a kind of relativism that may be a special "failing of the age" or "failing of reflection," one that has no benefits for humanity or even for the self. But once a person has "learned" skepticism, it is impossible to make her "unlearn" it. Once people have been "enlightened," they cannot be unenlightened.)

Moreover, the skeptics are very few in number. Most people never even consider this kind of doubt, and they have no need to be persuaded of the validity of moral rules or their obligation to follow them. So the only people moral philosophers can persuade are those who are already inclined to be persuaded. They already have the moral rules in their minds, but perhaps in a hazy, unclear form; philosophers just make clear to them what they already know. As for those people who do not share these beliefs, there is no way to persuade them through reflection on philosophy or rational argument. And there is no need to do so.

The reading above may have extrapolated too much from the text. Williams's arguments are indubitably rather different from those of previous skeptics, but he bases them firmly in human nature, noting the differences among people. In particular, he notices a distinction that I am very interested in: the distinction between the minority and the majority. So should moral philosophy stop making arguments for substantive ethical rules? At least stop making them to skeptics? But were these arguments aimed mostly at relativists in the first place? Because skeptics and relativists do not simply believe their viewpoints themselves, they also influence other people. Are many people undecided? And are moral debates and arguments in fact not aimed at our interlocutors but presented in an attempt to win over the audience that is still undecided on an issue? On every question, it is the vocal minority that influences the silent majority. How does moral philosophy respond to people who doubt its possibility on an epistemological level? And what can moral philosophy do about people who intend to reject and violate moral rules in their behavior? Can moral philosophy just ignore them as well?

It is worth looking once again at a rather extreme real example to see whether morality can have some force among people who totally reject moral rules for their behavior. These rejecters of morality present the greatest real threat to society, because skeptics like Williams tend to follow moral rules in real life, even to be rather honorable. But there remains a connection between rejecters and skeptics. Skeptics can deeply influence or even determine the behavior of rejecters. Think of Ivan in Dostoevsky's *Brothers Karamazov*, always pondering this question: If God is dead, is everything now permitted? Can we even murder? Even our own father? Of course, he never acts, but Fyodor Karamazov is killed by his illegitimate son, who has been influenced by Ivan's ideas and acts on them. So can we revive and maintain a moral theory and philosophy that may be more traditional but that retains some moral force? And can this moral philosophy have an impact on or improve the conduct of those who would violate the demands of moral rules?

Case Study: Fu Hegong and the Limits of Moral Philosophy

A story in the September 10, 2005, edition of the *Beijing News* reported that Fu Hegong, a thirty-one-year-old man from Miyun, had been brought before Beijing No. 2 Intermediate Court accused of committing the Beixin Kindergarten murders in Dongcheng District in October of the previous year, when a school was broken into and a teacher and student were assaulted and killed. He was found guilty of multiple counts of robbery, murder, theft, rape, and indecent assault and was sentenced to death. When Fu was led into the courtroom, observers noticed that he was wearing only a pair of shorts and a sleeveless jacket over his bare chest. He had orange flip-flops on his feet, and the expression on his bearded face was defiant. He was thin, but his arms were large and powerful. In the court, Fu's responses were very calm. He listened with eyes half closed as the court read out its verdict, occasionally looking to the left and right. But his expression remained impassive. When he heard the court sentence him to death, he responded briefly to the question of his appeal: "No appeal." Then he shrugged his shoulders and said a little louder, "The sentence is just right, not too heavy." According to his defense lawyer, in his testimony at the trial the previous month, Fu had requested that the court give him the death penalty.

There is no disputing that Fu Hegong was an incredibly vicious killer. He killed a woman and child in order to steal goods worth no more than a few hundred yuan, and he was a repeat offender. Since his eighteenth birthday, he had been jailed twice before. Each time he was released, he went back to his life of crime. Anyone who tried to stop him from stealing was killed without hesitation. His very existence was an affront to society. According to his own testimony, he did not want to be a public enemy, but at the very least, he had little regard for the values of his community. He clearly understood his own behavior and his situation. He was not deluded in any way.

After the sentencing, when Fu talked to the media, one phrase that came up repeatedly was, "No reason." He was asked, "Why did you kill people?" He replied, "No reason. I wanted to kill them so I killed them." "Why did you kill a child as well? How could you do that?" "No reason. I had to do it if I wanted them dead." "Don't you have any regrets at all?" "No reason to regret anything." "What do you want to say to the families of the victims?" "Nothing to say." "You'd been to prison before. Didn't you think of reforming yourself? Why did you go back to crime?" "No reason." To Fu, nothing seemed to matter at all. Nothing constituted a reason, nothing had any weight—not his own death, not his own occasional kindnesses, not the other crimes that he confessed to the police. None of them mattered, and he gave no explanations. He made no attempt to defend himself at all. Perhaps he knew that no defense would make any difference.[4]

We have seen many different levels of regret in people after committing a crime. Sometimes the guilt is so much that only death releases them.[5] This may be moral philosophy working upon them. Some even start to show an interest in ethics. Their moral philosophy or beliefs start to play an important role for them, even if they had never considered morality worth thinking about before. But what can moral philosophy do for someone like Fu Hegong? To be sure, it may be that nothing can be done—by moral philosophy or any other philosophy or even any beliefs. Perhaps his spirit was entirely insensible to them. Or perhaps he had his own ideas, maybe very specific ideas, but he was completely closed off to all communication on the moral level. In theory, of course, anyone may change so long as he is still alive. There is an optimistic theory of education that says that if we live long enough, anyone can become a good person. But this person, Fu Hegong, was to die very soon. He was to die defined by his crimes and perhaps carrying other secrets to his grave. And now, he is dead.

Fu's crimes do not seem to be obviously a product of their time or of our society. He just said that he was "the most defective kind of person." He said that he killed for no reason, not because of any kind of grudge against society. Miyun, the town near Beijing where he lived, is not especially impoverished. That means that his crimes are ones that could have happened in any society. Though people like Fu are only ever a tiny minority, antisocial ele-

4. On December 20, 2005, Fu Hegong was executed. He had remained unconcerned throughout, but in his last meeting with his mother, he broke down and cried. "Mom," he said to his white-haired mother, "I'm sorry." His mother comforted him. "I don't hate you. After you're dead, I'll take you home." Weeping herself, she urged him, "Be a good person in your next life. Don't do this again."

5. For example, I saw a case in which a father had killed his own son because he would not obey the father and was causing trouble in the village. After a month in prison, the father died of grief before he could even be sentenced. The differences in these cases make us think of the difficulty of achieving true "equality of punishment." This kind of equality is like a backward version of "economic equality." To achieve it, we would have to apply different sentences for the same crimes, because criminals will suffer the pricking of their consciences in differing degrees and because their sensitivity to punishment varies. The sensitive would have to receive lighter penalties, the hardened criminals heavier sentences. But this equality of punishment would be virtually impossible to put into practice, and it is not a goal as widely agreed upon and pursued as economic equality.

ments will exist in greater or lesser numbers in all communities. In a good society, most of them will probably never commit a crime, but however ideal the community might be, crime can never be completely prevented.

So at this point do we just turn the issue over to the law? Kill the criminal and get it over with? Perhaps, as the criminal's own behavior seems to indicate, for him this is not a moral case at all. It is just a legal issue: the law caught him, so he is ready to die. If the law did not catch him, then he would carry on with his life as heedlessly as before. He may even define right and wrong to himself in just this way: if the law catches him, he was wrong; if the law does not catch him, then he was right. Can we see law and morality in the same way? Can we ignore issues of justice and conclude that the law is effective because it ultimately has the power to compel? Is the reason that the law has no moral foundation just that morality itself has no foundation? But if laws like "thou shalt not kill" are valid only because people with power have made them—if they are not also absolute moral rules and commandments—then wouldn't their power be greatly diminished?

Moral philosophy may be powerless against the Fu Hegong that we saw in the courtroom. But there are two things worth noting. The first is that the police investigation showed that Fu had previously tried to throttle a child but stopped halfway through. He refused to explain his behavior in court. Later, he did reply to a question from the media about it: "I felt sorry for him for a moment." Was this real pity? Brief, but pure and moral? The second point of interest is Fu's answer to a journalist who asked what Fu thought of being given the death penalty: "You've got to pay for a life with a life, haven't you?" The journalist pressed Fu further: "How can you make up for your crimes?" Fu replied, "I'll pay for them with my life." The journalist persisted: "How many lives can your one life pay for?" For the first time, Fu gave no reply. He could not speak, and he gave no more answers. Does this show that the moral principles that he had absorbed over the years were now having some effect? That they did in fact have a place in his heart? Can we understand it this way: that a criminal guilty of such horrific crimes and apparently indifferent to them still at some level recognizes the rule "Thou shalt not kill"? That he still has some compassion in his heart, though it may be exceedingly weak and fleeting? If that is the case, if there is a possibility that this kind of criminal exists, then we must not underestimate the force of morality. If moral philosophy can help us do something, however little, then we should do that something.

Moreover, what we see here is the confluence of the emotional and the rational. On the one hand, moral philosophy is working to demonstrate and argue for the necessity of basic moral rules—to demonstrate and prove them to all people, including skeptics and immoral persons. On other hand, we may have hope that virtually every human heart has the capacity for compassion, which can be the motivation for acting on these moral principles, however weak and hazy these feelings and principles may be among this small minority. We have already noted that Fu Hegong represents an extreme case. If even this person, this perpetrator of revolting crimes, still possessed the smallest possibility of a turn toward the good, then we must not underestimate the role that moral philosophy can play and must not cast it aside too incautiously. If there is still the possibility that moral philosophy can be of use to a person like Fu Hegong, then is it not much more likely to be of use to others? It's true that what we have seen of Fu Hegong is a refusal to reflect. But could there be some connection between his refusal to reflect, on one hand, and excessive hyper-reflection (which leans toward relativism and nihilism), on the other?

The Usefulness of Moral Philosophy

The case of Fu Hegong shows that moral philosophy has much to offer. It can clarify moral concepts and moral language, and it can elaborate on the sources of morality, whether they are rational or emotional sources. Here we have to distinguish between two different levels: one, encompassing moral principles, rules, and standards; the second, encompassing moral reasons and motivations. The two levels should not be confused. The level of moral principles and rules is primary. That means that we should first consider whether or not there are universal rules and only then consider the question of motivation.[6] To put this in the language of Chinese philosophy, principles and rules are the *benyuan*, the substance of morality; motivation is *xiuyang*, or moral education, development, and technique. There is a school of psychological Confucianism that claims that "substance and application are the same." This school is much concerned with moral agency and the impor-

6. I recently read a passage by Thomas Nagel: "If your reasons for doing things depend on your motives and people's motives can vary greatly, then it looks as though there won't be a single right and wrong for everybody . . . if people's basic motives differ, there won't be one basic standard of behavior that everyone has a reason to follow." See Thomas Nagel, *What Does It All Mean?* (Contemporary China Publishing House, 2005), p. 88. While it is possible that universal standards can be refuted by the fact that people have different motives for their actions (motives will always vary), it remains true that the truth of a single standard does not depend on people's actual motives.

tance of moral practice. But I believe that the principles and rules have priority over the motivations. As I understand it, as our moral thought traverses these two levels, the first level of questioning is this: Are there ultimate standards or right and wrong, of good and evil? If there are, what are they based on? The second level explores moral motivations, including moral concerns, interests, benefits, and so forth. That is, it explores how to make people obey moral principles. Kant considered primarily the first level of questioning: he was concerned with the ultimate basis or foundation of morality. In theoretical terms, the first level seems to be more fundamental, or prior. It includes questions that the moral philosopher cannot ignore, and those questions are the more important and urgent for modern societies.[7] Of course we must bear the realities of practice in mind; we must be sensitive to reality. But practical questions of feasibility cannot be our standard for deciding whether a moral principle is correct. When we think about reality, we consider carefully the basic consensus that a society needs in order to exist and confront the diversity of values that modern societies must deal with.

The case of Fu Hegong hints at the two major directions in which moral philosophy can usefully take us. One direction is the grounding or arguments for moral principles and rules. We can still draw inspiration from Kant's principle of universal law. Today we may not have the same high expectation that the principle of universal applicability can be used to decide moral rules; we do not see it as the formative principle for moral rules, merely as an exclusionary principle. So instead we focus on the negative form and its ability to rule out moral rules, so that the most powerful moral rules may appear in the form of negative commandments like "Thou shalt not kill."[8] The other direction is moral motivations or wellsprings of morality. We can perhaps continue to attempt to stimulate a feeling of compassion toward other people, but this feeling of compassion is not, as Rousseau imagined it, based on self-love. Rather, it is as Mencius described it, unrelated to any self-love or self-interest. Moral philosophy cannot but aim for universality, and it may discover this universality in the compassionate heart that Mencius illustrated with his example of a child about to fall into a well.

But moral philosophy has real limits. The universality to which moral philosophy aspires will not receive assent from every person, and it is even less likely that every person will actually follow moral rules. Moral rules may be

7. See He, "Modern Ethics: Between Kant and Rousseau," *Du Shu*, no. 12 (2004).

8. His most persuasive example may be that "false promises" cannot be universalized.

proven, but proof will not be enough. Exceptions will always arise—but isn't that precisely why we need moral rules? Because there are always exceptions? Modern morality must cater to all people; it must achieve an objective universality to which all people will aspire. But in reality, the moral consensus that it seeks does not mean that every person will in fact assent. Assent may come only from a majority. The rule that "'ought to' implies 'is able to'" does not mean that all people are "able to." It may just be that most people are "able" under ordinary circumstances. The limitations of modern moral philosophy are the limitations of human nature, the limitations of crowds, and the limitations of society.

In the realm of knowledge, people can conduct unlimited experiments. But at the same time, we had best recognize our own limits. This admonition applies in particular to moral philosophy when it touches on other people and the community and even more on moral philosophy's most important subdiscipline: political philosophy. We are mortal beings, so our first priority is to consider the mortality of all, not personal immortality. In the philosophy of the good life today, it seems that we can no longer say to everyone that the unexamined life is not worth living. At most we can say that to ourselves, to lovers of knowledge, to philosophers. We also have to consider the fact that not everyone will, like Kant, perceive the "moral law within" that reflects the "starry skies above." Even all those who can perceive it will not experience the same "renewed and increasing awe and reverence."

Philosophy is a reflective exercise. The majority of people do not reflect but perhaps still follow moral rules or popular custom. Some of those people may even have a natural purity, conscience, and virtue. Of course, some of the nonreflective do not follow moral rules. The reflective minority also includes both those who become more committed to and those who become skeptical of moral rules as a result of reflection. The skeptics may continue to obey moral rules, or they may no longer obey them. One might ask exactly what it is that motivates some reflective skeptics to continue to obey moral rules. People come to moral compliance by a variety of routes, some rational, some intuitive, some emotional, and some habitual: fear of retribution—the concepts of karma or heaven and hell—or love of God, or some combination of those ideas. So do we also need to consider a multitrack approach to morality?

Arguments and constructions that pursue moral rules, like those of John Rawls, for example, are a form of philosophical reflection. So too is the work of Bernard Williams, attempting to cast doubt on and decompose moral rules. All such reflections have their limits. And in our modern society, with its democracy of ideas and highly advanced communications media, there is no distance between those who reflect and those who do not. Those who desire knowledge must therefore find a subtle balance between a rational individual honesty and a caring and concern for society. Today, we also need to be alert against "hyper-reflectiveness," which is corrosive to society's fundamental morality. We should consider doing some reflecting on reflection itself.

CHAPTER SEVENTEEN

The Intellectual Legacy of John Rawls

The best way to commemorate thinkers—particularly a great thinker like John Rawls—is to give due attention to their ideas, conducting a careful inventory of their legacy and thinking their thoughts for a while. That requires detailed analysis and discussion of their ideas from a range of perspectives, up to and including criticism and serious skepticism of those ideas. I myself have much to be grateful to Rawls for. In a sense, it was his ideas that cured or at least shifted my sense of pessimism and disappointment and corrected my excessive yearning for romantic, aesthetic individualism and personal redemption. But in this chapter, I would like to talk not so much about what Rawls has taught us, but about what we as scholars of China can say to his legacy. This is an attempt to achieve a "reflective equilibrium" on a larger scale, though for the most part I will be using Rawls's own concepts.

Rawls developed and painstakingly argued a theory of social justice, of "justice as fairness" (*A Theory of Justice*, 1971). He also tried to develop from it an "overlapping consensus" on the political level for societies with reasonable values pluralism (*Political Liberalism*, 1993) and attempted to extend it from domestic to international law (*The Law of Peoples*, 1999). Rawls argued for the application of two principles of justice in forming the basic structure of a society. The first is the requirement that all people should have equal basic freedoms; the second is that all people should have "fair equality of opportunity." There is also the famed "difference principle": that the only differences

This chapter is an edited version of an article first published in *Book Town*, no. 1 (2003).

allowed are those that bring the most benefit for the most disadvantaged. The first principle is a guarantee of freedom: freedom of conscience, belief, speech, and political participation. The second is about equality of livelihood and of wealth to the extent that it is possible. But the first principle must come before the second principle. Only after the first is satisfied can we think about satisfying the second. These two principles of justice do not allow for any exchanges of the goods involved. For example, it is not permissible to violate the basic freedoms of the minority in the name of the majority. Furthermore, the difference principle also demands that the interests of the most disadvantaged groups be guaranteed, because they must receive the maximum possible benefit from any difference in which they are the worse off.

Rawls saw his theory of justice as abstract and universal. It should apply to an ideal "well-ordered" society, one in which people would continue to obey his principles of justice once they had chosen and consented to them. In reality, the two principles of justice reflect the conclusions of American or Western society: that is, they are supported through a process of repeated reflection and judgment within those societies. But Western society, like any other, is a product of history. If we examine the two principles of justice in the context of the recent history of social systems and political thought in the West and then in the context of the rest of the contemporary world (particularly the harsh realities of non-Western civilizations such as China), we may find that we need to add an extra principle of justice prior to both of Rawls's principles: the principle of the preservation of life. This principle demands that the elements necessary for survival be provided before anything else. Of course, one can also argue that Rawls's two principles incorporate the preservation of life as a given, or even on some higher level. But we need to consider whether the preservation of life might in some particular circumstances conflict with the principle of equal access to goods or even with equality of basic freedoms. In such a case we would be forced to consider the ordering of these principles, and we would find that we need a principle of life and that it must be given the first priority. So taking into consideration both the ideal and reality, both Western and non-Western civilizations, we discover another set of principles, with three, rather than two, ordered rules: first survival, then freedom, then equality. Of course, my reason for bringing up the principle of life is not simply to construct another set of rules. I want to find a starting point prior to these rules.

Of the two principles proposed by Rawls, the one that demands more attention from Chinese thinkers is not the second principle, which has attracted so much discussion in the West, but the first. The principle of basic freedoms includes a number of freedoms, and equal freedom of conscience should be given priority over equal freedom of political participation. Similarly, within the second principle, we should be more interested not in the difference principle but in equality of opportunity—even in formal equality of opportunity. This cardinal ordering is consistent with Rawls's intentions, but because Western philosophers tend to agree on equality of opportunity, their debate has concentrated on the difference principle. This debate within liberalism is in fact an argument over the minimum requirements for liberalism—or over exactly where the smallest possible shared ground of liberalism lies. Nozick and Hayek argue for making that minimum a little smaller; Rawls wants to make it bigger, by bringing the greatest benefit for the least advantaged into the area governed by the principles of justice. But in a society that has yet to establish basic freedoms and rights, the most basic institutions of citizenship, and minimum material standards for its population, our attention and careful discussions should be focused firmly on Rawls's first principle of justice.

Even if we accept the difference principle, we should consider something that Rawls never thought of: how it might be applied in a different culture. Rawls proposed the difference principle in order to reduce differences, but in a relatively egalitarian but also relatively poor society (that is, where everyone is poor), the difference principle could actually be used to justify greater inequality: if this difference can bring greatest benefit to the least advantaged in the future, then why not allow it? This is somewhat like China's policy in the late 1980s: "Let some people get rich first." There is, of course, still room for much controversy and debate over which people should get rich, how they should get rich, and how rich they should get.

We should also notice that one of the reasons that Rawls gives for his difference principle is not so much that the poor "deserve" some compensatory benefits, that they deserve to be given more by the state; instead, it is that the rich, or the state, should provide those benefits. In fact, Rawls's theory of distributive justice virtually excludes the concept of "deserts," which is so central to Aristotelean virtue theory. So those who have a competitive advantage because of their natural endowments do not "deserve" their natural talent and therefore should give a part of the benefits that they get with their talents to disadvantaged groups. Moreover, this is not a question of voluntary or charitable giving. There should be redistribution through policies, such as strongly progressive taxation and social welfare policies, because a society is a collaborative system. If different classes do not pull together, the elite will not be able to generate the maximum returns, and the entire society may fall into turmoil and collapse.

Other reasons why the state ought to give more compensation to the more disadvantaged groups include economic reasons (giving guarantees to the rich is actually much more expensive than giving protection to the poor) and moral reasons (all people are of the same species, so there should be some solidarity among them). And now there is the sense that we belong not only to our own polity: the entire globe is becoming more and more interlinked, becoming a single commonwealth of which we are all a part, from cradle to grave. There is nowhere for either the strong or the weak to go to get away from others; we all share this one world.

Though Rawls is at pains to argue that society should be most concerned about its most disadvantaged, his reasons are cast in the form of "provision" and "cooperation," not as "deserts" and "conflict." The distinction is important. If the lower classes of a society deserve the lion's share of a society's benefits because they generated the wealth and are poor only because of exploitation, then any means of reclaiming that wealth is permissible. Even violent means are allowed, even considered just, because the wealth is being returned to its rightful owners. But if reducing the gap is seen instead as an obligation of the rich, then any plan to restore equality must be constrained in the means that it uses. At the very least, violence would be ruled out.

On a more holistic level, it is not only the difference principle that aims at equality. The principles of basic freedoms and fair equality of opportunity are also equality principles. In the areas of beliefs and political action, freedom means equality, and equality means freedom. And fairness of opportunity is another way of eliminating the differences that arise from social environment and family background. That means that the only inequality left for the difference principle to deal with is inequality that arises from differences in natural endowments.

Does inequality arising from differences in natural endowments have to be controlled by the state? This is the question that attracts the most controversy. It is much easier to build an "overlapping consensus" on the inequalities controlled by the two principles of justice. Rawls answers the question of state regulation of natural differences in the affirmative. Because of his understanding of the concept of justice, he sees justice as a counterweight to arbitrary or random factors. But it is not clear that justice must balance out *all* arbitrary factors. In fact, the birth and death of each person are effectively random events. One real factor that should be considered is this: the inequality caused by differences in natural endowments is very considerable, and the "Matthew effect" tends to amplify that inequality. This is true even when there is no violence, no fraud, and no other improper conduct. The gap between rich and poor continues to widen, to the point that people no longer have the will to stop the state from interfering, even though the gap is entirely a product of natural processes.

This discussion brings us to Rawls's understanding of society and human nature. These concepts are only implicit in his writing. Rawls understands society as a cooperative system. He sees people in the "original position" as naturally "rational"—in fact, as the rationally self-interested beings of economics. In the original position they are mutually disinterested, and they calmly calculate and weigh their gains and losses. Some critics believe that Rawls preloaded those in the original position with certain qualities, making them rather conservative, engaged in the pursuit of a "maximin" and not a true maximum. There is a clear distinction here with *homo economicus*, who always seeks to maximize.

Some critics may think that Rawls's understanding of society is overly naive, and those who research human nature may see his view of humanity as idealized in that he sees it as inclined toward a conservative rationality. People may in fact be inclined to take risks in pursuit of greater benefits, even to the point of not minding the loss of fundamental goods that they could have protected. Rawls would perhaps respond that the design of social institutions, particularly basic social structures, must be rooted in human rationality. The primary goal of social justice is to prevent the worst outcomes for everyone, not to pursue the best outcomes. This is not the only element in our social structure: plenty of space is left for individual passion, inspiration, and intellectual invention.

Rawls has left us a powerful intellectual legacy; the importance of his thought can be seen in many ways. He sparked a new focus in Western philosophy and ethics on substantive problems. He successfully established a deontological theory in the area of justice as a challenge to teleological theories such as utilitarianism. In his later work, he became more sharply aware of the divisions over values in modern society and worked tirelessly to find a consensus on justice. But his most important contribution was this: he created the most detailed model yet for the rational support of liberal politics and moral philosophy. In a sense, he can be seen as a spokesman for the values and approach to justice that hold sway in mainstream America.

Liberalism has been developed in the contemporary West by Hayek, Nozick, Berlin, Popper, and many other thinkers, with contributions from critics on the political left and right. This "owl of Minerva" started its flight early: these thinkers began producing their major works in the 1960s and 1970s. By the 1980s, history seemed to be confirming their ideas. Liberal democracy had started its triumphant sweep across the globe. That confirmation was celebrated in Fukuyama's concept of the "end of history," borrowed from Hegel and Kojève. Humanity seems to have found a way of political coexistence that best suits our character. It may not be the perfect political form, but it avoids the worst consequences of political conflict: it ensures that there is no violence and no blood-letting in our competition for goods and status and our political wrangling; it places limits on excessive power; and it ensures that no person ends up in circumstances too terrible or too desperate, no matter how disadvantaged their group or social status.

But this "end of history" is also linked to the "last man" (Nietzsche's "letzte Mensch" or de Tocqueville's "mediocrity"). Evening is descending for philosophy and perhaps for humanity itself. Maybe humanity is about to begin a long sleep, without the destructive struggles of daylight but also without its brilliant illumination. Liberal democracy may be a "permanent solution," and it seems to be consistent with humanity's basic morality. But will there be a new *Internationale*, calling on us to "thunder condemnation"? Will there be great, revolutionary changes to celebrate in which "twenty years is compressed into one day"? (Even if those changes bring about a state in which only a day seems to pass in twenty years?) Revolution and competition aside, will humanity's passion for struggle, for victory, and for excellence have space to express itself? How can we find a proper outlet for humanity's pursuit of excellence—an urge that is just as deeply rooted as the pursuit of equality? If historically people have pursued excellence at the expense of equality, then does our current pursuit of equality come at the expense of excellence? Will human culture wither and lose its spark? Will materialism and the gap between rich and poor rage beyond our control? Could they bring about a cataclysm sufficient to end humanity itself?

Of course, there are many more questions than I have listed here, and each of them links to a critique of liberalism. In a sense, liberal theory and liberal institutional practices have carried the day without ever being put to the test. In the process, liberalism made itself the most important political philosophy under consideration and the prime target for criticism. Liberalism is now often the shared ground on which thinkers can meet, and a target that every thinker can attack. We must remain sensitive and open to future, different political syntheses. But for the present, there is no visible competitor to liberalism for the central role. So until its critics can propose positive, constructive alternative institutional principles, attacks on liberalism will amount to no more than tinkering and updating. Liberalism may be an even more powerfully ecumenical and inclusive philosophy than Confucianism was in Chinese history. So long as liberal institutions and practices maintain their (sometimes exclusive) global dominance, we can be sure that in this new century, we will never be able to ignore John Rawls, the man who created the philosophical rulebook for political liberalism.

CHAPTER EIGHTEEN

THE APPLICABILITY OF THE PRINCIPLE OF LIFE TO INTERNATIONAL POLITICS

An indisputably essential precondition for the continuance of human civilization is that human beings have the ability to maintain certain states. For individuals, that state is *life*; for a nation, it is *security*; for the world, it is *peace*. This chapter examines some questions touching on this topic. How does "life" work as a principle? Specifically, how does it affect individuals and relationships between individuals? In international relations (particularly in the nuclear age, which we currently inhabit), how does it affect international politics? Can the principle of life attain moral status? How? Can we determine the content of a moral principle of life?

Russell on Nuclear War

Let us start with a very pointed perspective on how this principle might have an effect. In 1959, Bertrand Russell published a pamphlet titled *Common Sense and Nuclear Warfare*.[1] Russell said that the book was not "an appeal to this or that -ism, but only to common sense." It was an appeal "to human beings, as such, and is made equally to all who hope for human survival." A thermonuclear war would threaten the survival of the human race, so the interests of the entire human race—Western bloc, Eastern bloc, and non-

This chapter is an edited version of an article first published in *World Economics and Politics*, no. 1 (2004).

1. Bertrand Russell, *Common Sense and Nuclear Warfare* (George Allen and Unwin, 1959). The discussion here is based on the Commercial Press edition (1961).

aligned states—are served by preventing its outbreak. There is no need to appeal to any idealistic motives: "it is necessary only to appeal to motives of national self-interest." Ideological battles should give way to considerations of the survival of the human race. The West and East share certain interests, and the "first and most important of their common interests is survival. This has become a common interest owing to the nature of nuclear weapons." The danger now does not come from barbarians: "On the contrary, it is those who are in the forefront of civilization." The joint survival of both East and West should be the highest policy objective of both sides. And in the nuclear age, that can be refined to one explicit goal: nuclear war must be prevented at all costs.

Russell suggests as a condition for lasting peace the establishment of an international authority—in other words, a form of world government. But in urgent circumstances in which no other solution is available, he says that one side giving way or even surrendering to the other should be considered. If "one of the two blocs is so fanatical that it prefers the ending of mankind to a rational compromise . . . I think that the less fanatical bloc, if it had the welfare of mankind in view, would prefer concession to warfare." For example, the West could unilaterally disarm; the United States could voluntarily withdraw its forces from Europe, and so forth.

There seems to be some inconsistency here, because a decade or so previously, when the United States still had an absolute advantage over the Soviet Union in terms of nuclear stockpiles, Russell had argued that "it would be worthwhile to bring pressure to bear upon Russia, and even, if necessary, to go so far as to threaten war"—that is, he did not exclude the possibility of a preemptive attack on the Soviet Union. But ten years later, when the United States and USSR were in rough parity, Russell was arguing that the West should "make concessions" to the USSR to avoid war, despite the fact that Russell clearly endorsed the institutions and values of Western society rather than those of the Soviets. So why concede? Why did he not rule out surrender?[2]

2. In 1962, at the time of the Cuban missile crisis, Russell sent telegrams to the heads of both the United States and Soviet governments in an attempt to mediate, but the tone that he adopted toward the USSR was markedly more conciliatory. In his telegram to Nikita Khrushchev, he said, "May I humbly appeal for your further help in lowering the temperature despite the worsening situation. Your continued forbearance is our great hope." To Kennedy he wrote: "Your action desperate. No conceivable justification. We will not have mass murder. End this madness!" His approach was severe toward institutions that were open and flexible and gentle toward rigid, absolutist institutions. Another example comes from William Shirer, author of *The Rise and Fall of the Third Reich*. After

Russell notes two circumstances. First, he asks us to consider that "the great majority of mankind . . . are occupied throughout the greater part of their time with quite unpolitical matters. They are concerned to eat and sleep; they are concerned with love and family; they are concerned with success or failure in their work, and with the joy or pain of living, according to the state of their health." They would think insane any people who said that they would rather see the world destroyed than allow the triumph of foreign institutions and philosophies, even if they believe those institutions to be "unjust" or "evil." Now that we have nuclear weapons, human beings must learn to tolerate and accept each other.

Second, Russell also recognizes this: that even the most violent and despotic regime will not last forever. What is important is that humanity survives, that there are still people living on the Earth. To imagine that a tyrannical or autocratic regime will last forever because it has achieved global victory is to ignore the realities of history. But if humanity is exterminated, then its extermination is indeed permanent. Russell mentions the counterfactual suggested by Edward Gibbon: What would the world be like if the Christians had not defeated the Muslims at the Battle of Tours but had been defeated instead? He thinks that the differences would not be that great.

Today, after the end of the cold war, has history proved Russell wrong? Did Russell exaggerate the dangers of nuclear war? Politicians in the United States and the West did not take Russell's advice, but they did take a number of actions to ease relations between East and West, such as withdrawing troops from Vietnam. Or was there always another historical possibility: was it in fact only chance that prevented the outbreak of war when tensions grew? Of course, if that were the case, then there might well have been no one left to discuss the question. Human survivors (if there were any) might be looking back in wonder at Russell's prescience. Russell was a commentator, not a politician, and so his influence was limited, but he was important, nonetheless. Both those who speak and those who act have their limitations, do they not?

Russell's proposed permanent solution to the problem was a world government; his interim solution was concessions, up to and including surren-

---

World War II, he met with Raymond Aron in Paris, and from the balcony of an apartment they watched the celebrating crowds on the streets, particularly the happy young people. Aron, suddenly struck by a feeling, mused, "Perhaps, back when Germany invaded, non-resistance was actually right. These happy people wouldn't have lived to see this day if they were in the resistance." Of course, Aron was simply expressing a sudden impression, and he was talking about other people's lives, not his own. Aron was in fact a renowned resistance activist who deeply opposed the Vichy regime.

der. Are the two contradictory? Is world government too idealistic? Is surrender too realist? And can we agree that Russell's proposals seem to be supported by arguments from human nature and history? The debate over these questions continues. What we are concerned about today is this: can we find a single, unified principle behind the different positions that Russell held at different times?

We can. The principle is easy to spot. It is the principle of the survival of humanity. Russell's view was that nuclear war, which could wipe out humanity—or at least advanced human civilization—must be avoided at all costs. If that is what we want to do, then first we must control nuclear weapons. In his 1947 book, *Struggle for the World*, James Burnham suggested that the best and most feasible way to do that at the time was to have all of the nuclear weapons controlled by one authority only. Ideally, that authority would be a world government, but more realistically, it would be the United States or the USSR.[3] So in Russell's two apparently contradictory proposals, we can see an underlying consistency: the importance of survival. Everything can be abandoned for the sake of survival. And we need not be suspicious of Russell's motives. He was at the time nearly eighty years old, so any insinuation that he was merely trying to save his own skin is unwarranted. It was not a question of just his life; it was a question of the lives of people across the globe—perhaps of every human being. There may be those who do not agree with Russell's specific recommendations, and their doubts may be well founded. But we cannot deny the principle that lies behind them.

The Principle of Life and Its Moral Content

Can life, or the preservation of life, be a moral principle? The principle of life has a kind of intuitive (or commonsensical) appeal, witnessed by our survival itself. All people alive believe in this principle. Those who live under the most difficult circumstances believe it even more. The continued reproduction of the human race to the present time is an endorsement of this principle. Does there need to be any further argument for the principle of life? But then, is life a moral principle? Or rather, could it have moral content? If so, then how must we construe it so that it does have moral content?

First let us consider the survival of individuals. An individual seeks survival for himself or herself only. Both the everyday practice of "making a liv-

3. James Burnham, *The Struggle for the World* (New York: John Day Company, 1947), chapter 3.

ing" and the "fight or flight" reflex at times of stress are entirely natural actions. So long as the individual is not harming anyone else, then there is no moral blame to be attached to either, nor any particular moral praise. If the person was in a highly marginal state, in extreme danger or extreme deprivation, then survival—for example, after a shipwreck or a mine collapse— might be praiseworthy. Recall the lumberjack, who, rather than bleed to death after his leg was pinned by a fallen tree, chopped his leg off and then crawled to the road to call for help. Such people may be "heroes" because they display vital human traits: human potential, bravery, determination, and endurance. In holding their own lives dear, they represent a more general value: the value life itself. This is to view life in terms of values and duties. For example, many people believe that suicide is a violation of an individual's obligations toward others and toward the community. Kant saw the duty not to commit suicide under any circumstances as one that every person must act on (of course, this issue remains controversial).

Then there is survival within the context of personal relationships. Generally the drive to personal survival is a form of self-love. Self-love often stands in opposition to the interests of others, so it can lead to conflict. In fact, we can identify a "survival dilemma" for individuals that is exactly analogous to the "security dilemma" faced by states. The more a person makes his own life a priority, the more likely he is to infringe on other people's interests—or even on the survival of other people. The consequences could easily be damaging to that person's own interests. In the case of suicide, relations with other people seem implicit: suicide seems like an individual act, with only implicit links to others and the community. But the survival dilemma makes those connections direct and explicit. And this is where the moral element emerges.

Actions that are purely individual generally have no moral component. Actions that impact the lives of others indubitably have a moral dimension, and to such actions we would apply moral praise or censure. To say that the principle of life has a positive moral component is not to deny that individuals can seek their own survival. But it means that the principle of life must at least allow us to "live and let live." Our shipwreck survivors may be worthy of moral praise for their spirit, but if the survivors had not been alone—if they had had to battle with other survivors or even to eat human flesh to survive—then we would have a distinctly more negative view. We might turn away in disgust. But do people not have extraordinary rights to ensure their safety in times of emergency? In a life-or-death emergency, most people would agree that we have the right to interfere with the property of others, but can we violate the right to life of another person? In an emergency situation, does anything go?

Can any action be defended? In a time of urgent danger or urgent need, can we return to a state of nature, reinstating some dog-eat-dog law of the jungle? Is an emergency similar to Hobbes's description of humanity in a state of nature: with no concept of fairness, no good or evil, no right or wrong?

Of course, a civilized society with an established political order is not like that, even if its social institutions are powerless to take action. But when public authority loses its grip and people can act without any restriction at all, social order is ultimately doomed to collapse. This problem also reminds us that in practice our individual behavior and our personal relationships often reflect group relationships, in particular the relationships between the individual and the community, the individual and the state, and the state and other states. Let us now look at the principle of life in these relationships, and let us again examine a rather extreme situation. For example, picture two enemy soldiers who wake in a bomb crater between their respective lines. One is so severely wounded that he cannot move, but he is holding a weapon; he wakes to find that the other soldier has only been stunned unconscious but has no weapon. Can the injured soldier kill the unconscious soldier?

The world is a complex place. People often must make difficult choices in order to survive. But our focus is not on purely individual examples. We need to consider groups: under what conditions does a group's efforts to ensure its survival take on a moral dimension? Why? And what are the ethical duties of the leaders and decisionmakers of a group? In *Moral Man and Immoral Society*, Reinhold Niebuhr suggests that groups are more selfish than individuals. But for a decisionmaker, the "selfishness" of pursuing the interests of the group (within reason)—and particularly of protecting their lives—may also be a form of selflessness. If we compare a leader who works for the benefit of the group with the "let them eat cake" leaders that China has had in the past (the empress dowager Cixi is rumored to have said, "I'd rather give it all away to another country than let our wretched subjects have it"), then the difference is clear. We can distinguish a few different possible attitudes toward the group:

—Willingness to sacrifice one's own life for the good of the group. For example, the captain of a battleship who, in the face of overwhelming odds, orders surrender to save his men's lives but commits suicide himself.

—Equal consideration of the group's and one's own survival. For example, our captain may be willing to accept the stain on his honor and surrender along with his crew.

—No consideration of either one's own or the group's life. Imagine our captain just waiting to sink or boldly charging the massed enemy with no chance of causing them real damage.

—Concern only for one's own life. The captain abandons ship and flees in a lifeboat, leaving his crew to sink or swim.

We must not make simplistic judgments about these various actions. Many factors would play into this decision: whether the enemy would respect the conventions on war at sea, whether the crew would rather die than surrender, and so forth. But the fourth option is clearly shameful. The third option is the "bravest," but if the sailors prefer life, the captain has the problem of whether he can make this choice for them. This is similar to the first argument put forward by Russell. In a war that is not driven by religion or ideology or that is not a lawless tribal war or raid, either of the first two options could be considered. The first could be seen as quite honorable.

So the criterion that determines when the principle of life is a moral principle is the relationship between the self and others, or the self and the group. If the main object of concern is not the self, but others—not survival of the self, but survival of the group—then the Principle of Life takes on a positive moral value. After all, the value of the life of a leader—particularly the leader of a large country—is not very great at all. Leaders normally make their own survival a secondary concern in the nation's fight for survival, so the leader and the country share a common fate. At the level of leadership, the individual's life is often not the most important factor. Even though leaders are not average people, their mission is far more important than their own life. Sometimes we can completely ignore the issue of a leader's life. Then the focus is on the life of the group and on its other values: independence, dignity, freedom, honor, and so forth. The focus is on all the various issues within the group and on the group's relations with other groups.

Of course, moral scope also is important. We can see that over the course of history, the definition of moral subjects or moral agents has gradually expanded: the moral unit has expanded from the clan and tribe to the city and the state. Today, the largest unit in our moral practice is the state, but the concept of humanity—and even of all life—has started to gain currency on a moral level. Whatever the social unit used in a theory of ethics, it must still subscribe to core universal values. To be sure, the ethics of a single family and a single nation are still ethics; the partial democracy of ancient Athens was still a democracy. Humanity does not yet identify as one big, happy "family" nor as a single political entity. We live in more or less exclusive political groupings, and our ethics often reflects the in-group/out-group divisions that we observe. The groups within which we apply morality are growing larger, but it is still unclear whether we can achieve an all-inclusive "brotherhood of man."

So, for the time being, we must accept that the leader of a group will give priority and additional weight to the interests of his own group and that that priority is in fact legitimate. The only condition is that he must give *some* consideration to the equivalent interests of other groups. Decisionmakers will also face questions of how to negotiate the balance between their own group's security and the security of other groups: the classic "security dilemma." Blind pursuit of perfect security for one's own country—placing no value on the lives of citizens of other states while insisting that the lives of one's own citizens have the highest value—is a poor strategy. Moreover, it is morally warped. The only form of the principle of life that could claim an objective universality is full commitment to the life of one's own group combined with concern for the survival of people in other groups—for the whole of humankind. That is the only form that could be a moral principle.

The distinction between self and others means that individual reasonableness—that is, the kind of reasonableness and prudence that gives full consideration to the balance of long-term consequences—can also apply in international relations as a form of moral code, perhaps an extremely important moral code. Politicians and decisionmakers must take into account not just the consequences of their actions to themselves but also to their group, to humanity, and to all living things on this planet. That obligation gives their considerations a level of moral importance. We should pay particular attention to the shift from concern for one's self to concern for others. It is on this level that the prudence of national leaders can become a nation's morality—even a form of global ethics.

This argument applies equally to material goods and the good of survival. Consideration of the benefits of the group, not just the self, can be moral thinking. Even philosophies like Lord Palmerston's—"We have no eternal allies, and we have no perpetual enemies. Our interests are eternal and perpetual, and those interests it is our duty to follow"—can have moral force under certain circumstances. Enmities fixed for reasons of race, religion, or ideology often are more vicious than the cold calculation of interests. Of course, here the words "interest" and "benefit" are too vague. Survival may be counted as a type of "interest"—indeed, one of the most fundamental. But the concept of interest can easily become confused with others. Often it is mistaken for purely material or economic benefits; our interests in security and survival are forgotten. In international politics, moral relationships are primarily concerned with survival and security. A state may resist if its survival or security is threatened and may use violence in self-defense. But wars against other countries to obtain economic benefits or to support some ideology clearly would command little support in the modern world.

Let us return to the arguments of Bertrand Russell, discussed earlier. Russell presents arguments about an especially precarious situation. It is the application of the principle of life in extremely atypical circumstances. For Russell, there was one particular feature that made the situation different from any in history: nuclear weapons. Nuclear weapons changed the nature of warfare and geopolitics: for the first time, the destruction of the human race through war became a possibility. Russell himself never seems to speak of morality. He discusses only "interests": state interests and individual interests. But life-and-death decisions that have consequences for the entire human race are in fact the very first, most fundamental, most important moral decisions. Here we come to an extremely simple question: would you rather live in a world in which enemies coexist or in a world in which enemies drive each other out of existence? Would you prefer to have many people living under many pressures, perhaps under many threats, or to have no pressures, no threats, and no people?

Some people actually would prefer to have humanity destroyed than to allow regimes based on ideologies that they hate to come to power. But faced with the issue of human survival, the responsibility of politicians is to do everything in their power, to use every possible means possible, to prevent nuclear war. Politicians cannot get by with mere audacity. Even Khrushchev asked, "What good are principles when your head has been chopped off?" Isn't avoiding the option of chopping heads off a higher principle still? Isn't keeping all humanity secure a better option? And can't this kind of principle be given priority over our various ideologies? In addition to all of the ordinary principles of personal and international relationships, there should be another, higher principle: the principle of the survival of humankind. The principle of life should prevail over all conflicts of religious belief or ideology, over all conflicts of national interests. It should be able to bridge the gap between realism and idealism in theories of international relations and become part of a shared, minimum ethical consensus. There is room for debate over the strategies and methods used to keep the peace; reasonable people can differ over preferences and priorities. But on the principle of life itself there can be—and sorely needs to be—a high level of agreement. In a world in which groups and individuals are drawing closer together, we must try to ensure that closeness does not bring tension. We must seek the very best prospects for both our own country and the world. But we must also be prepared for the worst at any time.

An Initial Account of the Principle of Life

One conclusion that can be drawn from the previous discussion is this: there is a fundamental moral principle of life that is not necessarily clearly recognized by everyone. We may resist or refuse to properly recognize it as "moral." And yet in some cases, this principle is naturally incorporated into our behavior without any reflection—perhaps without any thought—at all. It emerges strongly whenever interests or beliefs clash, particularly in international relations concerning life-and-death matters. The morality of international relations is by nature not as broad as that of persons, and people might not normally think about everyday ethics in such situations, but they must in matters of vital importance. So when individuals falsely believe that they are ignoring morality or are unable to act morally, what they mean is that they are failing to act according to what they perceive as the higher standards of interpersonal morality. In fact, there is still a moral core to their actions, and that morality is the more universal. Of course, this division typically emerges only in highly marginal or extreme situations.

First of all, we must be clear on how it is that morality acts this way and exactly what moral principle it is that has this property of emergence in international relations. It must be the most fundamental of moral principles—and that, as I see it, is the principle of life. The principle of life, this moral principle that expresses itself so powerfully, rests unnoticed in the hearts of many, many people. And it acts through a deeply ingrained conscience or sense of compassion.

But can a morality of which we are barely aware—let alone have given full reflection to—really be sufficient to meet the challenges of our age? Is it stable and reliable? Do we not need to provide a clearer exegesis and focus for this principle? Philosophers including Rawls and Walzer have taken the example of U.S. president Harry Truman and his lack of hesitation before ordering use of the atom bomb on Japan to imply that in wartime we tend to act rather reflexively. If, in times of peace, we have not repeated and reaffirmed our principles many times over until they have become a fundamental constraint on our actions, then the urgent threat of the enemy and "military necessity" will certainly not allow us to do so in war. But as Kant wrote in the essay "Perpetual Peace," during war we must remember that peace will return again. That means that we should still make the effort to handle our interpersonal relationship according to normal moral principles. And in times of peace, we often encounter situations in which war could easily break out. At that point, we need to make decisions and act fast, and the presence or absence of some explicit moral standards will make a great difference in the decisions that we make. If we sink entirely into practical calculations of utility for our own state only, with no question of morality entering our thoughts, then we very probably will make decisions with disastrous consequences. When ordinary people make such decisions on the basis of their own experience, it is perhaps forgivable. When philosophers and politicians do it, it is terrible. So it is worth attempting here to sketch out an explicit version of the principle of life based on current philosophy and changes in modern society.[4]

I believe that from the social contractarians—Hobbes, Locke, and Rousseau—a series of ethical principles for society can be fairly easily derived: life, freedom, equality. The preservation of life was obviously the most fundamental principle. People would first ensure their own survival, then move to the other questions. Survival far outweighs any other consideration. For that reason, it is not just the first and most important for Hobbes, it is virtually his only principle. Other moral and political philosophers have been open to other principles, but the principle of life has always had priority.

As an expression of our values, if we look at it purely on the level of individuals, the principle of life says:

—first, that life is the primary and most fundamental value of humanity; it is the precondition for all other human values. As it is sometimes put: "Life is the greatest virtue"; "Life is better than death."[5] Some explanation of this has been given above, in the discussion on whether life is a principle for our age. This is the most basic and universal meaning of the principle of life.

—Second, that life is precious in itself—that is, it is precious as an end in itself, not just as a means. This aspect has been argued most forcefully by Kant in the three formulations of his categorical imperative: "universal law," "People are ends, not means," and "discipline of the will." The distinction is extremely important. Some moral viewpoints see humanity as the most precious thing on the planet but only because of its productivity or capacity to strive. This views humanity as an instrumental good.

4. When this principle is explicit and used with full awareness, I shall refer to it as the principle of life. That will help to distinguish it from the "survival principle," which is not fully explicit and is driven by circumstance. This principle can, of course, be explained in other ways. The explanation given here is just one possible version that tries to take into account both the core of the principle and the nature of our era.

5. In modern environmental ethics, many philosophers claim that human actions and decisions should take into account all life, including plants and animals. See He, ed., *Environmental Ethics: Spiritual Resources and Philosophical Foundations* (Hebei University Press, 2002).

—Third, that the life of every person is equally valuable, given that life is an end in itself, a completely free-standing value. Or, at the very least, that all lives should be seen as lives, that every person must be treated as a person. We should be concerned with every life; we should take "people as people" (that is, treat all people in a humane, or human, way). At this point, we can see that this principle now has moral content.

But because the principle of life is a deontological principle, it is easiest to explain it in the negative. It is most often expressed as a ban on certain kinds of action. There are two levels to the ban. First, do not harm life. That means to avoid killing or harming human lives whenever possible, particularly to avoid killing innocent people. Second, provide the conditions necessary for life. That means ensuring that all people have sufficient ability to provide for themselves. Basic material sufficiency is often reduced to "economic benefit." However, the provision of the basic necessities of life is not purely a question of fair distribution. It is an issue of fundamental morality.

The account of the principle of life given here is modern in character. That is most evident in the second and third values listed above. Because of differences in political institutions, the principle of life is instantiated at different levels in various states around the world. Elimination of every trace of in-group/out-group discrimination would be impossible. Ensuring a basic or decent standard of provision of material resources is primarily the state's duty. Citizens make that demand of the state to which they belong. But the injunction against killing is a transnational human obligation, an ethic for all the citizens of the world. It should become part of the duty ethic for decisionmakers in every country. Of course, "Do not kill" should not be understood too absolutely or mechanically. It does not rule out violence used in self-defense. This ethical duty expresses itself in international relations as the obligation to avoid violence and warfare and, if war begins, to avoid torture or unnecessary destruction. In particular, it is the injunction to avoid harming innocent civilians.

Nuclear weapons are currently the greatest threat to national security and to the survival of humankind. The twenty-first century began with two wars launched by the United States, against Afghanistan and Iraq, motivated in no small part by the fear that weapons of mass destruction (particularly nuclear weapons) would fall into the hands of anti-American terrorist organizations or the states that support them. More recently, there have been ongoing six-party nuclear talks with North Korea. These events remind us that though the threat of nuclear war has shrunk, it still casts a dark shadow.

CHAPTER NINETEEN

WHAT ARE THE DIFFERENCES?
AND WHAT CONSENSUS?

Since the publication in 1988 of Alasdair MacIntyre's *Whose Justice? Which Rationality?*, many philosophers have raised similar questions. Though this chapter follows in the same vein, it is oriented somewhat differently. Where I differ from MacIntyre is that I do not believe that different concepts of justice are incompatible, incommensurable, or devoid of shared ground. I think that developing some level of consensus on the question of justice is possible and necessary. To ask "whose justice" is to imply that justice is always the justice of some particular subject. But modern justice necessarily implies a universal, nondiscriminatory perspective. It is true that when we shift from a conception of justice shared within a single country to an international conception of justice, the need to strike a balance between rights and obligations implies that we see a reduction in the scope of justice. However, there are still core values that are held in common even at the international level, and we can appeal to a shared rationality as we seek consensus on those shared core values. Though I clearly have a view on the answers to the questions in the title of this chapter, I still present them as questions because there are many parts of my answers about which I still have doubts.

In today's world, as we accept and respect more and more of the differences among people, we are forced to make an effort to find areas of agreement. Difference is a fact, but it is also true that there is an objective basis for consensus. We just need to sort carefully through the concepts to decide which

This chapter is an edited version of an article first published in *Journal of Wuhan University of Science and Technology*, no. 5 (2010).

differences are not only important but also fundamental. Here I want to discuss differences that often are hidden: the differences associated with ethnicity and race. I discuss how we can achieve consensus between racial and ethnic groups, given that we want to accept reasonable differences and seek the Confucian ideal of "harmony, not uniformity." But what kind of a consensus will it be? In a multicultural world, can we really achieve consensus of this type? I accept that the most fundamental type of consensus has a scope that is defined politically. However, I think that in terms of its substance, it is still a form of moral consensus. And if even those thinkers who devote much of their thought to diversity and conflict will admit this moral consensus, then it is fair to say that seeking out moral agreement is both necessary and possible.

The Modern World: Globalization and Diversity, Difference and Equality

We live in an age of globalization. It is an age in which economic and social life have largely merged into one; it is an age of diversity, an age when "the Way has been torn into many pieces," as Zhuangzi poetically expressed the diversity of philosophies in his own age. On the practical level, we have a deeply integrated global economy and global society; however, we do not have globalized morality, politics, or beliefs. That is to say that humanity is growing ever closer and more similar on the substantial, tangible, and physical level while on the spiritual, cultural, and metaphysical level we are becoming more and more fragmented and more interested in differences. There is a "language" that all ethnicities can understand, that they all can use or must learn to use: the language of money and transaction. But the languages of culture, of values and beliefs, create a modern Babel.

The age in which we live is an age that demands equality, but it is also an age that honors difference. Is that a contradiction, or do the two contain each other? We demand equality precisely because differences exist. Different classes, groups, and individuals are not very equal; that is why we need to demand equality. People are not equal by the fact of their humanity. And the existence of differences is demonstrated by the demand for formal equality. That is why we have to make the effort to demand equal treatment for all in light of their humanity. The demand for difference is another feature of our age. In one sense there are infinite differences, but in another sense, there also seem to be only a few varieties. Values are diverse, but along the major fault lines of difference, they often present as two groups, those that hold certain values and those that do not, and in the mainstream, there is often a trend toward uniformity. Perhaps all questions of difference and equality are questions of scope and degree? But we also find some conflicts and differences that are deep rooted, irreducible, perhaps even necessary.

The countries of the world may be becoming more and more similar, and we may be required to accept more variety, but similarity and acceptance are not the same thing. Similarity is external, a natural trend. Acceptance is internal, a demand that we make on our own character. That is, on one hand all cultures, ethnicities, and even individuals are becoming more similar, particularly in their material lifestyles; on the other hand, we must accept all the subcivilizations, subcultures, and subgroups of humanity. Acceptance is about difference, even about making differences greater. The more we are urged to accept, the more the spiritual and cultural values of the world become unalike. This "unalikeness" is not merely a fact, it is a modern value, pursued and approved by modernity, which believes that differences should be seen as "normal." When difference demands acceptance, it is also demanding a kind of mutual equality. People are pursuing the acceptance of differences and respect for differences; at the same time, they are expanding circles of equality. So perhaps we are demanding equality on the material level while rejecting equality on the level of beliefs?

In fact, individuals do not pursue sameness in their lives nearly so much as they pursue difference. And so long as the possibility exists, they will pursue a higher "difference." But if only to ensure that this "difference" can operate normally, they must also seek convergence. That is, individuals must try to find consensus with other people so that they do not get in each other's way or undermine each other's pursuit of happiness as they individually understand it. The convergence that they seek will be a consensus on the political or moral rules governing their behavior and on permissible types of action.

Humanity may never have been in such a simultaneously promising and threatening situation. Our material and military power is at an extraordinary peak, but the spiritual and cultural bands that keep us connected to one another have never been weaker. There is a potentially fatal danger ahead of us. For the first time in our history, we are in a situation in which diversity means that even when faced with a "global catastrophe," we would be unable to create a genuine global authority. Even if, with the passing of time, we are able to build a real world authority, globalization and the convergence of humanity mean that in the event of the decline or destruction of our civilization, there would be no balancing resurgence elsewhere, as there has been throughout history. Now, we would all go down together. Humanity has certainly advanced since the end of the cold war. We no longer look first to military force to deal with difference, opposition, or conflict; we have learned to use the levers of economic competition, negotiation, and compromise. But the underlying problem has not been resolved. In a world of differences, a world that not only believes that difference is reasonable and normal but that it is actually moral and right, can we still pursue common ground in order to prevent the frictions and conflicts that differences inevitably bring from causing disaster? Even the collapse of society or the destruction of human civilization?

What Are the Differences?

In the human world, viewed from any number of perspectives, the range of differences is virtually limitless. As Montaigne said, humans are "infinite in substance, infinite in diversity." All difference is ultimately instantiated in the individual. But individuals have many different heritages and identities and are members of many groups. We can examine, summarize, recognize, and distinguish people not only as individuals but also as types—that is, members of a particular group. That brings us to the issue of similarity. A race, a nationality, a belief, a value, a lifestyle—all can be used to group people on the basis of their common elements, to distinguish them from other groups. Thus we create differences between groups.

Here, I naturally focus our discussion on group differences only. There are many historically familiar types of major difference. There are political differences, some of them even enshrined in laws governing social status. There are differences in economic class, as reported by Marx. These differences often are seen as being vast and fundamental, so much so that they generate the types of opposition that are the primary drivers of history. It is said that the standoffs and conflicts that arise from these differences can only be resolved through constant bloody clashes, violent revolution, or the dictatorship of one class over all others.

Changes in society can be traced in the differences with which that society concerns itself. Today, we talk more than anything about differences in culture. "Cultural differences" is a rather gentle, tolerant, and broad concept. There are many ways to read cultural differences: high versus low culture, popular versus elite pursuits, scientific versus humanistic views. Dostoevsky discusses an important quantitative difference that arises out of qualitative differences: the difference between the minority and the majority. As soon as we admit the reality of this difference, the concept of "liberation" (through revolution) becomes problematic; even "enlightenment" is revealed to have limits.

But here I would like to further limit the scope of this chapter to one particular type of cultural difference, though it is perhaps the most important type: the cultural differences tied up with historic civilizations, or nation-states. For example, the differences between Chinese and Japanese culture or those between Chinese and American culture. These differences can be examined independently of their context, but in reality we often refer to them directly as differences between the relevant civilizations, countries, religions, ethnicities, or races. The differences are not ancillary concepts, they are intersectional. And at the places where they intersect, they also delineate each other.

Among this most general genre of cultural differences, which are the most important? We might say that two types of cultural difference are most important. One is differences in religion or belief: these are differences in our highest or most fundamental pursuits—they are "top-end differences." The other is differences in the physiology, personality, or behavioral habits of ethnicities or races: these are "bottom-end differences," innate for each member of the group, so to some extent predetermined or inherited. Some of these differences cannot be changed or are highly resistant to change: skin color, physiology, and language, for example. These are very fundamental differences, but they are very rarely talked about these days; ethnic and racial differences are some of the world's great open secrets.

Here I would like to revisit some ideas proposed over a century ago by Liang Qichao. Chapter 4 of his book *New Citizen*, written between 1903 and 1906, is titled "On the Theory of Natural Selection as Evidence of the Need for New Citizens and Reform," and it includes a discussion of ethnic and racial differences. Liang looked at the five human races (black, red, brown, yellow, and white) and concluded that the whites were superior. Among the whites, he thought that the Teutons were the best; among the Teutonic peoples, the Anglo-Saxons were the best. The reason was that of the five races, the whites were the most motivated and ambitious. Of all the whites, the Teutonic people had the best political and organizational skills and the most self-restraint. The Anglo-Saxons were supposed to be the best Teutons because they were able to maintain their identity and were the most independent and self-sufficient.

Liang's discussion has the following features. First, the discussion is on race, but Liang does not focus on physical characteristics. Instead he looks at issues of personality, character, and ability. Whether there is any link between the two—natural characteristics and cultural characteristics—Liang does not discuss, but it is implied that some link exists. Second, Liang addresses racial differences without any equivocation. He actually ranks races in terms of overall superiority and finds his own race to be inferior. Third, his own race's inferiority is not, of course, total, and he later discusses the good qualities of the Chinese. But he looks at Chinese characteristics mainly in terms of national politics, an area in which he naturally finds the Chinese to be weak; however, he does not think that this is an immutable state. He hopes that the Chinese as a race will achieve greater fitness. He looks forward to the day when China will be prosperous and strong.

These views were not Liang's alone. They were the mainstream views at the time, but Liang, who was seen as one of the voices of his age, was more influential than most writers. Many Chinese people at the turn of the twentieth century felt that their country was in danger of collapse. They were searching for ways to preserve their "country, race, and traditions," and they were keenly interested in the differences between races, particularly in determining which were better and which worse. That was the source of analyses of the Chinese population and the urgent mission to improve Chinese citizens. The "self-improvement" meme lasted through the middle of the last century, with, for example, Pan Guangdan's *The Principles of Eugenics*.[1] There was a fairly fundamental change following World War II that was connected with the failure of the Third Reich. Before that time, there was no taboo on discussing these topics; to the extent that there was some political reticence, it would not be triggered by the ruminations of a "weaker" race, as it might by suggestions coming from the "stronger" race.

In the modern West, particularly in the U.S. academic world, the strictures of "political correctness" make it difficult to raise the issue of racial differences, particularly racial superiority. But does that mean that differences do not exist? Even if they do exist, it is seen as best not to mention them, and some have criticized Samuel P. Huntington, saying that his prediction of a "clash of civilizations" was self-fulfilling. Of course, our recognition of racial differences may be hidden in the terms "cultural differences" or "clash of civilizations." Whatever the case, if we recognize that racial and ethnic differences exist and that they are deep rooted, if we recognize that at least in the foreseeable future these differences cannot be bridged or eliminated, then they may force people to seek consensus with a new urgency: consensus on how to handle these differences.

1. Pan Guangdan (潘光旦, 1899–1967), a native of Baoshan, Shanghai, was one of the most distinguished sociologists and eugenicists of China. Educated at Tsinghua University, Dartmouth College, and Columbia University, he was also a renowned expert on education. Pan, who was labeled as a rightist and anti-revolutionary in 1957, died at the beginning of the Cultural Revolution.

And What Consensus?

As with many kinds of difference, there is consensus within many areas: within international politics, there will be agreements or consensus between two or more nations over certain issues. Those agreements may be political, but they are not limited to politics, if politics is understood in the narrow sense as the necessity of compromise ("We have no eternal allies, and we have no perpetual enemies"). Of course, if we follow that thought, a compromise that avoids purely zero-sum strategies has its own moral value (even if the ultimate aim is still victory over other parties).

But consensus cannot be just a temporary expedient. What we are seeking is a fundamental, lasting consensus, a consensus that has value as an objective in itself. That is the only way to properly protect cultural differences and ensure that nations can live peacefully with one another. That means that we need to find a political consensus with moral substance. A political consensus with moral substance should be consensus on political values of fundamental moral importance; it should be universal and permanent.

The scope of this consensus would be political, but its substance is moral. The limitation on the scope is important: we need, primarily and urgently, consensus on powers of compulsion, such as political authority, and violence. John Rawls's political liberalism gives the best account of this. Political liberalism is a moral philosophy within politics, or one that concerns politics—it can simply be called a "political philosophy." Isaiah Berlin recognized the relationships between these concepts when he called political philosophy a branch of ethics.[2]

Rawls believes that the goal of his political liberalism is to find an independent perspective on political justice. Political justice has three characteristics: it is a moral theory applied to politics; it is a moral theory that is independent of other general moral theories; and it is expressed through political concepts embedded in a culture of public, democratic politics. Rawls's justice is a form of morality, but it is morality applied in a particular sphere: a morality of political, social, and economic institutions. Calling this concept of justice "moral" means that its content is defined by certain ideals, principles, and standards that explicitly express some political values. But this kind of morality is not the same as traditional, general theories of morality. Political justice differs from other moralities in its scope: it is defined by the scope

---

2. Berlin: "political philosophy, which is but ethics applied to society," in Isaiah Berlin, *The Crooked Timber of Humanity,* translated by Yue Xiukun (Yilin Press, 2009), p.6.

of the politics to which it applies, while general moral theories are required to have much more general scope.[3]

As I understand Rawls's theory of justice—or the theory of "justice as fairness" on which he wants to build consensus—it is a theory whose scope is defined by politics but by moral substance as well. Rawls stresses that overlapping consensus is not a temporary arrangement; it is not a temporary expedient. That emphasis also shows the moral nature of his consensus: it is a fundamental set of rules. The reason that it can be accepted as a consensus is that its core content has an objective, universal basis.

Rawls proposes his two principles of justice as the content of his consensus. From the debates, criticisms, and responses that have followed in the forty years since the publication of *A Theory of Justice*, we can see clearly that most people in a democracy seem to be able to agree to the equality of freedom in the first principle and the equality of opportunity in the second. However, there is rather more controversy concerning the "difference principle" that forms part of the second principle of justice. Rawls himself thought that the difference principle, which demands that a society reserve its greatest concern for its least advantaged, was applicable within a polity but would not be applicable in international politics. The "Global Ethic" proposed by Hans Küng and others, with its four commitments, is an attempt to find a smaller area of consensus in international politics and also hopes to serve as the moral text of the consensus in international politics. Some may not be willing to settle for these lower levels of agreement. They may have higher aspirations or hopes; they may want more. But as I understand it, moral requirements must be moderated as we expand the scope to which they apply and the level of compulsion with which they are applied. We can put it this way: as scope expands, moral requirements shrink.

Some kind of moral consensus is necessary if we want to prevent racial and ethnic differences, ingrained as they are and further entrenched in state practices, from turning into bloody conflicts that damage or even destroy both sides. This moral consensus should be an agreement on the fundamental attitudes that we bring to cultural and ethnic differences: a basic consensus on how different ethnic groups and different states can peacefully coexist. This consensus on international justice will have at its heart the principle of life: a consensus on equality in terms of existence. Put in negative terms, it is the prohibition against killing, pillaging, and so forth. I believe that consensus can be found only on this minimal level, on this small range of shared

---

3. See John Rawls, *Political Liberalism*, trans. Wan Junren (Yilin Press, 2000), pp. 11–14.

rules, which fall almost entirely within the boundaries of politics and law. This level is the level of fundamental moral rules. The diverse civilizations and cultures, with their different values and beliefs, can come to agreement only on this limited set of rules, because the rules are in fact a part of the core rules of culture itself. They have an objective and universal logical rationale.

So can we actually realize this consensus? I believe that we can. But I do not go into the details here of how we can realize it.[4] Instead I present the ideas of two thinkers who gave much thought to the issues of difference and conflict. One is Isaiah Berlin. Berlin was extremely concerned with diversity of values and culture, but he believed that there was no need to dramatize the clash of values:

> There is a great deal of broad agreement among people in different societies over long stretches of time. . . . Of course, traditions, out-looks, attitudes may legitimately differ; general principles may cut across too much human need. . . . But, in the end, it is not a matter of purely subjective judgment. . . . There are, if not universal values, at any rate a minimum without which societies could scarcely survive. Few today would wish to defend slavery or ritual murder or Nazi gas chambers or the torture of human beings for the sake of pleasure or profit or even political good—or the duty of children to denounce their parents, which the French and Russian revolutions demanded, or mindless killing. There is no justification for compromise on this.[5]

Samuel Huntington, who coined the phrase "clash of civilizations" and who held out little hope for the rapprochement of different civilizations (or cultures), wrote this:

> Cultures are relative; morality is absolute. Cultures, as Michael Walzer has argued, are "thick"; they prescribe institutions and behavior pat-terns to guide humans in the paths which are right in a particular soci-ety. Above, beyond, and growing out of this maximalist morality, how-ever, is a "thin" minimalist morality. . . . There are also minimal moral "negative injunctions, most likely, rules against murder, deceit, torture,

---

4. One of the major reasons why it is possible is that the consensus is on only a very restricted, small class of fundamental rules. In my essay "Some Possible Arguments for Global Ethics," in *Modernity and China* (Guangdong Education Press, pp. 105–30), I dis-cuss related arguments, and in my book *What Is Ethics* (Peking University Press, 2008), I propose three possible directions of argument for global ethics.

5. See *The Crooked Timber of Humanity*, p. 22.

oppression, and tyranny." What people have in common is "more the sense of a common enemy [or evil] than the commitment to a common culture." Human society is "universal because it is human, particular because it is a society.". . . Yet a "thin" minimal morality does derive from the common human condition, and "universal dispositions" are found in all cultures. Instead of promoting the supposedly universal features of one civilization, the requisites for cultural coexistence demand a search for what is common to most civilizations. In a multicivilizational world, the constructive course is to renounce universalism, accept diversity, and seek commonalities.[6]

The universalism that Huntington says here that we should renounce is the pursuit of universalism in cultural values: using the patterns or values of one civilization to unify the world. The commonalities that he says that we should seek are a fundamental set of ethical rules. Thus, I think we can say, not without some irony, that if intellectuals, who have traditionally been the least able to find common ground, can come to an initial agreement on this kind of morality, then we have real hope that the consensus can be extended to the far larger group of humanity.

6. Samuel P. Huntington, *The Clash of Civilizations and the Remaking of World Order* (Xinhua Publishing House, 1999), pp. 368–69. Of course, I agree with the concept of "minimal morality" that Walzer proposes in his book *Thick and Thin: Moral Argument at Home and Abroad* (University of Notre Dame Press, 1994), but I do not agree with the link that he draws between maximal and minimal morality. This question can be followed up elsewhere.

Further Reading

The Writings of He Huaihong, 1983–2013

Books

2013

《独立知识分子》*Duli zhishifenzi* [Independent intellectuals]. Chongqing: Chongqing Press.

《新纲常》, *Xin gangchang* [New principles]. Chengdu: Sichuan Renmin Press.

2011

《世袭社会》, *Shixi shehui* [The hereditary society], revised ed. Peking University Press.

《选举社会》, *Xuanju shehui* [The selection society], revised ed. Peking University Press.

《生生大德》, *Shengsheng dade* [The great virtue of life-giving]. Peking University Press.

《中国的忧伤》, *Zhongguo de youshang* [The sorrow of China]. Beijing: Law Press.

2010

《道德·上帝与人》, *Daode shangdi yu ren* [Morality, God, and man], revised ed. Peking University Press.

2009

《良心论》, *Liangxin lun* [A theory of conscience], revised ed. Peking University Press.

2008

《平等二十讲》, *Pingdeng ershi jiang* [Twenty lectures on equality], editor. Tianjin: Tianjin Renmin Press.

2003

《比天空更广阔的》, *Bi tiankong geng guangkuo de* [Wider than the sky]. Shanghai: SDX Joint Publishing Company.

2002

《公平的正义—<正义论>导读》, *Gongping de zhengyi: Zhengyilun daodu* [Justice as fairness: Introduction guide to A Theory of Justice]. Jinan: Shandong Renmin Press.

《生态伦理: 精神资源与哲学基础》, *Shengtai lunli: jingshen ziyuan yu zhexue jichu* [Ecological ethics: Spiritual sources and philosophical foundation], editor. Baoding: Hebei University Press.

《伦理学是什么》, *Lunlixue shi shenme* [What is ethics]. Peking University Press.

2000

《自选集》, *Zixuanji* [Selected works]. Guilin: Guangxi Normal University Press.

2001

《生命与自由—法国存在哲学研究》, *Shengming yu ziyou: Faguo cunzai zhexue yanjiu* [Life and freedom: Research on French existentialist philosophy]. Wuhan: Hubei Education Press.

《西方公民不服从的传统》, *Xifang gongmin bufucong de chuantong* [The Western tradition of civil disobedience], editor. Changchun: Jilin Renmin Press.

1999

《道德、上帝与人》, *Daode shangdi yu ren* [Morality, God and man]. Beijing: Xinhua Press.

1998

《底线伦理》, *Dixian lunli* [Minimalist ethics]. Liaoning Renmin Press.

《选举社会及其终结—秦汉至晚清历史的一种社会学阐释》, *Xuanjushehui ji qi zhongjie: Qinhan zhi wan Qing lishi de yizhong shehuixue chanshi* [The selection society and its end: a sociological interpretation of the history from Qin-Han to later Qing]. Shanghai: SDX Joint Publishing Company.

《尊重生命》, *Zunzhong shengming* [Respect life]. Guangzhou: Guangzhou Jiaoyu Publishing House.

1996

《世袭社会及其解体—中国历史上的春秋时代》, *Shixishehui ji qi jieti: Zhongguo lishishang de chunqiushidai* [The hereditary society and its collapse: the Spring and Autumn period of Chinese history]. Beijing: SDX Joint Publishing Company.

1994

《良心论—传统良知的社会转化》, *Liangxin lun: Chuantongliangzhi de zhuanhua* [A theory of conscience: the transformation of traditional morality]. Shanghai: SDX Joint Publishing Company.

1988

《生命的沉思—帕斯卡尔评述》, *Shengming de chensi: Pasika'er pingshu* [Contemplating life: comments on Pascal]. Beijing: China Federation of Literary and Art Circles Publishing Company.

Book Translations

2009

《正义论》（修订本）*Zhengyi lun* [A Theory of Justice], revised ed., by John Rawls, cotranslated with He Baogang and Liao Shenbai. Beijing: China Social Science Press.

2006

《论僭政》, *Lun jianzheng* [On Tyranny], by Leo Strauss. Beijing: Huaxia Press.

1991

《无政府，国家与乌托邦》, *Wuzhengfu guojia yu wutuobang* [Anarchy, State, and Utopia], by Robert Nozick. Beijing: China Social Science Press.

《帕斯卡尔文选》（合译）, *Pasika'er wenxuan* [The selected works of Pascal], cotranslated with Chen Xuanliang and others. Beijing: SDX Joint Publishing Company.

1989

《沉思录》, *Chensi lu* [Meditations, by Marcus Aurelius]. Beijing: China Social Science Press.

1988

《伦理学体系》, *Lunlixue tixi* [A system of ethics], by Friedrich Paulsen, cotranslated with Liao Shenbai. Beijing: China Social Science Press; Taipei: Shuxin Press.

《正义论》, *Zhengyi lun* [A theory of justice], by John Rawls, cotranslated with He Baogang and Liao Shenbai. Beijing: China Social Science Press.

1987

《伦理学概论》, *Lunlixue gailun* [Introduction to ethics], by Frank Thilly. China Renmin University Press.

《道德箴言录》, *Daode zhenyan lu* [Moral maxims], by Francois de La Rochefoucauld. Beijing: SDX Joint Publishing Company.

Selected Articles and Book Chapters

2012

"青年罗尔斯批评自然主义的伦理学涵义," "Qingnian luoersi pipan ziranzhuyi de lunlixue hanyi" [The ethical meaning of the criticism of naturalism by young Rawls]. *Journal of Tsinghua University*, vol. 2: 104–08.

"知识分子，以独立为第一义," "Zhishifenzi yi duli wei diyiyi" [Independence as the prime object of the intelligentsia]. *Dushu*, vol. 5: 3–10.

"王道之始与义利之辩," "Wangdao zhi shi yu yili zhi bian" [The beginning of the Tao of ruling and the debate on justice and interest]. In *The Culture of the Tao of Ruling and a Society of Justice*, edited by Liu Zhaoxuan and Li Cheng. Taiwan: Central University Publishing Center and Yunaliu Press, pp. 141–56.

2011

"未来十年的中国与美国," "Weilai shinian de Zhongguo yu Meiguo" [China and America in the next ten years], with four other scholars. *International Economic Review*, vol. 3: 15–35.

"汉立六十余年之'更化,'" "Hanli liushinian zhi genghua" [The transformation of Xi-Han in its first six decades]. *Leadership*, vol. 42: 157–65.

"青年罗尔斯论共同体及对自我中心主义的批判," "Qingnian luoersi lun gongtongti ji dui ziwozhongxinzhuyi de pipan" [Young Rawls on community and his criticism of egoism]. *Journal of China Renmin University*, no. 5, pp. 43–48.

"正义在中国：历史的与现实的," "Zhengyi zai Zhongguo: lishide yu xianshide" [Justice in China: history and reality]. *Review of Public Enforcement*, vol. 1: 2–15.

2010

"底线伦理的概念、含义与方法," "Dixian lunli de gainian, hanyi yu fangfa" [The concepts, content, and method of minimalist ethics]. *Morality and Civilization*, vol. 1: 17–21.

2007

"柏拉图《理想国》中的四隐喻," "Bolatu Lixiangguo zhong de siyinyu" [The four metaphors in Plato's Republic]. *Journal of Peking University*, vol. 5: 33–38.

2005

"现代伦理学：在康德与卢梭之间," "Xiandai lunlixue: zai kangde he lusuo zhijian" [Modern ethics: between Kant and Rousseau]. *Morality and Civilization*, vol. 1: 35–39.

2000

"全球伦理的可能论据," "Quanqiu lunli de keneng lunju" [Some possible arguments for global ethics]. *Modernity and China*. Guangdong: Education Press, pp. 105–30.

1999

"儒家的平等观及其制度化," "Rujia de pingdengguan ji qi zhiduhua" [The Confucian conception of equality and its institutionalization]. *International Journal of Research on Confucianism*, Issue 6, China Social Science Press, pp. 266–81.

1995

"从传统引申：和平与政治秩序的关联," "Cong chuantong yinshen: heping yu zhengzhizhixu de guanlian" [A justification from Chinese tradition: the correlation between peace and political order]. *Xueren*, Issue 7, Jiangsu Literature and Art Press, pp. 469–99.

1994

"关于'civil disobedience'的翻译," "Guanyu civil disobedience de fanyi" [The translation of civil disobedience]. *China Book Review*, vol. 2: 63–72.

1989

"自然状态与社会伦理," "Ziran zhuangtai yu shehui lunli" [Natural state and social ethics]. *Intelligentsia*, vol. 1: 97–100.

1985

"自由的概念: 萨特自由哲学的再考察," "Ziyou de gainian: Sate ziyouzhexue de zaikaocha" [A reexamination of Sartre's philosophy of freedom]. *Modern Foreign Philosophy*, Issue 7, Renmin Press, pp. 161–79.

1984

"试析萨特的自由伦理学," "Shixi Sate de ziyou lunlixue" [An interpretation of Sartre's ethics of freedom]. *Modern Foreign Philosophy*, Issue 5, Renmin Press, pp. 62–82.

1983

"试析萨特的自由本体论," "Shixi Sate de ziyou bentilun" [An interpretation of Sartre's ontology of freedom]. *Modern Foreign Philosophy*, Issue 4, Renmin Press, pp. 55–72.

INDEX

Adorno, Theodor W. (writer), xxxiv
Afghanistan, 219
All-China Federation of Trade Unions, 103
Analects, The (Confucius), 10, 158
Anarchy, State, and Utopia (Nozick), xxxi
Anger. *See* China
Anglo-Saxon and Teuton people, 224–25
Anthropocentrism, 177, 178, 182
Archimedean point for philosophy, 191–92
Aristotelian philosophy and theory, 190,
 203
Aristotle, 175, 192
Aron, Raymond-Claude-Ferdinand
 (philosopher, political scientist), 209n2
Aurelius, Marcus (emperor, philosopher), xvii

Ba Jin (pen name of literary figure), xxiv,
 109
"Balls under the Red Flag" (song; Cui), 84–
 85
Bans, 128–32
Beccaria, Cesare (legal philosopher), 153–
 54
Beijing, xviv, 111
Beijing Cultural Review, 95
Beijing News, 194
Being and Nothingness (Sartre), xxx
Beliefs. *See* Value-based beliefs
Bell, Daniel, 45
Berlin, Isaiah (philosopher), 205, 226, 228

Blau, Peter, 60
Book of Changes, 14–15
Book of Documents, 17
Book of Han, 57
"Bottom-Line Ethics" (newspaper column;
 He), xxxiii–xxxiv
Bourdieu, Pierre, 45
Bo Yang (Taiwanese author), xxv
Braudel, Fernand, 45, 60
Brecht, Bertolt, 71
Brothers Karamazov (Dostoevsky), 193
Buddha, xxvii
Buddhism, 171
Bureaucracy: in China, 42, 47, 47n12, 56,
 65, 111; as an institutional model, 42–
 43; Weber's model of, 42. *See also* Gov-
 ernment; Officials
Burnham, James (philosopher), 211

Cai Yuanpei (scholar), xxxii
California School (school of thought), 67
Callicles (philosopher), 191
Camus, Albert, xxx, 148–49
Capitalist-roaders, 101
Capital punishment. *See* Death penalty
Carson, Rachel (writer, conservationist),
 184
CCP. *See* Chinese Communist Party
CCTV. *See* China Central Television
Cen Chunxuan (viceroy), 54